McMillion$

McMillion$

THE ABSOLUTELY TRUE STORY OF
HOW AN UNLIKELY PAIR OF FBI AGENTS
BROUGHT DOWN THE MOST SUPERSIZED FRAUD
IN FAST FOOD HISTORY

James Lee Hernandez and Brian Lazarte

GRAND
CENTRAL

NEW YORK   BOSTON

Grand Central Publishing
Hachette Book Group
1290 Avenue of the Americas, New York, NY 10104
grandcentralpublishing.com
@grandcentralpub

First Edition: August 2024

Grand Central Publishing is a division of Hachette Book Group, Inc. The Grand Central Publishing name and logo is a registered trademark of Hachette Book Group, Inc.

The publisher is not responsible for websites (or their content) that are not owned by the publisher.

The Hachette Speakers Bureau provides a wide range of authors for speaking events. To find out more, go to hachettespeakersbureau.com or email HachetteSpeakers@hbgusa.com.

Grand Central Publishing books may be purchased in bulk for business, educational, or promotional use. For information, please contact your local bookseller or the Hachette Book Group Special Markets Department at special.markets@hbgusa.com.

Library of Congress Control Number: 2024935037

Interior book design by Timothy Shaner, NightandDayDesign.biz

ISBNs: 9781538720110 (hardcover), 9781538720103 (ebook)

Printed in the United States of America

LSC-C

Printing 1, 2024

To all those who played McDonald's Monopoly in the '90s and never won anything more than free fries. And to our parents.

CONTENTS

BEFORE WE GET STARTED ...

I n the summer of 2017, we began making the six-part HBO documentary *McMillion$* about a long-running fraud perpetrated against McDonald's and its incredibly popular promotional contest based on the Monopoly board game. For some reason it struck a nerve in the fast-food–clogged hearts of Americans and triggered countless mind-blown emojis on X (then known as Twitter).

Perhaps it was nineties nostalgia or how we revealed that of the billions served, close to zero had a chance to win a million bucks, a new car, or any high-value prize. Perhaps it was the shock of learning for the first time that a criminal conspiracy and the FBI were involved—the FBI even went undercover as a video production company working for McDonald's in order to crack the case. Perhaps it was the cast of colorful characters, many of whom didn't know one another, sharing their stories for the first time that caught the public's attention. Whatever it was, we had no idea so many people would "eat it up."

A 2012 post on r/todayilearned on the website Reddit—*TIL No one ever won the McDonald's Monopoly game*—kicked the whole thing off for us.

If you grew up going to McDonald's in the eighties and nineties like we did—you played the McDonald's Monopoly game. But nowadays, most people don't remember the scandal around the game and the arrests that followed. Why? To put it bluntly: 9/11. The first wave of indictments happened in the weeks right before America changed forever. It was lost in the ether . . . until we unearthed it almost twenty years later, thanks to the Reddit post.

Sure, you can watch the documentary series and listen to the companion podcast, which we hope you all do. (And if you did, thank you!) But there's only so much we could cover in those formats, and we felt the story needed a deeper dive. At some point, we realized if we didn't write the book, who would? As obsessed as we were with this story, we wanted to document it in print and hopefully blow a few more minds.

Since we are first-time book writers, we enlisted the help of Los Angeles–based writer and journalist Michael Albo. In filmmaking, it may appear that the directors do it all, but they work with other creatives to challenge ideas and collaborate to tell the best story possible. We wanted a similar experience writing this book.

Much like the documentary we couldn't tell the story of every person involved in this crime, so we focused on those who were willing to share their story with us. Yes, there were many who didn't want to talk to us, and—no surprise—there were also many who wanted money. For the record, nobody was paid to participate in this project and we want to give our sincere thanks to all those who chose to let us into their homes or offices to share their experiences. For some it was one of the most challenging parts of their lives and we are grateful they trusted us with their story.

We are also incredibly thankful to our good friends Mark Wahlberg, Stephen Levinson, and Archie Gips at Unrealistic

Ideas along with the executives at HBO who believed in two (at the time) unknown directors to bring this story to life.

To the McDonald's employees who, twenty years later, are mostly still working for the corporation, we thank you for participating. We know that wasn't an easy corporate decision.

Mark Devereaux, this wouldn't have happened without you.

To the FBI agents, since you've already hacked our emails—Kidding! Kidding!—you already know what we think of you.

And, last, we are thankful to the millions of people around the world who watched *McMillion$* . . . and now we thank you for picking up this book.

When we began putting together the pieces of this story, it always played out like a movie. At times we'd imagine what might have been said behind closed doors. At times we were given what was said by those who were there (to the best of their recollection). Throughout this book we want you to experience the best of both.

We'll spare you all the numerous "Mc" references and puns—we've heard them all.

We just hope you enjoy the read, eating an Egg McMuffin with cheese, some hash browns, and a cup of piping hot coffee with ten creamers and five sugars, a Colombo staple. (This will make sense later, we promise.)

McMillion$

INTRODUCTION

I n March 2001, the phone rang in the office of Rob Holm, the director of Global Security for McDonald's Corporation. "Holm," he said as he picked up the receiver. He didn't expect what followed.

"Hi, Rob. This is Special Assistant United States Attorney Mark Devereaux calling from Jacksonville, Florida."

Holm stammered, "How can I help you?"

"I'd like to invite you to come down here from Oak Brook to have a little chat with us here at the FBI's field office."

"What's this about?" asked Holm.

"I'm not really at liberty to discuss that with you over the phone. We can talk about it when you guys get here."

"You want to talk to me about something but you can't tell me what it's all about? When?" asked Holm.

"Now," answered Devereaux. "Oh, and Rob? I really have to emphasize that you need to keep this quiet. Nobody other than yourself and your team can know about this, okay?"

"Uh, sure. Okay," answered Holm. "But can't you give me some clue as to what this is all about?"

"I apologize. Everything will be explained once you get down here. I look forward to meeting you in person. Thanks." Devereaux ended the call.

Faced with this mystery, Holm and two of his colleagues—McDonald's in-house legal counsel Kathryn Mlsna and communications head Jack Daly—made the flight from Chicago to Jacksonville.

When the plane touched down and the trio stepped onto the concourse, they were met by a sharp-dressed man. He introduced himself as Mark Devereaux, and he wasn't what they had been expecting. With his slick, double-breasted suit and salt-and-pepper hair and mustache, he looked more like a well-heeled yacht owner than a Fed. He led them to the short-term parking lot where his government-issued Ford Crown Victoria was parked. "Welcome to Jacksonville," Devereaux said as they climbed in.

The ride to FBI headquarters was tense. Devereaux tried to make small talk, but it wasn't clicking with his captive audience. The question hanging heavy in the quiet interior of the car was *What are we doing here?* Devereaux ignored it and instead offered trivia about the city of Jacksonville. As they crossed over a bridge, Deveraux said, "See that? That's the St. Johns River. It's one of the very few in the country that flows south to north. Unbelievable, right?"

The trio of McDonald's executives smiled politely and nodded, feigning interest. *What is with this guy?* They were high-powered corporate people. They weren't used to being treated this way.

As Devereaux wheeled the big black Crown Vic into the parking lot for the Jacksonville office of the FBI, the mood in the car began to change. The McDonald's execs' sense of dread and suspense was turning to irritation with the well-dressed man behind the wheel.

At the entrance to the blocky, completely ordinary-looking building, Devereaux drew his badge and led his guests past the FBI seal inlaid on the lobby floor. An escort of agents met them and led the group through sets of security doors—"man traps" as they were called—where they had to wait, stuffed into a cramped chamber, until the door behind them closed with a *whoosh* of recycled air. Once the door closed, the escort would key in a code to open the door in front of them.

Was there a more streamlined way to do this? Of course, but Devereaux was invested in ratcheting up the tension. With nearly twenty years of prosecutorial experience, he hadn't given them the long tour for kicks or to annoy them. He had been watching them carefully the whole time. The agents who had been escorting the executives used the opportunity to study them as well. They looked for body language and any other little tells that might indicate guilt. To Devereaux, these execs were all potential suspects.

Were any of these people starting to sweat? Anyone looking flushed or flustered? Any nervous laughter? Any inappropriate attitude? Did they do anything that might be the manifestation of a guilty conscience? To Devereaux's eyes, they showed nothing other than a growing sense of frustration with him.

They entered a nondescript conference room where they were soon joined by a trio of agents. "Hi, thanks for coming," said a trim, sharp-featured man. "I'm Chris Graham, white-collar crime squad chief. These are Special Agents Rick Dent and Doug Mathews."

The executives politely shook hands all around, gave their names and positions, and sat on one side of the conference table while the FBI took the other. All of them wondered about the young-looking agent, the one introduced as Doug Mathews. He stood out, impossible to miss or dismiss. While everyone else in the room was dressed for serious business in dark suits, Mathews's suit was gold. He looked like a cross between Graceland Elvis and a McDonald's French fry. It seemed incongruous for the seriousness of the situation, but nobody commented on it and Mathews offered no explanation. It was just *there*.

The two teams could have almost switched sides—except for Doug Mathews and his gold suit—and nobody would have been the wiser: buttoned up, buttoned down, and every hair in place, these were the representatives of two towering cultural symbols: the FBI and the Golden Arches. Both were woven into the fabric of the country. G-men and fast food.

Devereaux moved to the dry-erase board. He paused— again for dramatic effect—and wrote down a name. "Ring any bells?" he asked the execs.

They glanced at the name, turned to one another with confused looks on their faces before they shook their heads. "No. That name means nothing to us."

"Okay," said Devereaux. He wrote another name below the first. "How about this one?"

Nothing.

Devereaux continued the parlor game for several more rounds. The whiteboard was starting to fill with names . . . absolutely none of which meant a thing to the McDonald's executives. Devereaux started to feel confident that these people weren't part of any criminal scheme. He felt relatively convinced their reactions were genuine.

McDonald's in-house legal counsel Kathryn Mlsna finally spoke up, a hint of annoyance in her voice. "Is anyone going to tell us what this is all about?"

Devereaux answered, "These are all names of some of the top prizewinners in your Monopoly promotional games."

If the execs had a readable reaction, it was "So what?" The fast-food giant had, by this point, been running the promotional Monopoly games at least once, if not multiple times a year since 1987. Hundreds of contestants had claimed the top prizes: Dodge Vipers, Sea-Doos, trips to the Super Bowl . . . and cash, lots of cash. The monetary prizes ranged from as low as $50 all the way up to $1 million. Each time the game was run, there were at least two million-dollar winners. If the game was run twice within a year, there were four million-dollar winners.

Devereaux, always the showman, picked the precise moment to drop the reveal. "Do you realize that some of these people are related or connected to each other in some way?"

The surnames on the board were all different, but Devereaux started drawing lines and filling in information. "This guy, William Fisher? He's the father-in-law of this winner, this Jerry Colombo fellow." Deveraux continued drawing lines connecting the names.

The McDonald's executives were caught off guard.

The prosecutor continued. "We ran the numbers. The odds of anyone winning any of the big prizes are about one in a hundred million," Devereaux said.

The executives shot glances at one another, unaware of the specifics. Devereaux went deeper. "The odds of three people from the same family or group of friends winning"—he pulled a small notebook from his jacket and flipped to the page he was looking for—"are one in a hundred and twenty *trillion*. You have a better chance of growing a third eye or acquiring superpowers from a mosquito bite. But maybe this is just one, singularly lucky family. Maybe it's coincidence. But in my business, there's no such thing as coincidence. I'm sure it exists somewhere, but in my world, it doesn't factor in." With finality, Devereaux stepped away from the whiteboard and took a seat. Silence again swallowed the conference room.

Devereaux broke it with his kill shot. "The suspect game pieces go all the way back to 1989. That's two years after you launched the Monopoly promotion. It's entirely possible that the last twelve years of the game have been tainted by fraud."

The execs were dumbfounded. They were not babes in the woods. They were experienced people. They had *seen some shit* over the course of their careers. Mlsna had been solving company problems with McDonald's in-house legal department since 1977, when she was recruited by the company fresh out of Northwestern University's law school. Jack Daly ran the comms team and was such a company man, he wore a Golden Arches pin on his lapel. If the company had an image problem—or anything else—he was the fixer. There was never a shortage of problems. He'd recently reassured a world rattled by reports of "mad cow disease," traced to British beef, that McDonald's did not use any meat products from the UK. There was no time to rest. As soon as he handled that bit of business, he was busy dealing with the fallout from the book *Fast Food Nation: The Dark Side of the All-American Meal* by Eric Schlosser, which decried fast food in general but reserved its most potent venom for McDonald's. Rob Holm had been the director of McDonald's global security for four years. Tall with strong features and a commanding presence, he had a voice to match. He was, as they say, "always on it." Problems rarely fazed him. Now though, after hearing Mark

Devereaux's summary, these three execs were absolutely speech-less. How did they miss this? They had so many questions. And for good reason. The McDonald's Monopoly game was no inconsequential promotion. It was big voodoo. There was a rea-son the game had been around for fourteen years . . . and was set to begin a new cycle in just a few short weeks and run until June. The FBI realized it was on a ridiculously tight time line.

Without fail, every time McDonald's ran its Monopoly pro-motion, there was an almost unbelievable 40 percent jump in sales. Those kinds of numbers were unheard of in the world of retail promotions. The Boardwalk Avenue game piece—the one that matter-of-factly read "$1,000,000 cash"—was a real-life version of Willy Wonka's Golden Ticket. More than that, the television commercials hyping the game ran virtually non-stop during prime time—"Do not pass Go, go directly to McDonald's!" After fourteen years of this, McDonald's Monopoly game was wedged into the brains of even the most casual consumer of mass media. Beyond that, McDonald's itself was Americana. It was pop culture. It touched everyone.

The game also brought the promise of fame and celebrity. Maybe not anything huge, but winners got play in regional media where they were often seen hobnobbing with Ronald McDonald—who was definitely a celebrity—and holding com-ically huge cardboard checks, each made out for a cool "One . . . Million . . . Dollars!"

But the hoopla wasn't always confined to small-town newspapers and TV stations. Sometimes it went national. On a chilly December day in 1995, as the holiday season was beginning to ramp up, Tammie Murphy was in the mailroom of St. Jude Children's Research Hospital in Memphis, Tennessee, opening donation envelopes. She came across an unusual one and almost trashed it. For one thing, it only had the hospital's address handwritten in black ink in big block letters. There was no return address. It wasn't freaky-weird to get an envelope like that, but it was unusual enough that Tammie took note. After opening the letter, she got the surprise of a lifetime. Instead of the typical five-or ten-dollar donation, the envelope held a McDonald's Monopoly game board. In addition, there was a winning game piece. Tammie didn't look at it too closely—how much could it possibly be worth?—and wondered if she could even accept such a donation. Tammie called her supervisor, twiddling the game piece as the phone rang. She studied the piece a little more carefully as she waited. She almost choked when she saw the piece was worth a million dollars. It was a "holiday miracle."

The national news media had a field day. Audiences loved mysteries and they loved the feel-good vibe of some selfless person out there doing something for nothing. It was a story that lent itself to many angles, and it seemed every outlet had one. There was Tammie who nearly trashed the prize thinking it was junk. There was the hospital director who broke out in tears of gratitude and sobbed, "Whoever you are out there— thank you. You are an angel." *CBS Evening News* anchor Dan Rather closed out a broadcast by using the story to assure his audience that there was still some good in the world: "Odds of finding this winning piece were one in more than two hundred and six million," he intoned in his best grave, trusted broadcaster's voice. "Odds of someone giving it away . . . heaven only knows." Ultimately, the money was delivered as a "donation" rather than a "win" to keep everything ethical and upright, but a million dollars is a million dollars.

Back in the FBI's conference room, the McDonald's execs had to ask themselves, "Did we overlook an obvious scam because we were caught up in the thrill and excitement of the game and the attending hype ourselves?" That seemed impossible. They had been around. They had seen real winners. People had been on TV, smiling from ear to ear, jumping up and down with excitement. That had been genuine, hadn't it?

Despite their initial findings, it was still unclear to the FBI if the fraud was limited to Devereaux's examples on the dry-erase board. Given past experience, they doubted it. But even armed with cops' suspicion and cynicism, they hadn't yet discovered just how deep the scheme had gone: that over a twelve-year period from 1989 to 2001, virtually none of the winners of any high-value prizes were legit.

Every man, woman, and child who had excitedly peeled a game piece off a box of fries or a soda cup; who had clipped a piece from an ad in a magazine or a Sunday newspaper; or who had walked up to a McDonald's counter worker and asked for a game piece (for legal reasons, no purchase was necessary to play the game) had almost no chance of winning.

All of the winners who walked into various McDonald's restaurants across the country, waving a winning game piece and claiming a victory over the gods of chance, were cogs in a skillfully crafted conspiracy of fraud. From the start of one of the longest-running promotional games in the country, just about every single big-ticket game piece—including the one an anonymous do-gooder sent to St. Jude Children's Hospital—was stolen.

Unfortunately, by the time the McDonald's executives arrived in Jacksonville, the FBI's limited amount of hard evidence wasn't enough to warrant the resources needed to launch an official, honest-to-goodness, get-shit-done investigation. The list of potential suspects kept metastasizing. Attempts to break down how the fraud worked were still only theories, which only led to more questions. Were the game pieces being manipulated at their place of manufacture? How many people were involved in *that* process? Who were they? Considering all the cash and prizes that had been paid out over the years, one thing was certain: the scheme, however it worked, was successful.

Back in the Jacksonville conference room, with the McDonald's execs no longer suspects, Mark Devereaux had a question for them: "What are the nuts and bolts of the game? How does that little game piece that we peel off a box of fries get there in the first place?"

It was a good question. A simple question. And it was a question the McDonald's execs had no idea how to answer. They looked nervously at one another. They didn't have a clue about the inner workings of the game.

This was unexpected. McDonald's founder Ray Kroc had put a system in place that was brutally efficient, unwaveringly consistent—when you ordered a hamburger in Phoenix, Arizona, it was the exact same burger you'd get in Beijing, China, right down to the placement of the pickle slices—and clearly understood by every employee from the high schooler working the counter part-time to the executives sitting in the conference room talking with the FBI. This was accomplished by a company policy that required every corporate executive to put in a week doing grunt work at one of the company's restaurants.

Before she got settled into her role as the company's promising legal star, Kathryn Mlsna's first week was spent at a McDonald's in Darien, Illinois, frying spuds, mopping floors, and unintentionally messing up customers' orders. But to truly get granular with all aspects of the company's workings, all managers and executives had to attend Hamburger University where they earned advanced degrees in Hamburgerology. In reality, though, Hamburger University was more boot camp than ivy-covered halls. The training was intense. Every McDonald's executive in the conference room that day could tell the agents the incredible minutiae of constructing a Filet-O-Fish sandwich or the correct method of cleaning a McDonald's restroom, but not one of them knew a thing about the workings of the company's biggest sales generator.

That was because the game was outsourced.

It made sense, though. Devereaux rationalized, "McDonald's makes French fries and hamburgers and milkshakes and apple pies. It doesn't make marketing."

However, the McDonald's team did know one thing: McDonald's was planning to gear up a new Monopoly game in a few weeks. After that, they'd launch in Europe. They were concerned. Rob Holm, the director of global security, spoke up. "So . . . maybe we should cancel this thing." His team nodded in agreement.

The FBI saw things differently. Calling off the game would be counterproductive to an investigation. Devereaux explained, "The best way for us to try to pull the rope in and figure out what's on the other end of this is to have another game. We want to catch the perpetrators in the act." And then he made a request: "We'd like McDonald's to run the game—just as was planned—one more time."

There was an uneasy silence from the McDonald's side of the table. Was running the game—with full knowledge that it was rigged—the best plan of action? McDonald's had a reputation to protect. The company was iconic. Like Disney, its reach was global, but its face was a sunshiny, idealized version of the US of A. Smiles were bright, family was paramount, and there was cultural harmony. The McDonald's experience was woven into the fabric of everyday life. McDonald's *was* America.

Not surprisingly, the McDonald's execs knew they had a lot to protect. Each head at that table started to fill with images of scandalous headlines, lawsuits, and all the ensuing problems that could follow if this thing went public. The damage could be beyond repair.

On the one hand, the company was under no obligation to honor Devereaux's plea to run the game again. Sure, McDonald's had to provide properly requested materials, but it wasn't required to participate in a sting operation with the FBI. There was always the option of just walking away and filing the entire thing in a folder marked "Forgotten."

On the other hand, the company wanted to find out who was behind the fraud. Was anyone from corporate involved? Devereaux and the FBI mostly felt confident that was not the case, although Doug Mathews remained skeptical. Rick Dent explained to his rookie that they had to be open with McDonald's if they expected information and cooperation. Mathews sighed. "Sometimes you just have to roll the dice to move an investigation forward."

McDonald's wasn't in favor of condoning crime, but the company had to look at this as a business issue. There was always the strong possibility McDonald's might get sued once word got out about a possibly rigged game, and whatever fraud had taken place over the course of the promotions, it hadn't really cost the company anything. The prizes and cash would have been awarded to somebody—or nobody in the event of a winning game piece being tossed in a trash bin. So was this strictly about ethics? McDonald's took them seriously. All employees, top to bottom, were given a standards of business conduct under which they were expected to operate. The document was forty pages long and covered almost every aspect of working for McDonald's. All employees were required to read the document, know the document, and sign the document to affirm they'd read it. But how did ethics help the bottom line? Game winners, legitimate or not, created lots of buzz and the company couldn't buy that kind of PR and advertising. There was a lot to consider. A decision couldn't be made on the spot.

The execs flew back to Chicago to take the FBI's findings to then-CEO Jack M. Greenberg. They knew that McDonald's— like any other corporation—would go to great lengths to shield itself from negative publicity . . . and in the past, there had been some stunningly bad press, including a mass shooting.

When James Oliver Huberty, a forty-one-year-old firearms enthusiast, was laid off from his job in the private security sector, he reacted in a way that would become increasingly common in the United States: random violence. Armed with a Browning Hi-Power handgun, a semiautomatic Uzi, and a Winchester 1200 pump-action shotgun, Huberty walked into a San Ysidro, California, McDonald's on July 18, 1984, and murdered twenty-one people and injured nineteen others. Why he chose McDonald's—a business to which he had no connections—remains a mystery. The company had a serious problem on its hands.

At the time, it was the deadliest mass shooting by a single gunman in American history. Before a police sniper took out Huberty with a chest shot and ended the carnage, it was already being called "the McDonald's massacre." Pictures from the crime scene broadcast on the world news all seemingly managed to get in the Golden Arches. Sick jokes riffed on McDonald's ads and messaging. "Over 50 billion served . . . and only 21 murdered!" These spread like wildfire in an age when the closest equivalent to the internet was the CB radio. This was McDonald's. Everybody had a hot take on the story. McDonald's vowed to reopen the San Ysidro store. That didn't sit well with the community.

A petition opposing its relaunch circulated and gathered thousands of signatures within hours. McDonald's was out. Within a week of the tragedy, Joan Kroc, the recent widow of company founder Ray Kroc, personally donated the location to the city. By late September, the restaurant was demolished. Gone without a trace. McDonald's one stipulation to the city was that no other restaurant of any kind could ever be built at the location. Agreed. By that October, it was as if nothing had ever happened at the site.

The Monopoly fraud case certainly didn't rise to the level of what happened in San Ysidro, but there was still the strong likelihood that the McDonald's board would just toss the Monopoly fraud down the corporate memory hole, never to be seen or heard of again.

It wasn't a snap decision; nothing in the corporate world ever is. Whether or not the company would cooperate with the FBI wasn't Rob Holm's decision. Personally, Holm was against running the game due to the level of risk it presented. The question was: Would Jack Greenberg take the easy way out or would he do what the FBI wanted?

The following week, Mark Devereaux had just about written off the company's cooperation. He was at his desk when the phone rang. "Hey, Mark. It's Rob Holm. McDonald's Corporation is all in. The game's set to start next month, so we'll go from April through June."

Devereaux hung up the phone. The clock was ticking . . .

- 1 -

"McDONALD'S MONOPOLY FRAUD?"

March 2001...
Two weeks prior to the Jacksonville meeting...

nother beautiful day in Jacksonville, Florida! thought Special Agent J. D. "Doug" Mathews, twenty-nine, as he approached the entrance to the Jacksonville field office of the Federal Bureau of Investigation. Forever, it seemed, he had harbored fantasies of being a hard-charging, door-kicking, fire-spitting undercover agent, the kind he had seen in countless movies and TV shows ever since he was a kid. He dreamed of being on a long stakeout, stuck in a parked car with another agent, living off black, barely warm thermos coffee, cold cardboard-like pizza, and half-melted candy bars.

His professional training was in accounting, though. He had initially been a tax cop for the North Carolina Department of Revenue's Criminal Investigation Division where his skills with numbers and accounting helped him go after what he called "tax cheats." His work in the area of white-collar crime put him on the radar of the Charlotte, North Carolina, office of the FBI after Mathews's specialized skills stood out during a joint task force operation with the bureau. At the time, the Jacksonville office was concerned with healthcare fraud and a man with Doug's skills would be welcomed. But even within the FBI, he was a numbers guy and thus confined to a desk. The reality of the job was a lot different from what he had pictured.

Jacksonville itself didn't help. It was sleepy and quiet and Doug longed for the kind of action he wasn't likely to find there, despite all the things Jacksonville did have to offer. The place was, as municipal boosters put out in promotional brochures and websites, the largest city by landmass in the entire country and boasted more shoreline than any other city in Florida. If that weren't enough, it was the birthplace of the Allman Brothers Band and Lynyrd Skynyrd.

There was also the Jacksonville Zoo that claimed to have 2,400 rare and exotic animals—and some common ones, too— as well as a veritable riot of 1,000 plants from all over the world that thrived in Jacksonville's sultry tropical weather. For high-minded visitors, there was the unfortunately named Cummer Museum of Art & Gardens. For those with less lofty taste and interests, there was the Catty Shack Ranch. Because this was Florida, with its lax rules for acquiring and housing exotic animals, roadside attractions featuring big cats were popular up and down the length of the state. Lions, tigers, leopards, and jaguars—along with hybrid species like ligers, tiglons, and liguars—were crammed into cages and put on display for gawking tourists. But as the popular Netflix documentary *Tiger King* later showed, what really brought in the rubes were the tigers. They were big business in Florida, and Jacksonville wasn't immune to the phenomenon. Doug Mathews wasn't the target audience for any of it, although his cheery demeanor, quick jokes, and boundless energy might lead one to think he was.

Still, it hadn't been a straightforward route to the Big Show for Mathews. Or for anybody. The FBI was special, elite. The bureau didn't take just any old number cruncher—no matter how good—who might harbor a desire to be a G-man. If you were in law enforcement, being an FBI special agent meant you were, indeed, badass and nationwide. And to become one, you had to be tested, trained, and approved before you got a badge and a service weapon. While Doug had thought about applying to the FBI, his work as a tax cop had kept him pretty busy. His performance on the joint task force had not gone unnoticed by the bureau though.

Doug Mathews was at his desk at the Department of Revenue when he got the call.

"Doug Mathews?" asked the voice on the other end of the line.

"Yes, that's me," answered Mathews, peppy, in his mild Southern drawl. The voice sounded authoritative and businesslike, so he refrained from the usual gabbing and joking.

The voice continued, "This is the Charlotte division of the FBI. We'd like you to come in for a quick chat." Apparently, this was common practice.

Not knowing what was up—but hyperaware it was the FBI—Mathews agreed to the meeting. He hoped the voice on the other end of the line would let him know why they wanted to talk to him, but they just said, "Great. See you tomorrow."

The next morning, bright and early, Doug Mathews piloted his car—a red two-door Honda Accord (which he was still driving as of 2024)—through traffic from Raleigh to Charlotte. He arrived early and paced; he was a perpetually tightly wrapped package of energy. Despite that, he couldn't help but be somewhat in awe. This was the FBI. He wasn't sure what they wanted with him, but it was a rush just to know that the agency knew his name.

He was led into an office and, again, suppressed his instinct to be the class clown and took a seat while the agent behind the desk got right to the point.

The agent opened a manila folder and looked through some papers before he lifted his eyes and asked Mathews, "So you've got a degree in economics and training in accounting? I see you're a certified public accountant."

"Yes."

The agent shuffled through some more papers before once again looking directly at Mathews. "Okay, here's the deal," he started. "We're looking for people with backgrounds in white-collar crimes. Number crunchers. Guys who can read ledgers and records. Does that sound like anything you'd be interested in?"

It was an opportunity Doug Mathews wasn't going to pass up. "Yes."

He was shuffled off to a room full of other applicants. They sat at little desks like they were back in high school. They were handed a test sheet and sat scratching out answers with no. 2 pencils. When Mathews finished, he handed in his pages and went home.

A few phone calls and follow-up steps later, Doug Mathews found himself in Quantico, Virginia, at the famous headquarters of the FBI Academy, the campus housed on the grounds of Marine Corps Base Quantico. Over the seven-week training program—filled with obstacle courses, weapons certifications, and pen-and-paper testing—Doug Mathews saw the weak and unqualified choke, perish, and leave the program. He thrived in this environment. Always a bit of a fitness enthusiast, Mathews was hard-muscled beneath his nineties-style baggy clothes. He had the build of a shortstop or second baseman—he had played ball in both high school and college—and he was all quickness and coordination.

At the end of those seven weeks, Doug Mathews was accepted into the FBI. He was allowed to request the top three places he'd like to be assigned. There were no guarantees. The bureau could send newly minted agents wherever it wanted. Doug Mathews's main criteria was to go somewhere warm so he picked Jacksonville. He knew that office did a lot of casework; besides, Florida seemed like it might be fun and Jacksonville was Southern, so Doug Mathews wouldn't have to make many cultural adjustments. A recruit from Los Angeles or New York might have had second thoughts, but not Mathews. He was primed. He made the move to Florida.

He immediately made an impression at the Jacksonville office. His ebullience and tendency to "mess with" his coworkers—and superiors—got him noticed. People liked the new kid and the energy he brought with him.

The four-story pale yellow stucco building with dark, tinted windows wasn't an intimidating temple of law enforcement. It had a friendlier, if nondescript, utilitarian vibe. The FBI had a long presence in the city that went all the way back to 1924 when Jacksonville first established an FBI field office. Outside of the occasional glamour cases like civil rights violations, espionage, and cocaine trafficking, Jacksonville was quiet to the point of being boring. The bulk of the cases in the office involved insurance fraud—which would never be as exciting as Klansmen, spies, and dope.

Mathews had been placed under the supervision of an older, straitlaced agent named Rick Dent. He was the polar opposite of Doug Mathews. Quiet, conservative, and religious, Dent regularly attended church, and while he never wore his faith on his sleeve or made much of a show about it, his beliefs did inform his professional decisions. People in the office referred to Dent as "the human lie detector." His superpower was his way of looking through anyone and getting directly to the truth.

Their first case was a healthcare scam that involved breast augmentation surgery. By 1999, healthcare fraud had become the meat-and-potatoes of the Jacksonville office. It was quiet, low-key work, investigating bankers and insurance execs. The cases often involved vast amounts of money, but they weren't always filled with the kind of world-shaking, cops-and-robbers excitement that Mathews craved.

As the new kid on the team, Mathews should have been deferential to his older and more experienced partner: seen but not heard. That just wasn't Doug's way. While Mathews respected his partner, there was a lot about Rick Dent he just didn't understand. Some people would take you into their confidence if they liked you. Doug Mathews would "mess" with you. It was never mean or cruel, and Rick Dent immediately recognized there was affection behind it, even if it did tend to exasperate him. Dent also saw that Mathews was not intimidated by him or any of the other senior agents in the office, and he liked that. The kid was bold.

However mismatched they may have been in temperament, it became clear to the office that the pair worked well together. They could often be seen conferring in Dent's cubicle clearing the deck on whatever case they were on.

The older agent was patient with his young protégé. The kid was like a puppy: undisciplined but trainable. Dent liked to act more disapproving than he actually was, in hopes of bringing the kid along in the ways of an FBI man. When Mathews wasn't acting silly and trying to get a rise out of Dent, he showed flashes of brilliance. Dent could see Mathews had potential if only he could keep a lid on the antics. Despite Doug Mathews's natural inclination toward a certain kind of boisterous humor, Dent's tutelage had an effect on the younger agent.

Although Mathews often described his supervisor as being "like a piece of wood, just not as exciting," he also had major respect for Dent's experience and wisdom. He appreciated that Dent "messed with" him, too, by constantly slowing Mathews's role and cautioning the young agent that he "wasn't ready" to start grabbing his own cases just yet. The pair had the attention of the office. Not only were they highly entertaining to observe, they were also tops in the Jacksonville office when it came to clearing cases.

It was an impressive feat for a field office that had only about fifty agents. By comparison, the Miami office had over four hundred. Despite the great record he was building for cracking cases, Doug Mathews yearned to do more than be a glorified CPA. He constantly threw out ideas and suggestions that would allow him to go undercover, just like in the movies. As he entered the office that morning in March 2001, Mathews grabbed some coffee and made his way to his desk. This could take some time because his personality demanded that he stop, chat, and joke with his coworkers.

The stream of banter continued until Mathews reached Rick Dent's cubicle. He blew in like a summer squall. "What's new in the world of healthcare fraud today?" Mathews asked as he leaned against Dent's desk.

The older agent held up a file.

As he reached for the file, something caught Doug Mathews's eye. On Rick Dent's well-organized desk Mathews noticed a bright yellow Post-it stuck to the corner of Dent's computer monitor. On it, in Rick Dent's neat and precise handwriting, was a phone number and three words in the form of a question: "McDonald's Monopoly fraud?"

It caught Doug Mathews's eye. "What's that?"

Without looking up, Rick Dent said, "Just something someone called in. The question mark's there for a reason." That reason being that the tip line civilians used to report crimes to the FBI wasn't always that reliable. While people would call in with valid tips—suspicious packages left in public places and things like that—there were also a lot of calls simply designed to attempt to manipulate the FBI to hassle and harass former spouses, bosses, and coworkers.

The FBI being the FBI, a simple phone call alleging a crime isn't enough to launch an investigation. The bureau is thorough. The bureau is precise. There must be some very concrete reasons for an actual, official investigation to formally begin. Calls must be made. Records need to be obtained and looked into. Supervisors have to sign off on things. Go-aheads are required. A potential case needs to be nurtured like a hothouse flower. And it all has to be kept quiet. Suspects can't be alerted by intrusive and suspicious calls or visits to acquaintances. Investigations are always a process. For Doug Mathews, that kind of thoroughness could be incredibly frustrating. His primary instinct was to jump in with both feet. And as he had experienced firsthand, a rookie agent could stumble onto a case, do the legwork, make the calls, and take it to the next level, but as soon as all that hard work started to pay off, the senior partner would usually say, "Okay, good work, rookie. Now, stand down and let the big boys handle this thing." Mathews sensed Rick Dent might not be as sold on the idea of looking into the McDonald's Monopoly tip as he was. He was also aware that since he was the junior partner, it was going to have to be Dent who pulled the trigger on moving ahead with any investigation into the potential case.

"You're not curious to look into this?" Mathews asked Dent.

"It's likely nothing," assured the older agent.

"But what if it isn't?"

"Well, you don't use an elephant gun when you've got ants, do you?"

"Ants?! This is the McDonald's Monopoly game. It's huge! You've never played?"

"I played Monopoly when I was a kid, sure," said Dent.

"No, no, no. Look, this is a promotional tie-in kind of thing. Like, you buy some fries, right?"

"Not the healthiest thing on the menu," said Dent.

"Yeah, yeah, yeah. Put that all aside for a minute. You get a large order of fries, right? They come in that happy little red box with the famous Golden Arches logo. Well, when they run the game, there's a little tab you pull off the box that says if you're a winner or not. But it could also just be a piece for filling out the little Monopoly board."

"What do you win? More fries?"

"Sure. Maybe, but free food isn't the only prize. The contest has some big-ticket stuff, too: cars, boats, cash. Like, up to a million dollars. And it's nationwide. Hell, this is McDonald's. Mickey D's."

Rick Dent was listening.

- 2 -

YOU DESERVE A BREAK TODAY

R ick Dent was, in the eyes of many, a square. He had a degree in mathematics from Tulane University. Those who knew him best would tell the story of how, as an RA in his college dorm, Rick quickly built a reputation for being a strict enforcer of the rules: no loud talking, no boisterous behavior, no horse-play or roughhousing, no loud music, no pot-smoking, no underage drinking. Somehow, he made it to graduation with-out being killed by his fellow students. If we had to guess, it was thanks to his wit. He was sharp.

The squareness was even apparent in his day-to-day look: Rick Dent may have only been about ten years older than Doug Mathews, but it was as if they came from two different eras. Dent was Christian-themed pop music and buffed wing tip shoes. Mathews was rock and roll, polo shirts, and well-worn Adidas. Suits obviously on days of official business.

Always methodical and cautious, when Dent got the call alerting him to possible fraud involving the McDonald's

Monopoly promotional game, he dutifully made note of it on a Post-it and slapped it to his desktop computer. Maybe it deserved a deeper look, or even more likely, maybe it didn't. In all likelihood, he thought, this was some kind of hoax, a dead end. Right now, though, there was the prime directive to work the healthcare fraud cases, an unenviable mandate handed down to the Jacksonville office from the highest reaches of the agency. The note was there to remind him to eventually get around to it.

But when Doug Mathews saw the Post-it, there was immediate excitement. Like a kid on Christmas morning, he was ready to tear into the mysterious gift under the tree.

Despite Mathews's jubilance, cases aren't built at the FBI on one agent's enthusiasm. It's a process.

Mathews, whose desk was piled high with paperwork, sighed. Doug Mathews's actions had long been directed by what he called his "fun meter." This was an internal mechanism, a sense that rang like an alarm whenever he encountered something promising any level of excitement. When he saw the Post-it on Rick Dent's desk, the fun meter redlined and he went into action.

First, he called the number and contacted the anonymous confidential informant. The informant had a lot to say. Very chatty. Mathews soaked it all in, busily writing down names and dates.

Rick Dent was in his cubicle, at his carefully arranged desk, an open manila folder before him. Mathews busted in.

"You're not going to believe this." Mathews came around the desk and slapped his own stack of papers on top of Dent's desk.

"What's this?" Dent asked.

"From the Post-it you gave me. The McDonald's Monopoly thing."

Mathews began to lay out the broad strokes of what he'd found.

"See? This guy is the first winner. Just like the confidential informant said. He won a Dodge Viper. You ever seen one of those? Never mind. Not sure why I asked."

"So he won a car?"

"Yeah! A Viper."

"Isn't that what's supposed to happen in a game of this type?"

"Well, yeah, but check this out." He grabbed a legal pad and started inking in a rudimentary map. He had Dent's attention. "Okay, we got this person, this one, and this one . . . ," Mathews continued. His pen scratched down four names.

Rick Dent shifted in his seat and leaned in a little closer.

"The source who called in said three of these people are related and won. We're talking million-dollar winners and they didn't just walk into a McDonald's and get lucky, they got the game pieces from a guy called *Uncle Jerry*. I went through a bunch of public records associated with these people and guess what?"

"What?"

Mathews blurted out, "They're all related. And all three live in the same area! They claimed various addresses throughout the Southeast, but they all live in Jacksonville."

If Rick Dent had been a fish, this would have been the moment that Mathews set the hook.

Rick Dent took a deep breath. "We got something here," Mathews said. "I think we really got something."

Dent could see that, so far, Doug Mathews appeared to be correct. There was something here. "Who's this 'Uncle Jerry' guy you've got written down?" Dent asked.

"Good question."

"Good work," said Dent, who took Doug's notes and placed them neatly into a manila folder.

Doug Mathews had a moment of panic. Was Dent taking the case for himself?

"Relax. You're going to need some help with this. I'm in," announced Dent.

Quietly, without causing too many ripples, Dent reached out to the company and obtained a subpoena to acquire a list of all the winners from the McDonald's Monopoly promotional game since its debut. If this raised any alarms within the company, it wasn't evident. When he received the requested records, it was abundantly clear that the informant wasn't just making something up for his own amusement. The questions were endless. How many more could be involved? How far back did it go? Who was this Uncle Jerry? Was McDonald's in on it?

And just like that, the two most mismatched agents in the history of the Jacksonville office were ready to chow down on some McDonald's Monopoly fraud. Now the real work could begin. The first thing they needed to do was to link up with a federal prosecutor to share their findings, confirm they had a viable case, and convince them to take it on.

Rick Dent knew the right man for the job. Prosecutor Mark Devereaux was a graduate of The Citadel—the military college of South Carolina—where he earned a bachelor of science degree in business administration, accounting, and finance. He acquired a law degree from the University of Tennessee's College of Law. Later, Devereaux had served as a military lawyer as part of the Judge Advocate General's Corps—better known as "JAG" to the general public. He carried himself with a military bearing. Like Rick Dent, he was a stickler for tradition and decorum. Once, after a judge instituted a "casual Friday" in his courtroom, Devereaux showed up in a sharp, bespoke tuxedo to protest. He was not exactly familiar with the concept of "casual."

Doug Mathews and Rick Dent took Devereaux down to a conference room and laid out what they knew about the McDonald's case. This was an important part of the process. Both Dent and Mathews were aware that if they didn't present this well, if they failed to intrigue Mark Devereaux, the case was dead in the water and there was no going forward. The investigation would die then and there. Devereaux sat quietly until the two agents finished. They looked at each other nervously. Had they presented things well enough to convince Devereaux to proceed? The two agents were relieved when Devereaux removed his shades for the first time since he'd entered the field office. "Let's do this," he said.

The next step—and potentially the most difficult one—was to get the full weight of the FBI behind an investigation. Basically, they needed approval to dedicate time and resources to this. It would first require a meeting with their squad superior, Chris Graham, the head of the white-collar crime squad. Graham was clean-cut and fit with the spirit of a well-mannered football coach: he was a great listener who was incredibly efficient with his words. Graham's mandate from his superiors was to work those insurance fraud cases. Those were the spine of the Jacksonville office, not some scam involving fast food. He was going to need an okay from up high to allow Mathews and Dent the resources they'd need for an investigation. Mathews softened his opinion of Graham when the supervisor said, "What we have here is a high-profile case, fellas. I'm going to kick this upstairs."

Any investigation into a company as high profile as McDonald's had to be undertaken with care and precision. Graham went to his boss, Special Agent in Charge Tom Kneir.

Another meeting was called in the conference room. Once again, the whiteboard was soon a tangle of names, lines, arrows, and questions: "How are the game pieces distributed?" "Where do the game pieces come from?" "How do the game pieces get onto the fry boxes?" "Are McDonald's counter people involved?" As the meeting went on, the whiteboard became dense and barely readable. There were a lot of moving parts to this thing. The conference table, at first neatly set up with coffee service and cookies, was now in worse shape than the whiteboard: broken cookies, crumbs, crushed Styrofoam cups, and some McDonald's—for research, of course.

"We're going to want to talk to whoever's in charge of this thing at McDonald's," said Kneir. Most SACs don't insert themselves into investigations, but Kneir was different. He had started out as a street agent. His biggest claim to fame was that he had been an integral part of the team that broke open the Iran-Contra scandal. Kneir was a man who liked to get his hands dirty even in his ranking position.

Mathews was not a fan of this idea of contacting McDonald's. As a rookie, decorum dictated he sit quietly, defer to the more experienced agents, and above all keep his mouth shut. But that wasn't Doug Mathews. "What? We can't do that! You can't be serious! That's going to tip them off!" In Mathews's rookie eyes, everyone at McDonald's was a suspect, including the executives up to and including the CEO.

Faces turned to Rick Dent as if to say, "Hey, man. Control your boy."

Rick Dent held out a hand, palm facing down, and slowly lowered it as if to indicate, "Bring it down, kiddo."

Doug smiled, nodded, and quietly said, "Sorry, sorry . . . You guys know I get excited."

"Mark, why don't you get the execs down here to talk?" said Tom Kneir.

Chris Graham agreed. "Make the call."

Devereaux nodded.

The next day, Mark Devereaux placed his call to Rob Holm, the head of security for McDonald's Corporation and requested Holm and his team come to Jacksonville.

When the meeting was over, they told Devereaux they needed to consult with CEO Jack Greenberg before they could proceed—*if* they could proceed.

A few days later, the McDonald's execs informed Devereaux that the company would assist the FBI in whatever ways it could. The fast-food giant already had plans in the works to launch a new game, but time was tight. The new McDonald's Monopoly game was set to kick off in April—just a few short weeks away—and run until July. Which meant the FBI would have a mere four months to catch whoever was behind it.

– 3 –

PIECE BY PIECE

The conference room was quiet. Rick Dent, Chris Graham, and Tom Kneir sat patiently. Doug Mathews, on his third cup of coffee for the day, was pacing.

"Where is he?" asked Dent.

"Devereaux sent word he's running late," answered Graham. "Probably shining his shoes or trimming his mustache."

Devereaux had already entered the building. In the men's room, he washed his hands and stood before the mirror to give himself one last look before entering the meeting.

Like a skilled actor portraying a prosecutor, Devereaux opened his briefcase and took out papers, folders, and various items before he took a seat.

To Mathews, it felt like everything was moving in slow motion. "So, get to it?" he blurted out.

Devereaux, seemingly for dramatic effect, or just to irritate Doug, placed both palms on the table. "Gentlemen, McDonald's is all in," he said. Relief gave way to smiles.

"So . . . now what?" asked Graham. "Ideas? And Mathews, don't say 'undercover.'"

"Undercover!" said Mathews.

They all laughed. "Rick, thoughts?" asked Kneir.

"Well, we have our work cut out for us. I think we should do what we usually do with any white-collar case: roll up our sleeves and get to work on our research. We need to know everything we can about how these game pieces get made, how they get distributed and attached to the fry boxes and cups. Beyond that, let's try to get our hands on as much paperwork as we can from McDonald's. Tax records. Invoices. Receipts. Basically, any paperwork tied to the game." As Mathews would put it, "the boring stuff." For Dent, this was the fun stuff.

Devereaux reminded everyone of the time frame. "Remember, McDonald's is running the game one last time for us. We have about three months and change to get this thing figured out. After that, we're not catching anyone in the act."

"Undercover!" said Mathews as he slapped a hand on the table.

"Doug . . . ," said Kneir.

"Look, we need to find a way to get in there, beyond burying our heads in paperwork. Who knows what we might find or how long it will take? We got to move quickly, like if this were a drug case," Mathews said sulkily.

At that moment, the clouds parted, the sun broke through, a thousand light bulbs switched on, and trumpets blew a stately alarm—and all of it contained within the mind of squad chief Chris Graham.

"Bingo! Kid's right," said Graham.

"What?" asked Kneir.

Even Mathews uttered a halfway stunned "Huh?"

"We should approach this like a drug case," said Graham. "You know, with dope, we have a product we can track. With this McDonald's thing, we have the game pieces. We can follow those. What's one of the first things we'd do if this were about dope?"

Devereaux spoke first. "Phone records. We'd comb through phone records and see who's talking to who. See if there are any commonalities, see if there's anything—and I mean anything— unusual or even slightly out of the ordinary. From there, we can go deeper, but phone records of past McDonald's Monopoly winners is where I'd start. I can get those records released to you right away."

"Okay, so here's what we'll do," Tom Kneir quarterbacked. "Mark, you'll get those phone logs to Rick and Doug, they'll give them a look. In the meantime start finding out everything you can about the process from McDonald's and—"

"Undercover!" interrupted Doug Mathews.

"—we'll meet back here in a couple of days. Okay?"

There were general nods as the men picked up their folders and pens. Just like that, the first piece on the FBI game board was in play.

Doug Mathews and Rick Dent looked particularly bleary-eyed. Since the last meeting they had been on several calls with McDonald's learning what they could about who managed the game. Additionally, they were digging through phone records of all the past winners, combing through the months surround-ing each of their respective wins, trying to find a common denominator. It was like trying to find a four-leaf clover in a field of shamrocks.

"My eyes are going to start bleeding here pretty soon," Mathews complained.

"This is the job, kiddo," said Dent.

The younger agent straightened his posture and stretched. His mind wandered but was snapped back into focus when Rick Dent said, "Well, look at this . . . I've seen this number before." Mathews studied the number as Rick pulled out another phone log from a previous winner. There was a match. Doug took a giant sip of his coffee and grabbed another log. With a number in his mind, he ran his finger down page after page, Rick doing the same with another log. Mathews's finger stopped. "Oh boy!" he screamed. For the rest of the day, they pored over log after log, discovering the same number appearing again and again. "You don't make these kinds of discoveries going undercover," quipped Dent. Mathews just smiled.

When the wider team assembled in the conference room, Mathews was eager to share the news that a common phone number had been found among almost all the winners' logs they'd searched. There had been several calls going both ways heavily before and after a win, and then they just stopped. Even more concerning was that the number of connections far exceeded the number of winners first given by the informant.

Dent wrote a single name on the board with a black dry-erase marker. In bold block letters he neatly spelled out a single name: Jerome Jacobson.

There was not much reaction to the revelation. The team exchanged looks.

"Who's Jerome Jacobson?" asked Kneir.

"What Tom said," chimed Chris Graham.

It's somewhat disconcerting to learn how much of our lives are readily available for anyone's consumption through public records, but as the kids say, "That's the price of freedom." Doug Mathews and Rick Dent put in the shoe leather, learning as much as they could from public records, the FBI database, and various phone calls.

"Jerome Jacobson is the absolute head of security for Simon Marketing," said Dent.

Blank faces all around the table as if to say, "So what?"

Sensing the confusion, Rick Dent brought everyone up to speed. "Simon Marketing is the outsourced company that actually runs the McDonald's Monopoly promotional game."

Located about an hour outside of Atlanta, Simon Marketing handled promotions for a number of large companies, but the company's account with McDonald's was special. The two organizations had a long history of working together successfully. Simon Marketing had developed the toys that came with the hugely popular McDonald's Happy Meal.

Simon Marketing was also responsible for the development of the promotional Monopoly game. Starting out as a simple scratch-off ticket, the concept evolved into fold-up game pieces, and, finally, it became the familiar instant prize pieces affixed to the sides of French fry boxes, soda and shake cups, and the familiar cardboard container of the company's flagship burger, the Big Mac.

And the lord of security at Simon Marketing was Jerome Jacobson, more familiarly known as "Jerry." Could he be the mysterious "Uncle Jerry"?

Again searching the databases, Dent and Mathews discovered little. They learned Jacobson was in his late fifties and had started his career as a police officer in Hollywood, Florida. He hadn't been on the force long before he left, citing an injury that prevented him from holding a gun. There were no documents indicating trouble. No citations for heavy-handedness or brutality against citizens, nothing. Jerome Jacobson's record as a cop in Hollywood, Florida, was clean. There's nothing suspicious about someone leaving a job. It happens every day.

There was a seemingly long break in Jacobson's employment history following his exit from the force. Maybe he was being supported by a spouse or living off a trust. Maybe he just couldn't find a job. Whatever it was, it was strange, a possible red flag that could mean something bigger was going on with the guy. The records indicated that Jacobson eventually reentered the workforce and remained in security, although he was now involved in the corporate arena. His first gig was as a security official at a small accounting firm. From there, he'd springboarded to Dittler Brothers, a secure printing facility that also made tickets for scratch-off games, raffles, and various state lotteries. In the late 1980s, he took his current position with Simon Marketing. He had been there for over a decade.

Incidentally, Dittler Brothers was the company that printed the game pieces for the McDonald's Monopoly game.

Red flags fluttered in a stiff breeze. Did the FBI now have a suspect? The information was enough for Devereaux and Rick Dent to begin the long, involved process to acquire a wiretap on Jerome Jacobson's home phone line.

In the normal course of things, the FBI might embed an undercover agent as a newly hired employee at Simon Marketing where the agent could then observe and, possibly, develop a relationship with Jacobson, but the agency had a ticking clock, and there just wasn't the time to invest in this plan. It was now April and the game would be over—for good—in June. If the perpetrators of this scheme were to be caught in the act, the FBI needed to get busy.

"Undercover!" said Doug Mathews.

Rick Dent had a better idea. For now. "Let's try this first," he advised. Mathews's shoulders sagged in defeat as Dent got on the phone and punched in a number.

"Rob Holm? It's Special Agent Dent calling from the FBI's Jacksonville office."

"You find something?" asked Holm.

Dent replied, "We're still just at the beginning of our investigation. What can you tell us about Simon Marketing and Dittler Brothers?"

Holm didn't know really anything, as they were not directly a part of McDonald's. He admitted as much. Dent continued, "Mr. Holm, we obviously wouldn't want to walk in there, start asking questions ourselves, and arouse any suspicions that there is an investigation underway. We would like you to go and give us a clear picture of the mechanics of the Monopoly game. How does it work from start to finish? How does a game piece get from the printer to a box or a cup and finally to the consumer? From there, if the piece is a winner, what happens? I need all the steps and all the people and departments the game pieces pass through in this process. We also need to know what their security looks like."

"Yeah, sure. That's not going to be a problem," assured Rob Holm.

"Rob, I can't emphasize this enough. You have to be subtle about this. You can't let anyone know that you're in contact with us."

Dent ended the call and Doug Mathews groaned. "Did I hear that right?"

"Hear what?" asked Dent. He suspected what came next.

"So we're sending the McDonald's guy undercover, but I'm stuck here in the office looking at phone numbers?"

Dent just looked at Mathews for a moment before responding, "Yes."

Under the ruse of a company audit of the processes involved in the life cycle of the game pieces in preparation for the impending launch of McDonald's European Monopoly game, Rob Holm arrived in Atlanta and was given a guided tour of the highly secure processes undertaken by both Dittler Brothers and Simon Marketing.

As a security man himself, Holm couldn't help but be impressed by the operation. Both companies utilized the latest in high-tech corporate security. Not a single move in the process went unobserved. "We have a great team," Holm was repeatedly told. "And our process is proprietary. Developed right here in-house by our own guy. He's a real genius." Holm could believe it. From the videotaping of the printing process through the multilayered security protocols and multiple eyes—always the eyes—on each step taken, the count room of any Las Vegas casino would admire the precision of what was going on at both Dittler Brothers and Simon Marketing.

At one point, observing yet another step in the process, Holm asked, "Isn't this . . . overkill?"

One of the Dittler Brothers people explained, "This is McDonald's, man. *McDonald's.* We go the extra mile."

"Who developed the system?" Holm wanted to know. It seemed bulletproof. "Who's the one with the final say on all these processes?"

"Oh, that'll be Jerry Jacobson," he was told. "He's, like, the Einstein of security."

"Impressive. I'd love to meet him," said Holm.

Holm didn't get a chance to meet this security savant.

He also had no idea Jerry Jacobson was the FBI's prime suspect in the McDonald's Monopoly scheme. He was so in the dark that when he finally met with Doug Mathews and Rick Dent following his investigatory trip, all he could do was talk about how secure the process was and how glowingly everyone spoke about this Jerry Jacobson. Most of all, Rob was impressed by the system Jacobson had set up for McDonald's promotional game. "They've really got it wired," Holm told Special Agent Dent.

Holm's trip also took him to Los Angeles where the Simon Marketing home office was located. This was the end of the line for winning game pieces to receive final verification. From the time the piece arrived in its envelope, its journey was tracked on video. From the opening of the envelope to the examination of the winning piece under a magnifying glass. As another level of security, the winning game pieces all featured a tiny printing anomaly. A letter on the piece may have a clipped line or some other imperfection designed to weed out fakes, forgeries, and fugazis. On top of that, there were various layers of different designs on the pieces. The troubling thing was that all the winning game pieces since 1989 checked out as clean and legit on Simon Marketing's security videotapes. Every single one.

With their deeper knowledge of Jerry Jacobson, Rick Dent, Doug Mathews, and the FBI team received approval to get a wire on Jacobson's home phone line. It wasn't an easy process. Getting approval for wiretaps never is. Rick Dent's "affidavit in support of application" requesting the interception of "wire communications" ran a full sixty-two pages. Once approved by a judge, a subpoena to route incoming and outgoing calls on Jacobson's line through the FBI's wire room was faxed to the regional manager of the Southern Bell phone company.

What nobody in the Jacksonville office knew was that the regional manager didn't pick up his own faxes. His assistant handled mundane tasks like that. Every morning, before the regional manager arrived at the office, his assistant would grab any faxes that had come in and direct them to their proper destination. If they were for her boss, they went on his desk and would be waiting for him when he arrived precisely at nine a.m.

The secretary's name was Linda. Linda Jacobson. In an incredible turn of circumstance, Linda Jacobson was Jerry Jacobson's wife. Despite the team's thorough look into Jerry Jacobson, this little nugget had slipped through the cracks. Had Linda picked up the fax, she could have tipped off her husband and the investigation would have been over. But in another incredible turn of circumstance, Linda Jacobson was out sick on the morning the subpoena arrived. A temp handed the fax to the manager and the wire was up and running.

At the Jacksonville office, the FBI tech crew had set up the wire room: a tangle of cables, plugs, headphones, and recording devices blinking red and green lights. Here's a secret: despite what you may have seen in movies and television, monitoring phone calls is the most boring job in the world. Watching paint dry is probably more exciting because the observer is actually doing something. That's not the case for 99 percent of the time spent in the wire room. Doug Mathews would have ended up in a straitjacket had he drawn the assignment. He was a rookie, but there were even newer "baby" agents who were given the task. Agents Tim Adams and Sean O'Donovan drew the short straws and were sentenced to "the room."

Rick Dent, who had done his own time in wire rooms, sympathized with Adams and O'Donovan and made sure there were always delicious freshly baked cookies and brownies—supplied by Mrs. Dent—in the wire room.

As the calls began to mount and the agents listened, they discovered something odd. Several people referred to Jerry Jacobson as "Uncle Jerry."

"Damn. This guy can't have that many nephews and nieces," said Doug Mathews.

"You know who calls everyone 'uncle'?" asked Dent. "Mob guys. It's a show of respect."

"So you think Jacobson is connected to organized crime? His name doesn't end in a vowel," said Mathews.

"Crime is an equal opportunity employer, kiddo. Let's look into this angle," advised Dent.

He and Mathews began assembling a "murder board" to keep everything in focus. It was a thing we've all seen in movies and television: a cork board dotted with pictures of the suspects, notes, and connections made with red twine held by colorful pushpins. Murder or not, they still call it that. At the very top and center was the name JEROME JACOBSON/UNCLE JERRY.

– 4 –

OPERATION FINAL ANSWER

APRIL 2001...

Rick Dent had started to worry about his rookie partner.
Doug Mathews, ever since getting on the trail of the McDonald's Monopoly fraud, had developed a singular, laser-like
focus: undercover work.

To some of the FBI team, Mathews's desire to go undercover became annoying. His constant refrain of "Undercover!"
had become old and tiresome. He used it whenever he'd pass
squad supervisor, Chris Graham, in the office. He'd hurl it like
an epithet at the big boss, Tom Kneir. Rick Dent had learned
to tune out and squelch a lot of the rookie's verbal output—the
jokes, the japes, the folderol not becoming of a "traditional"
FBI man—but this was something new altogether. It was
obsessive.

The rookie was so insistent, Dent decided to give him a
chance and make a pitch for an undercover operation to the
team. Let him finally get it out of his system. Why not?

It was set for the next strategy meeting. The agents, Mark
Devereaux, the supervisors, all filed in at their leisure and took

their seats around the conference table that took up most of the space in the office. Support staff—what non-agents are called within the FBI—set up water bottles, snacks, and coffee to sustain the team during the session. As Doug Mathews arrived, Graham was about to say, "No, Doug," but Dent spoke up.

"Let's hear him out," he said.

Every face at the table turned to him, perplexed and somewhat off guard.

"What?" said Graham. "Are you kidding me?" He was going to say, "Are you *fucking* kidding me?" but since he was addressing Rick Dent, he corrected course even though technically he was Dent's boss.

"He's obviously got some ideas," said Dent. "I say we give a listen."

"Okay," said Graham. "Let's hear his idea . . . and then I'll tell him no."

"Wouldn't Tom Kneir be the one to tell me no?" asked Doug Mathews in a tone that said "You're a butt-munch, Graham."

"If we're going by the book, yeah," said Kneir. "But who knows? Maybe Doug's got something that we could use. Something we haven't thought of."

"Thanks," said Mathews with all sincerity.

"Don't embarrass me, rookie. Go."

Mathews picked up his manila folder and tapped it against the table so that the pages it contained lined up neatly. He stood and made his pitch. "This is what we do," began the rookie FBI agent. It was his moment to shine. "We tell all the past winners that McDonald's is hosting a big reunion of past winners in Las Vegas, all-expenses-paid. We fly them to Vegas and put them up at Embassy Suites—nothing too fancy, but take over a whole floor. Once we get all these people under one roof, we kick down the doors to their rooms and bust everyone at the same time." Mathews was on fire. Excited to finally have the stage.

Tom Kneir laughed. "Are you crazy, Doug? I mean, seriously. Are you crazy?"

Mathews was perplexed. He looked to Rick Dent, but there was no help coming from his partner. Mathews was alone on this one. "What?" he asked Kneir. The rookie was genuinely confused.

Tom Kneir filled in the blanks. "First of all, what kind of money do you think the FBI has that we can just fly every past winner to Vegas and put them up? But secondly, and even more concerning since you should know this, we can't just arrest people without evidence."

"Well, those are just the broad strokes," Mathews said. "That part still needs to be worked out."

Rick Dent sighed. Had he misplaced his trust in the rookie?

The meeting that had started with such promise for Mathews now ended in utter disappointment for him. Not only was he not going undercover, he may have just made a serious career misstep with the brass. He picked up his folder and slinked off to his desk.

Things were trending down for Doug Mathews . . . but they were definitely on the upswing for a man named Michael Hoover.

The call had come into the prize redemption center in Simon Marketing's Los Angeles office on a hazy, too warm afternoon. Matilda Dahahn picked up the call on the second ring. "Redemption," she said.

"Uh, hello?" The voice at the end of the line sounded a little confused.

"Redemption Center, Simon Marketing," Matilda clarified.

"Is this the place I'm supposed to call if I got a McDonald's Monopoly winner?" asked the voice on the end of the line.

"Yes, it is," answered Matilda. "How can I help you?"

"Well, I'm the manager here at a McDonald's in Rhode Island . . . and some guy just walked in with a winning game piece for the Monopoly game. A winning piece for the million-dollar prize! I was told that if this ever happened, I was supposed to call your number."

Matilda Dahahn had handled the phones in the Redemption Center for the past twelve years, and she had heard it all before. The excitement was expected. A winner meant lots of local and regional coverage of the event, and that drove sales. Naturally, the stores' managers were always hyped as if they themselves had won. At its most basic level, a customer claiming the big million-dollar prize was an extremely rare occurrence. A store manager could spend an entire career without ever seeing one. When one did show up, there was intense focus on the restaurant in the local and regional press, sales went through the roof, pictures and blurbs went into local papers, and area news crews rolled up in their vans. If a manager of a McDonald's in East Boondocks, South Carolina, hosted a big winner, that manager got on the radar of corporate in the best way possible.

The manager continued. "This guy Michael Hoover just walked in and presented the piece! Can you believe it? And you know what? He didn't even get it here. He says he found it in a *People* magazine insert. How's that for luck, huh?"

Matilda Dahahn carefully took down all the manager's information—as well as giving him a few instructions about how to properly handle the winning game piece and get it sent over to Simon Marketing. Then she called McDonald's corporate offices to inform them that there was a potential million-dollar winner. These steps lined up with the mechanics that McDonald's Corporation security chief Rob Holm had learned doing his own deep look into the process. They did not seem suspicious. In fact, they tracked without registering an alarm. Still, as soon as Holm heard the news, he was on the phone to the Jacksonville office of the FBI.

Graham relayed the news to the team. "We just got a call from Rob Holm at McDonald's corporate. We have our first million-dollar winner in the new Monopoly game." It was all-hands-on-deck strategizing how to take advantage of this new information. Everything they did from here had to be precise in service of obtaining evidence that could help lead them to prove Michael Hoover and Jerry Jacobson were committing fraud. One misstep and they might get nothing.

Mathews raised his hand as he took the floor.

"No!" screamed Chris Graham.

"You don't even know what I'm going to say," said Mathews.

"You're gonna say 'undercover.'"

"You don't know that."

"Okay fine," Graham relented. "Just don't say 'undercover.'"

Rick Dent just ignored them. He was deep in thought, writing out an idea.

"Alright," started Mathews. "Before you say anything, just hear me out. These winners have to sign paperwork and waivers before they can collect their winnings. As you already know, buried in all the mumbo jumbo is a clause that states the winners all agree to participate in whatever promotional events McDonald's comes up with to publicize the company, the game, whatever. That includes showing their faces and doing televised promos. Sooo . . . I think we can do an undercover operation where we pretend to be a production company for McDonald's and show up at Michael Hoover's house, all Publishers Clearing House–style, like get him on camera with balloons and the big check. We film him telling us all about his winning ticket, tap his phone, and see if we can't just tickle the wire." Graham couldn't believe Mathews was this relentless. He just shook his head. Dent stopped writing and looked up at Mathews. Seemingly intrigued, he asked, "Who's going to do this, you?"

Without a beat Mathews replied, "Yes. And I'll get someone from McDonald's to come with me. I'll pretend to be the director because they don't do shit."

Dent just replied with a "hmm" and went right back to writing.

Later that day, hours after Mathews had retired to his cubicle, he heard the announcement over the intercom: "Doug Mathews please report to the SAC office immediately." *Uh-oh.* Doug Mathews didn't like the sound of that. A call to the boss's office was never good, no matter where you worked.

He stood and made the steps to Special Agent in Charge Tom Kneir's office—the Walk of Shame. As he threaded his way through the floor, his fellow agents took the opportunity to needle the rookie. They could tell he was a little shook by the summons and it was their turn to pull jokester Mathews's chain for a change.

"Pink slip . . . "

"What did you do, kiddo?"

"Oooooooooooh, boy, you're in *trouble.*"

"Be sure to ask if you can get a recommendation. Jacksonville PD's looking for some good traffic guys."

Mathews knocked on Kneir's door and heard the boss's voice: "Come in, Doug." Mathews pushed open the door and his jaw nearly hit the floor. Sitting there with Kneir were squad chief Chris Graham, Mark Devereaux, and Rick Dent. If this were a mob movie, and these were mobsters, this would be the scene where some hapless goombah notices the plastic tarp on the floor seconds before a .22 bullet is pumped into the back of his head. Sensing impending doom, Mathews threw up both hands and jokingly said, "Whatever I've done, I'm sorry!" But in the back of his mind, he still worried about what might unfold in the moment.

Kneir, Graham, Devereaux, and Dent, their faces turned to granite, sat unmoved. They maintained the stony silence for as long as they could, but it was impossible. Mathews looked so desperate, so pathetic, so . . . sad. Graham was the first to break. "Oh, fer cryin' out loud, Doug. Relax."

"Y'know, Doug, that, right there, is conduct unbecoming of an FBI agent," said Kneir.

Rick Dent, always the straight arrow, gave a little smile.

It registered with the rookie that his colleagues were giving him a little taste of his own boisterous medicine. "You got me," said Mathews.

"What we got is good news for you," said Kneir. "You're going undercover."

"Wait. What?" asked Mathews.

"This just might work," said Dent.

Mathews's fun meter was pegging max, but he played it cool. The general protocol for undercover work within the FBI is that all agents undergo a rigorous two-week training and certification process at the agency's training facilities in Quantico, Virginia. The agents were all aware of this, including

Mathews. "When do I head out to Quantico?" he asked. Kneir, aware that under special circumstances, SAC authority could allow an agent to bypass the training, responded, "You're not. There isn't time."

"Just want to make sure you guys realize Doug doesn't know anything about undercover other than what he's seen on TV, right?" asked Rick Dent.

The plan was to have Mathews get a crash course on going undercover from Janet Pellicciotti, the head of the undercover division at the Jacksonville office. They wanted to surround Mathews with other agents who had done undercover work before to fill out the production team. Jan Garvin was called in to be the videographer. He was a twenty-year air force vet who'd joined the FBI in 1992. Prior to working several undercover operations, he'd been responsible for filming training videos for the bureau. In addition to Garvin, two other seasoned agents would take on the roles of sound and lighting.

Even with the crew now in place, there was still the concern that none of the agents had ever posed as part of a film crew representing a major American corporation. The FBI was going to need someone with actual experience in the world of corporate publicity to help guide the sting. To make it real.

Amy Murray, the twenty-eight-year-old head of press and publicity for the Monopoly winners, was working quietly at her desk when her immediate supervisor entered and asked her to come with him to the security department. *This can't be good*, thought Amy. Like Doug Mathews, Amy Murray made her own Walk of Shame.

It was a rare thing for the FBI to go outside the agency on something like this. It was even more rare to involve a civilian.

And it almost never happened that a civilian with absolutely no prior experience was drafted to go undercover as part of a sting operation. It could be dangerous.

When Rob Holm laid out the plan to the young publicist, he cautioned her, "Amy, you don't have to do this. I don't want to scare you or discourage you, but the reality here is that things could go sideways. People facing arrest, people facing doing time, they can all get desperate and when desperation sets in, anything can happen."

Amy Murray, despite a blond, bubbly exterior—like so many of the happy, happy people who work in communications and publicity—had some steel in her spine. After a night to sleep on it, she called Holm first thing the next morning. "I'll do it," she told him without hesitation. "I mean, there's going to be FBI agents with me. What could possibly go wrong?" She had not met Doug Mathews yet.

Back in the Jacksonville office, the bones of the sting in place, a brainstorming session was underway to name the operation. For all kinds of reasons, these things were always given some sort of official designation. Agents tried to come up with cool, catchy names for whatever they were working on. Dent, Mathews, Kneir, and Graham sat in Kneir's office and kicked around several potential names: Operation Hamburglar, Operation Stale Fries, Operation Fallen Arches, Operation Unhappy Meal. As they bounced the names around, Dent brought up a good point: "Hey, we're going to be working *with* McDonald's. Let's make sure we don't piss them off with a stupid name involving their company."

At the time, a new game show had recently debuted on television and had captured the nation's attention. It was called

Who Wants to Be a Millionaire and it was so popular, it ran nightly over a two-week, heavily hyped prime time period. It was hosted by beloved presenter Regis Philbin.

The format was simple: contestants were asked a series of fifteen questions, each more difficult than the last, and were then asked to pick a response after being presented with multiple-choice answers. Host Regis Philbin came armed with a phrase that caught on immediately. As the contestants mulled over their choices, a countdown began until Philbin demanded the player's "final answer." It was dramatic.

The current McDonald's Monopoly game was tied in and branded for the then-popular TV game show *Who Wants to Be a Millionaire*. The show's tagline had wormed its way into the national consciousness, and now into the FBI's naming convention. It worked.

Operation Final Answer was a go. It was official.

– 5 –

'CAUSE YOU'RE JUST LUCKY!

APRIL 2001...

Despite being given "SAC authority" to go undercover, Doug Mathews—and civilian Amy Murray—still had to undergo an intense compact training session. Nobody was going into the field without at least a few hours of training. It wouldn't be safe. Of course, there was always the risk—no matter how small—that things could spin out of control in an instant.

Doug Mathews—now "video director Doug Dewitt"—was amped for his very first undercover assignment. He was practically vibrating with excitement. He wanted to get this thing right. Mathews, armed with a new persona, had been bitten by the acting bug. He wanted to play his role as the bogus director of a bogus film crew to the hilt. And this portrayal had to be seamless and bulletproof, he thought. He wanted people to see him and say, "That Doug Dewitt. Now *that's* a video director!"

The only problem was that Doug Mathews didn't know diddly about video production or video directors.

He wondered what he should wear. "Clothes make the man." He couldn't sell his undercover identity without looking the part. He conferred with Amy Murray, who knew everything Doug Mathews did not.

"I have this really great gold suit," Mathews told her. "It's like I'm a giant golden French fry or the Golden Arches King. It's pretty versatile."

Amy was skeptical. "That's really not the norm, Doug. I mean, you *could* wear something like that, but it would be . . . unusual."

"Well, okay, Amy," said Doug. "You're the expert. What do you suggest?"

Amy smiled. "Most directors dress like they just stepped off a golf course. A pair of comfortable shoes, a pair of khakis, and a polo shirt is kind of the standard uniform for directors in this industry."

Doug Mathews feigned disappointment to learn he was going to dress like an average Joe. "Can I at least pop the collar of the polo shirt?" he asked.

"Yes, that would be perfect," allowed Amy and Doug visibly brightened.

"Great," said Mathews.

Amy knew she was integral to the sting. With the armature of the plan in place, it was imperative to craft the magic that would make it believable to anyone on the outside. In Amy's hands, they might be able to pull it off. She would be able to make this thing look like the real deal.

"So how does a video crew travel around?" wondered Mathews. "Does the director travel in a different car?"

"We can all drive together. Usually, a video crew travels around in a van because you can fit a lot of stuff in there: your props, if any, your crew, your equipment, all the stuff you'd normally use to complete a shoot: the cameras, the sound stuff, microphones, all that stuff," Amy told him.

"Video crew's like a crack commando unit: it's small, it works fast, and it travels light. Self-contained. In and out."

Doug Mathews liked the sound of that. He was impressed with Amy's skill set.

"The other thing is that, with McDonald's anyway, we don't have an in-house team. We outsource."

"So we need to set up an entirely fake video company?" asked Mathews. He was thrilled. He had ideas how to approach this.

"Yes," Amy confirmed.

"I'm on it!"

Following his conversation with Amy, Mathews went back to Rick Dent. "We're going to need a few things," Mathews told his partner. "We have to invent a whole video company because McDonald's uses outside contractors."

The FBI also had another task for Amy. Since they needed as much evidence as possible, Mathews gave Amy a briefcase. Inside it was a large tape recorder that hooked directly to her cellular phone. "If any winner calls, you need to tape it," he said. Everywhere she went, the trusty Samsonite was by her side. Even when she went to Jackson Hole, Wyoming, for a friend's wedding. When a call came in, she snuck into the bathroom in her bridesmaid's dress.

Back in Jacksonville, Tom Kneir, Chris Graham, and Mark Devereaux were called in and apprised, and another brainstorming session began. They, too, were unfamiliar with video teams and film crews.

"So, as Amy explained it to me, what they do is, they cram into a van and go where they're needed. Like a SWAT team or a cavalry unit. Mobile. Highly mobile. We're going to need a van," Mathews explained.

"That won't be a problem," said Special Agent in Charge Kneir.

Chris Graham had a concern. "What are we going to call it?"

"Call what?" asked Kneir.

"The company," said Graham.

"Yeah, we gotta build this up from the tires. It's got to seem real," said Mathews.

"Suggestions?" asked Dent.

They all sat in silence, thinking.

"C'mon, guys, how hard is it to come up with a name for a sham production company," said Chris Graham.

"That's it!" said Mathews. "It's perfect."

Everybody else in the conference room looked confused.

"Shamrock Productions. It's perfect," he said.

"It's Irish?" wondered Rick Dent.

"No. It's a reference to McDonald's Shamrock Shake," explained Mathews, who was an expert in all things McDonald's.

In fact, the Shamrock Shake came into existence through Amy Murray's dad Jim Murray, the former general manager of the Philadelphia Eagles. When the daughter of one of the team's players was diagnosed with leukemia, Murray created a promotion with McDonald's with a portion of the funds raised going to what became the Ronald McDonald House, the company's charitable arm. Because the shake sprang into existence right around Saint Patrick's Day—and as a nod to the Eagles' team colors—it was green.

"Don't you ever eat at McDonald's? Think Saint Patrick's Day. McDonald's does a seasonal promotional item called the Shamrock Shake. It's green. It's super popular," explained Mathews.

"It's green?" asked Dent, somewhat incredulously. Mathews couldn't believe he had to explain what he considered a pop culture sensation. "Is it mint flavored or something?"

"No. It's just a vanilla shake with green coloring."

"So a green vanilla shake?"

"Yes. A green vanilla shake."

"Are they good?"

"If you like vanilla, Saint Patrick's Day, shakes, or green, then yes they're good."

"You two are giving me a headache with this," said an exasperated Tom Kneir.

"Let's just go with Shamrock Productions, can we?" suggested Chris Graham. "Doug's got a good name for our production company here."

"You're going to need a slogan to go with that," said Mark Devereaux. "Company branding, let's say. I'm seeing something in my mind like 'Because You're Just That Lucky!'"

"You know when we get magnetic signs to put on the van, we get charged by the letter," noted Graham. "Let's remember taxpayer dollars. We can cut that down. I'm thinking ''Cause You're Just Lucky!' That's six letters we don't need. Save a few bucks."

"That actually works better," said Mathews. "It's more casual. It's friendlier. It'll put everyone we talk to at ease!"

"That's it, then. We got it. 'Shamrock Productions. 'Cause You're Just Lucky!' I'll get you your van," said Tom Kneir.

Found in the Rhode Island FBI office's motor pool, the van was a well-used, white 1997 Ford Econoline fitted with ordinary Florida-issued license plates instead of the US government plates typically found on FBI vehicles. Depending upon the location of the targets, the team would pull the vans from the nearest field office rather than bouncing all over the country in a Jacksonville-issued vehicle. A sign that read SHAMROCK in a black serif font and PRODUCTIONS, curiously in black sans serif letters within a clover-green rectangle. It looked like about fifteen seconds worth of thought went into making it, but it was a rush job and there wasn't time to get too artistic with it. "Quick and dirty," is how Mathews put it. They were ready to roll.

Michael Hoover had no idea that a Category 4 shitstorm was brewing and tracking straight for him.

– 6 –

A DAY AT THE BEACH

Heard of a van loaded with weapons, packed up and ready to go.
—TALKING HEADS, "LIFE DURING WARTIME"

MAY 2001...

This was no party. This was no disco. And there certainly was no foolin' around. This was serious business as the white, somewhat beat Ford E-150 van, marked "Shamrock Productions" bounced down a boulevard in Westerly, Rhode Island. If this were a movie, the Talking Heads' song "Life During Wartime" would pump on the soundtrack as the team rode silently—and a little jittery—on the way to its first assignment: an interview with McDonald's Monopoly newly minted millionaire, Michael Hoover.

Westerly was close to some of the best tribal gaming in New England. It was only a thirty-minute drive to the vast Foxwoods Resort Casino, one of the biggest on the East Coast and just over the state line in Connecticut. Million-dollar McDonald's Monopoly winner, Westerly resident, and prime suspect Michael Hoover was the pit boss at Foxwoods.

Amy Murray had other things on her mind. She had volunteered for this operation, and even with her crash-course training and her faith in the skills of the FBI team, she wondered what lay in store. She kept reminding herself to be sure to always address Doug Mathews as "Doug Dewitt" instead of "Agent Mathews." She was nervous. She didn't show it, but she felt it. She was a civilian and about to engage in her very first and likely only undercover operation. She could almost hear her own blood pumping through her ears.

Mathews's nerves were running hot too, but like Amy, he tried to present a cool exterior. Field agent and videographer Jan Garvin was calm. However, Doug wasn't aware that on one of his last undercover assignments Garvin had mistakenly brought a sandbag to "set" that was labeled "FBI." Luckily before anyone caught it, Garvin grabbed a Sharpie and quickly turned it into "ABC." The other undercover agents—whose identities remained hidden—handled the lighting and sound. The truth was that the van was full of a palpable electric energy. While trouble or violence seemed unlikely in this instance, there was always the chance something could go wrong and the whole operation could spin off into any number of dangerous situations.

After all, what did they really know about Michael Hoover? They were going in with only some very basic knowledge about the man. The casino complex, located just across the Rhode Island state line in Ledyard, Connecticut, in the Mashantucket Pequot Tribal Nation, boasted two hotel towers with over two thousand rooms, and several restaurants and buffets including a Hard Rock Café. But the real draw was the gaming and Foxwoods boasted 250 tables for blackjack, poker, roulette, and craps. If table games weren't your thing, there were 5,500 slot machines and video poker terminals to choose from.

As pit boss, Hoover managed a collection of gaming tables on the casino floor aka "the pit." The job generally broke down so that the typical pit boss oversaw a collection of eight to twelve blackjack and poker tables or six to eight craps and roulette tables or some combination of the two.

A pit boss didn't just step into the position. There was a career arc that generally required several years spent as a dealer, followed by another few years as a floorman. The floormen supervised the table games and settled any disputes that might arise among the players. They were also responsible for keeping the tables filled because an empty chair loses money for the house. After five to seven years of supervising dealers and tables, a good floorman might move up to pit boss where they could make about $70,000. While dealers could receive tips from players, it was considered a major breach of etiquette to tip the pit bosses. Despite earning a decent wage, the team learned Hoover had a mildly checkered financial history, which included bankruptcy.

It really wasn't much for the team to go on to get a measure of their target, but it was better than nothing. Still, to Doug Mathews, it felt like going in blind. Amy had been brought aboard partly because she was the main corporate contact for the "winners" and was familiar to all of them, including Michael Hoover. She assumed that the undercover agents had concealed weapons on them or in their equipment cases, which gave her some comfort. Truth be told, they didn't, which is more common than one might think. Even a gun in an ankle holster could be visible when sitting and make things more dangerous.

As the Shamrock Productions van turned onto Michael Hoover's street, the agents knew that the battered brown Extreme Plumbing panel van parked a few doors down from

Hoover's address wasn't there to fix someone's clogged drain. This was their backup. Sitting inside was a group of well-armed agents who would monitor the situation remotely. If they heard the phrase "I don't feel that great. Might be something I ate," they would come in like a cavalry charge.

They parked the Shamrock Productions van in front of Hoover's small, nondescript, completely average brick house and began to offload personnel and equipment.

Amy smoothed the fabric of her slacks and blouse and Mathews asked, "Are you feeling okay? Good to go?" He was normally a joker, but now Mathews was all business and coolly professional. "How do I look? Directorial?" he asked Amy.

"Here," she said as she reached up and popped the collar of his polo shirt. "Now you're a director," she said. Mathews couldn't help but smile. Amy had just made a joke. *This civilian was alright*, he thought. She was calm under pressure and was, apparently, on his wavelength when it came to humor. "Alright, everybody. Showtime!" said Mathews and the team approached Michael Hoover's front door.

Just as Mathews was about to knock, the door opened and he was face-to-face with his quarry. Up close, Michael Hoover was far from intimidating. He was middle-aged and heavyset, and seemed to be flushed and out of breath just from the exertion of answering the door.

Mathews and Amy slipped into character. "Michael Hoover, the Million Dollar Man!" crowed Mathews, his naturally boisterous personality now front and center. Amy, holding a clipboard with notes like she normally would, was a little more low-key but still perky. "Congratulations on your win, Mr. Hoover. Where can we set up?" Behind her, Garvin and the other agents carried camera, cables, sound equipment, and a giant cardboard prop check from McDonald's made out to Michael Hoover in the amount of one million dollars. It was signed by McDonald's spokesmodel Ronald McDonald. They shifted placidly under the weight of their loads like draft horses . . . just like a real-life, silently surly, nonunion video crew would do.

Hoover ushered them into his tiny living room and the crew went about setting up their equipment. Mathews and the team scouted all potential exits. If things went south, Amy had been told to get behind Mathews and follow him. But as they made small talk with Hoover, the potential for anything popping off did not seem likely.

"Why don't we do the interview right here on the couch?" Amy proposed.

"Will we have enough light here?" asked Mathews, now fully invested as Shamrock Productions director Doug Dewitt.

"Oh, this'll be perfect," assured Amy. Garvin set up the camera. He was rolling. Everything was ready. She turned to Michael Hoover. "Are you good to go?"

"Uh, sure. Yeah," said Hoover, sounding a little unsure and hesitant. Was he just suffering from a case of stage fright or was he nervous because he had committed a crime?

"Uh, Amy? Why don't we start by having Michael here tell us his story?" Mathews began to feel his way into the role of video director. Amy and Hoover, scrunched knee to knee across from each other in the cramped living room, made small talk while Doug Mathews set up the shot with the giant cardboard check behind them. "We all good?" asked Mathews. Before anyone could answer, he said in a loud, confident voice, "Action!"

Amy faced Hoover and began. "Well, why don't you tell us the story about how you won at the Monopoly game? In your own words." Michael was ready.

"Day started out pretty peaceful. It was a day off, went to the beach for a while, fell asleep, and when I woke up, the wind picked up and I was covered in sand, not a lot, just a little so I picked up my belongings to head down to the water to wash my legs off and I was a little klutzy, the *People* magazine and towel fell out of my bag, fell into the water and got all wet." Mathews noticed that as their suspect hesitantly told his story, Hoover's face grew redder. Hoover had also started to glisten with a sweaty sheen. He stumbled through odd details of his story, claiming to throw away his ruined magazine and stop at a store for food, seeing the same *People* magazine he never had a chance to read, getting home, finding the insert and peeling off the million-dollar instant prize. His reaction was unenthusiastic, forced. "Wow. Is this for real?" he flatly exclaimed.

Mathews interrupted. "Okay, that was great. Now, you mentioned that you stopped at the store. Is that nearby?"

"Uh . . . yes. Not far from here," said Hoover.

"Can you take us there? Let's go to the store. Maybe we can reenact it. This will be great!"

Amy and the crew looked at one another. Making a side trip—making any kind of trip—was not in the playbook. The crew broke down the equipment and gathered up the giant cardboard check. "Michael, we'll follow you."

This was extremely unusual. The veterans on the crew were hesitant, but there wasn't much they could do in this situation but play along. Outside in the brown Extreme Plumbing panel truck, the FBI agents who had been monitoring the audio looked at each other. "What the fuck is this crazy Mathews guy doing?" Mathews had been "trained" for this assignment by Janet Pellicciotti, the head of the undercover division at the Jacksonville office, but Doug was being Doug and played things his own way. Everybody else was just along for the ride.

They watched as Hoover rolled his nondescript sedan down the street followed closely by the Shamrock Productions van. They gave them a little space before they pulled away from the curb to go after them.

Hoover led them to a nearby McQuade's Marketplace. Owned by Michael J. McQuade, the market was part of a three-store New England chain with the two other stores in Mystic, Connecticut, and Jamestown, Rhode Island. In addition to groceries, McQuade's also featured an on-site bakery and a hot foods deli that specialized in New England delicacies like lobster rolls, battered and fried clams served with coleslaw and lemon wedges, and root vegetable hash. And, of course, it sold *People* magazine.

Once again, the crew set up in front of the store in the parking lot. Shoppers entering and exiting the market slowed to see what the commotion was when Doug Mathews, who had really started to get into the role of director, shouted, "Action!" Garvin quickly interrupted, "Hold on, I haven't started rolling." He quickly hit record.

"Michael, for the camera, tell us what we are doing here and what you are holding," prompted Amy.

"This is where I got the . . . uh . . . *People* magazine. And inside was the Monopoly game with the instant million-dollar winner. And it was great. Fantastic," said Michael, with feigned enthusiasm while holding the magazine.

It was obvious he was nervous and uncomfortable. Like a bad actor reading a line, it felt canned and rehearsed. Mathews tried to put him at ease telling him he was doing great, but he also had him repeat his story, to see if he'd mess up.

"Now what beach were you at when you ruined your original copy of the magazine?" Mathews asked.

"It's right down the street," said Hoover. "Not far at all. It's a . . . uh . . . nice beach."

"Do you know the name of the beach?" asked Amy.

"Uh . . . well, you know, I . . . uh . . . I just call it 'the beach.' I'm not sure what the official name is supposed to be," answered Michael Hoover. He seemed to be getting more rattled as Doug Mathews and Amy Murray continued to ask him the little details about his supposedly unexpected and sudden windfall.

"Why don't you show us? I'd love to see the beach, wouldn't you, Amy?" Mathews asked. She did not want to see the beach and was hoping this was the end of the field trip.

As Michael Hoover slipped the key into his ignition to lead the team to the beach, he was a little bugged that in order to collect his money he had to sign a waiver that would allow McDonald's to use him for promotional purposes. He couldn't refuse. He had to play along. He led the team from McQuade's Marketplace down Beach Street for a couple of miles until he took a slight jog to the left onto Winnapaug Road through the dunes, marshes, and sparse seagrasses of the Lathrop Wildlife Refuge until Hoover hit Atlantic Avenue and made a right that took them all—including the backup agents in the Extreme Plumbing vehicle—into the parking lot of Westerly Town Beach.

Amy was struggling to walk in the sand in her heels, so she took them off. The wind was strong, blowing her hair everywhere. She managed to keep her cool as Garvin got the camera ready. "Is this the trash can where you tossed your original magazine?" asked Amy.

"Oh, that's a great question, Amy!" said Mathews. "Hey, Michael, tell us the story again about how you ruined the magazine and threw it away. And, if you can, really lean into it. Make it exciting!"

Hoover, standing next to a trash can, retold his story in his hesitant, unsure manner.

"Okay, gang!" said Mathews. "Let's get some stuff with Mike holding the big check. I want to get that in the shot."

Once again, the crew set up and Amy and Michael Hoover—now holding the million-dollar prop check—took their marks on the sand. Just as Garvin finished grabbing some artsy shots, they were interrupted by a blur of stringy hair, pasty white skin, and faded denim. A drunken beachgoer in a pair of cutoff jeans bum-rushed Hoover, ripped the check from his hands, and ran off down the beach with a loud "Whoo!"

Acting more on instinct than anything else, Mathews stopped pretending to be a video production director and went into full law enforcement mode. Without hesitation, he took off after the thief. His loafers slowed him down, but having spent a fair amount of time in the gym lifting weights and doing cardio, it didn't take him long to catch the young man. He tackled him and wrested back the check.

"What the fuck, man?" slurred the would-be thief.

"What are you doing, dude?" asked Mathews, genuinely wanting to know.

"Those were a lot of zeros. I'm drunk as hell. Whoo!"

Mathews realized he was dealing with an idiot. He also realized that video directors normally didn't go into cop mode to chase after prop checks. That was probably what the crew guys were supposed to do, he thought. He brushed himself off, helped the drunk to his feet, and walked back to the group like a bantam rooster with a huge grin on his face. "Did you get that on camera?" he asked. "Okay. Let's go back to Mikey's place and shoot some wraparounds and pickups and we'll be done."

Once again, everyone piled into their vehicles and took another drive. "This fuckin' guy!" muttered the exasperated backup agents in the Extreme Plumbing van. This wasn't exactly what they were used to.

Now set up on Michael Hoover's front lawn, with Hoover holding the giant check, Amy asked him a few more questions and received halting, hesitant answers from the target. Mathews popped the last question. "Michael, you've won one million dollars. What on earth do you plan to do with all that cash?" he asked.

Hoover thought about it for a second and then answered for the first time without any stumbling. "I'm gonna buy a boat."

"Boat's gotta have a name," said Mathews trying to make some small talk. "What'll you call her?"

Again with no hesitation, Hoover blurted out the name he planned to christen the as-yet-to-be-acquired boat with: "*Ruthless Scoundrel!*"

Figuring it had been a wildly successful day—they had Hoover on tape telling his improbable story of how he "won" his prize, which could be used as evidence in court as soon as they figured out how he had *really* gotten the winning game piece—the team packed up and headed home.

Meanwhile, back in the wire room in Jacksonville, Florida, baby agent Tim Adams captured a call from Michael Hoover's phone. Hoover had rung up an acquaintance, a colorful character named A.J. Glomb that the team would soon learn had a long criminal history that included convictions for drugs and smuggling during South Florida's "cocaine cowboys" years and several years of prison time.

Agent Adams heard Glomb ask Hoover, "How did it go?"

Hoover, the hesitancy he had shown during his interview with the team now gone, laughed and said, "I got one over on those idiots."

"So it went good?" asked Glomb.

"Yeah, it went great." Michael Hoover went on to say how attractive he thought Amy was and how much she liked him.

In a debriefing meeting back in Jacksonville, Tom Kneir, Chris Graham, Mark Devereaux, and Rick Dent listened to Doug Mathews once again tell the story of how the local drunk snatched the prop check and how Mathews—more like Superman than an ordinary FBI agent—ran him to the ground. Everyone had a laugh. Mathews most assuredly knew how to tell a funny story.

"What we really need to do now is get the past winners of the game on camera. There's no telling what we'll find out," said Mathews. "I'm more than happy to go back undercover. That shit worked!"

Rick Dent suppressed a smile. His rookie had done good.

"That's not a bad idea," agreed Mark Devereaux.

"You're going to go around to all these people's houses and talk to them? Won't that take a lot of time?" wondered Rick Dent.

"Like I've been saying," said Mathews, "how about we hold a super reunion of past winners in . . . *Las Vegas* . . . and let them come to us?" asked Doug Mathews.

Special Agent in Charge Tom Kneir still didn't like the idea. "Doug, do you have any idea how expensive that would be?" Chris Graham began to riff on the proposal. "Maybe we're looking at it wrong. Who says we actually have to go to Vegas?" he said. "We just have to pretend there's going to be a reunion of winners there."

Mathews, spitballing off Graham, said, "Yeah, we can tell them we need to come to their house before that and film them telling the story of how they won, so we can put it up on the big screen at the reunion with balloons and confetti."

Graham liked where this was heading. "You can have all the confetti and balloons as you want there . . . because 'there' is just in your imagination. So many of them are right here in Jacksonville. This won't require much to make it happen," he said.

Kneir couldn't help but join in. "We'll print up some post-cards with, 'Reunion of Champions' or something like that. 'McDonald's wants you for an all-expenses-paid Las Vegas weekend. Come celebrate with all the winners.' We'll have them RSVP or call us to confirm, and then we'll schedule the interview."

"What if they don't come?" wondered Chris Graham.

"Too bad," laughed Doug Mathews. "They signed the waiver. They *have* to. We can have Amy at McDonald's talk to all these past million-dollar winners and get them on board!"

"Unless they ignore the postcard."

Mathews didn't think that was possible. "They claimed a fake game piece for a million bucks, there is no way they'll pass up a free trip to Vegas. Hell, I was hoping for a free trip to Vegas. But I'm a team player. After they get the postcard, we'll just call them up and remind them it's required."

"Alright, then. Excellent work, guys," added Kneir, ending the debriefing.

As the agents gathered up their belongings, Rick Dent asked Doug Mathews, "Why are you so hot for Vegas?"

"Because people love Las Vegas, Rick. It's *fun*. Same reason you all love having me around."

- 1 -

MEET THE COLOMBOS

1995...

There was a whole lot of bad news in 1995, and if you watched television, there was no escaping it: Tejano superstar Selena was murdered by the president of her fan club. Anti-government terrorists Timothy McVeigh and Terry Nichols set off a truck bomb at the Alfred P. Murrah Federal Building in Oklahoma City, Oklahoma, and took 168 lives and injured 680 more. The Unabomber claimed another victim, Gilbert Murray, a lobbyist in Sacramento, California. Former football star O. J. Simpson was found not guilty of the murders of his former wife Nicole Brown and her friend Ronald Goldman. In the San Diego suburb of Clairemont, methamphetamine-addled army veteran Shawn Nelson stole an M60A3 Patton tank from the local National Guard armory and went on a twenty-three-minute, televised rampage of destruction. The ride didn't end until San Diego Police Department officers managed to climb atop the tank and open the hatch with a pair of bolt cutters. When Nelson still refused to surrender, his command was terminated with extreme prejudice.

75

However, the unrelenting bad vibes floating over the air-waves were punctuated with an exclamation point of relief in the form of a happy, uplifting, almost inspirational TV com-mercial from McDonald's. It was a spot for the company's McDonald's Monopoly promotional game.

In the commercial, the near-orgasmic joys of American consumer culture were on full display: a blond woman grin-ning from ear to ear on the saddle of a speeding Sea-Doo as it spewed an impressive rooster tail of water; an excited kid enthusiastically playing the difficult-to-acquire Sega Genesis video game console; a portly Italian-looking guy wearing a silly grin and waving a giant cardboard key over a brand-new Dodge Viper. The TV spot held open the possibility that any-one—even you—could be a winner.

And who wouldn't want to win a Dodge Viper? It was *the* hot car to have in the mid-1990s: an American-made, two-seat super car. Everybody wanted one. On the West Coast, there were stories in the press about how Jenna Jameson somehow jumped the waiting list and managed to land a blue Viper—much to the despair of many car enthusiasts who lacked the juice that came with being the number one porn star in the entire world.

The Viper featured Dodge's V10 engine, a ten-cylinder monster developed with input from Lamborghini. There was no air-conditioning, a canvas roof, and vinyl and zippered win-dows like on a Jeep Wrangler. It was a street-legal version of a GT racer, but did include a few creature comforts like adjust-able seats with lumbar support, an AM/FM in-dash cassette deck, and carpeting. To save on weight, there were no airbags. That may have been a mistake since the Viper's basics made it an awful lot of car for the average driver to handle. It was tricky—and potentially dangerous—for untrained motorists to take the car up to high speeds.

The excited winner in the McDonald's commercial—who looked like he might have trouble fitting himself into the driver's slim-fit cockpit—was Gennaro Colombo. Going on camera as the purported winner of a flashy car in a TV commercial that played nonstop across the nation was probably not the best decision he could have made for himself. There was a reason.

Gennaro "Jerry" Colombo was mob royalty.

The Colombos were one of the infamous Five Families, a cartel of New York City's most powerful Italian Mafia organizations. Originally known as the Profaci family, its roots could be traced back to the late 1920s when it was formed as a bootlegging enterprise under Joe Profaci during Prohibition. Profaci's insistence on all members paying him tithes and tributes led many in the family to become disillusioned with his managerial style. By the late 1950s, the Profaci gang was torn apart by an internal war. It was resolved in the early 1960s when family member Joe Colombo Sr. reunited the feuding factions, took the reins of power from Profaci, and rebranded the family with his own name under the approval of the other four outfits. Out of the ashes of the Profaci family, the Colombo family was minted.

Low profiles and tight lips are the norm for mafiosi. Joe Colombo was different. He was a showman. He wasn't afraid of appearing in the press. He wasn't afraid of being identified as a Mafia chieftain, but that didn't mean he liked it. In 1970, with ethnic minorities forming anti-defamation groups to protest unfair treatment by law enforcement and negative portrayals in the media, Colombo formed the Italian-American Civil Rights League (IACRL). One of the group's first acts was to organize about thirty protesters to picket outside the FBI's

New York City office after Colombo's son Joe Colombo Jr. was arrested for melting coins into silver ingots. The league increasingly garnered press attention.

Joe Sr. was also instrumental in the filming of Francis Ford Coppola's adaptation of Mario Puzo's sprawling best-selling mob novel *The Godfather*. The production team found themselves up against New York City's byzantine filming regulations and mob-affiliated unions to say nothing of negative reactions from Italian Americans over what they imagined their portrayal in the movie would be like. Joe Sr. smoothed things out by acting as a liaison between the Italian American community and the film's producers. After persuading the filmmakers to remove the words "Mafia" and "la Cosa Nostra" from the script, the IACRL threw its support behind the production. Joe Sr. also aligned the group with radical Rabbi Meir Kahane's Jewish Defense League and even went so far as to provide bail for jailed JDL members.

It was astonishing. Mafia dons did not swan through the press as civil rights activists. They operated in the shadows and always did so quietly. On June 29, 1971, as Joe Sr. delivered remarks to a crowd gathered at Columbus Circle for the second Italian Unity Day rally, a gunman shot him three times with one round catching the Mafia don in the head. Amazingly, he survived. The shooter was immediately killed by Joe Sr.'s soldiers. Joe Sr., paralyzed and unable to speak but a few words, lingered on for the next seven years before he finally passed from a heart attack.

Jerry must have inherited some of that razzle-dazzle from his great-uncle. No longer based in New York City, Jerry was living in South Carolina where he ran an underground casino and had fingers in a lot of different pies, some legal, some not. Like Joe Sr., Jerry didn't believe in keeping a low profile. Jerry appeared in a television commercial that showed him as the winner of a Dodge Viper in the McDonald's Monopoly game. In our 2020 HBO documentary series, his wife Robin Colombo said, "My husband almost died from that commercial," implying that the McDonald's ad let his enemies know where Jerry was and that he had recently come into some money.

Gennaro still made frequent trips back to New York City on family business and was particularly close to his uncle Dominic, a top-ranking and influential member of the Colombo family. Robin Colombo speculates that it was Uncle Dominic who saved Jerry from being whacked when his public antics drew unwanted attention to the family. "He just couldn't help himself," said Robin Colombo.

Jerry cemented his reputation as the black sheep of the Colombo family when he married Robin. She was definitely not the traditional mobster's wife. For one thing, she wasn't Italian. For another, she was Southern.

It's helpful to remember there are two Souths. One is genteel: stately mansions framed by cypress trees and Spanish moss, sweet tea served on the verandas, and cotillion balls. The other is a little more relaxed: fuzzy slippers at the Waffle House, bourbon whiskey in a porcelain decanter that looks like Elvis, and WrestleMania. Robin really wasn't the cotillion type.

Robin Fisher came with some baggage. She was a free spirit with a pretty deep dating history that included an affair with guitarist Allen Collins of the band Lynyrd Skynyrd. But Robin was too independent and too much of a free spirit to settle down with a touring musician and become a "road widow," so she hustled when and where she could and took a job at an optical store in Daytona Beach, Florida.

One day, bored out of her mind—the world of eyeglass frames and progressive lenses was not as exciting as she had been led to believe—a big man, approximately the size of a deluxe refrigerator and definitely a Yankee, entered with a group of other large appliance–size men, also Yankees. Suddenly, Robin was no longer bored. *Who are* these *guys?* she wondered, intrigued. She'd never seen anyone like these fellows with their thick forearms, gold chains and crucifixes, diamond pinkie rings, and wildly colorful, extravagantly patterned, oversize sport shirts. They weren't local boys, that was certain. They walked in like they owned the place, and they deferred to the biggest among them, who just happened to be a patient. From the looks of it, though, he was a very special one.

Robin couldn't help but notice how her boss, the store manager, reacted to the entrance of this alien crew. "Oh my God! Do you know who that is?" he whispered. Robin watched as he greeted the group with a combination of friendliness mixed with obvious fear and panic. Robin noticed how the manager's reaction amused the visitors.

He quickly locked the front door, put the CLOSED sign in the window, and scurried to the back room of the store. Robin made eye contact with the group's leader and she felt an internal shiver of excitement. She tried to play it cool. She was not the type to chase after a man. With her big hair, high heels, and short skirts, men chased after *her.* She watched as the manager, still a nervous wreck, emerged from the back room with the patient's latest pair of eyeglasses and a brown paper sack stuffed full of what Robin suspected was cash. She acted like she didn't care when the big guy who had been handed the sack smiled at her and winked before leading his crew out the door. Robin swears to this day she heard Jerry say to his gang, "I'm gonna marry that girl!"

Once they had gone, the manager sagged. "That was Jerry Colombo!" he said.

Robin stared blankly. "Who?"

"Jerry Colombo! He's a gangster!"

"He didn't seem so bad," said Robin.

"You don't know. You've never heard of the Colombo crime family? From New York?"

"Maybe. I guess. That stuff doesn't impress me."

Later that evening, as Robin and the store manager began to close the place, the phone rang.

Robin answered. "Jacksonville Optics."

"Is this the good-looking, sexy lady who was working the floor this afternoon?" said the voice.

Robin knew who it was, but she played it close to the vest. "Maybe."

"I came in with my boys to pick up . . . an order. My name's Jerry Colombo and I was wondering if I can take you out some time."

"Tomorrow at eight," said Robin. "Pick me up at the store."

The following night, Jerry arrived and took Robin out for steaks and cocktails where he charmed her. He may not have been the best-looking man she had ever seen, but he had charisma and Robin was hooked. Their courtship was exciting. Robin was no stranger to the wild side of life, but she had never seen anything like this. At the time, Robin was carrying on a long-distance affair with a federal agent, but she was growing increasingly bored with him. Jerry was fun, although there was a little red flag, once out to eat, when he told her, "Let's switch seats. I can't sit with my back to the door."

She would accompany Jerry on his collection rounds to various businesses. People reacted to him with fear and respect. At a jewelry shop one day, after receiving his plain brown bag full of cash, Jerry reached in and peeled off a few dozen hundred-dollar bills for Robin. "Go nuts," he said. She soon found she was running out of room to store her growing collection of luxury shoes, clothes, and jewelry.

For his part, Jerry was intrigued by his little whirlwind of trouble. She was spunky and, as they said down South, "didn't take no mess." He had found his match . . . but Robin was going to be a difficult sell to Jerry's traditional Italian parents. He worried that Robin's sass would not be well received by the folks.

On their drive to their first family dinner, Jerry tried to prep Robin. "Look, you need to understand just how traditional and conservative my family is. In our culture, women act like women. They keep their eyes down and their mouths shut. They don't wear sexy clothes, they don't wear fuck-me high heels, and they do not smoke cigarettes."

Robin proceeded to crack a window and light her twelfth cigarette of the day. "Didn't you just hear what I said?" Robin didn't care and laughed, "Do they expect me to be a fucking virgin too?" They did.

The dinner went as well as could be expected.

Robin found herself frozen out of any chance at conversation when Jerry's parents refused to speak English at the table. Robin didn't speak Italian so she couldn't really tell if they were arguing or if this was just how Italians speak in their native tongue. That is until Jerry crashed a meaty fist on the table and said in English, "Fine. We'll leave." He got up and pulled Robin along with him to his car.

"What was that all about?" asked Robin.

"My dad smelled cigarette smoke on you. He's not happy. I fuckin' *told* you!"

"What about your mom?" asked Robin.

"She likes you even less—if you can believe such a thing is even possible."

"So they can kill people, but I can't smoke?" Robin wondered.

Jerry just shrugged as if to answer "Well, what can ya do?"

It all balanced out when Robin brought Jerry home to meet the Fisher family. If Jerry's family disliked Robin, the Fishers matched their disdain when it came to Jerry.

Faced with such disapproval from their families, Jerry and Robin did what any couple in a similar situation would do. They got married. The wedding could have been lifted straight from a Mafia movie. There was even an Italian flag hanging behind them at the dinner table. Despite their disapproval, both sets of parents attended the wedding and reception.

They soon became parents when Robin gave birth to their first child, a boy they named Gennaro Jr. This violated an Italian tradition in which the firstborn son is always named after the paternal grandfather. Jerry's parents reacted as expected. They were outraged to the point of cutting off all contact with their son and grandson. For Robin, this was ideal . . . until she saw the emotional toll it took on her husband. He may have been a mobster and tough as nails, but when it came to family, he was emotionally vulnerable. Robin could see the hurt in his face.

"If it's going to be this big of a fuckin' deal, let's just name the kid after your dad. Jeez," she said.

"Really?" said Jerry. He was surprised. His wife tended to dig in her heels when she felt she was being pressured. "You'd really do that for me?"

"Absolutely, baby. This is no way for you to live. This is no way for *us* to live."

And just like that, Gennaro Jr. became Francesco Gennaro "Frankie" Colombo. Jerry's parents immediately became doting grandparents. They even started treating Robin—as the mother of the beloved child—with some measure of respect. They may not have liked her, but they tolerated her.

"Your family is nuts," Robin advised her husband.

Robin was now a mob wife. She learned that the role included a frequently absent husband. Jerry's work kept him on the move. When he wasn't running collections, managing the underground casino in South Carolina, or doing whatever else a mobster below the Mason-Dixon Line did, he was making trips to visit Uncle Dominic "back home" in New York City.

On one of the trips, the older Colombo told Jerry, "I got this thing goin', and I could use some help."

"Always. You know that. What do you want me to do?"

"You ever heard of this McDonald's Monopoly game?" asked Uncle Dominic. "You see the commercials all the freakin' time."

"Oh yeah. I know what you're talking about."

"Well, I have a connection to the winning game pieces. What I need you to do is find people willing to be winners, collect the cash and prizes . . . and then kick back a taste to us because we're the ones who made it all possible."

"C'mon, Uncle Dominic. Is this legit? You have access to the real game pieces? Not some kind of fugazis. How?"

"How do we ever do anything? I know a guy."

"Who's this guy?"

"Just somebody I know. Do you think you can find people?"

"Why don't we just keep all the money for ourselves?"

"You want to pay taxes on a million dollars?"

"No."

"Look, if you're worried that it's bogus, take this game piece down to a McDonald's and see what happens." Uncle Dominic slid a game piece across the table with a finger.

Jerry left the meeting with it and found himself the winner of a brand-new Dodge Viper the very next day. To collect, of course, he had to sign a waiver that said he would go on camera to promote the game. "You probably shouldn't do that," cautioned Uncle Dominic.

"Too late now," said Jerry.

He knew Uncle Dominic was right to be cautious, but that just wasn't Jerry. He appeared in a commercial for McDonald's that was shown all over the country. People recognized him because of it. As far as the Viper went, Jerry opted to take the prize's $53,000 value instead and never actually took possession of the Viper. It was a cool car, but it was difficult for his three-hundred-pound frame to fit into such a tight space, and, as he told Robin, "I gotta give a taste to a guy and I can't chop up the car. What am I gonna do, give him a muffler?" It didn't matter. He still had his beloved red Corvette . . . until it "mysteriously" blew up in the Colombos' South Carolina driveway one day. Luckily, Jerry Colombo was not behind the wheel when it happened.

Jerry, now convinced his uncle Dominic had access to legitimate game pieces, was all in. What he wanted to know was who was Uncle Dominic's connection and, more important, if he could meet him. Uncle Dominic remained tight-lipped, while Jerry kept finding new "winners," and a steady flow of tax-free cash made its way into their pockets.

It was a good hustle. But Jerry wanted to meet the connection, and he wouldn't let it rest.

"So, c'mon, who is this guy, Uncle Dom?"

"You don't need to know, smart guy."

"You're kind of hurtin' my feelings here, Unc."

"Look, it's not you. It's him. Don't get me wrong, I love the guy—and I trust him—but he's goofy, this guy. Real careful about who he meets."

"What is he, some kind of cop?"

"Don't you worry about it."

"What if something happens to you, God forbid?"

"What are you sayin', kid? Your ol' uncle Dominic's healthy as a horse." To prove it, Dominic threw a lightning-fast left jab into Jerry's fleshy biceps.

"Ow," said Jerry, rubbing his sore arm with a hurt look on his face. "I'm just sayin' you never know. I mean, you're a very robust guy and whatever."

"Jerry Jacobson."

"Huh?"

"You wanna know my guy, that's my guy. Jerry Jacobson."

"He ain't Italian?"

"It's a big world out there, bambino."

Not long after their talk, Uncle Dominic was dead—of natural causes, it should be noted—and Jerry Colombo was partnered with Jerry Jacobson. Robin was brought into their confidence. It was a cozy relationship. Jerry and Robin had started calling Jacobson "Uncle Jerry" as a sign of respect and trust and it wouldn't be an exaggeration to say they had become friends. Several nights a week at the Colombo house in South Carolina, with little Frankie taking his first steps, the phone would ring. Robin would light a cigarette and grab an ashtray before answering.

"Uncle Jerry!" she'd holler. "Hold on, let me get him."

Jerry Colombo would lumber into the kitchen and take the phone. The two Jerrys would speak frequently. But Jerry had all kinds of side hustles Robin knew little about. Jerry Colombo at one point bragged of another food promotion that he supposedly got his hands on: M&M's.

The success McDonald's had with Simon Marketing's Monopoly did not go unnoticed by other big corporations. Mars Inc., the multinational candy conglomerate was gearing up for a Simon Marketing promotional game that was similar in some ways to the McDonald's Monopoly contest. The company was known for classic candies like the 3 Musketeers bar, Skittles, and chewing gum like Wrigley's Spearmint and Hubba Bubba as well as a freight load of others.

The contest involved finding an "imposter" M&M in a bag of the colorful hard-shelled chocolate candies. The winning candy was gray and instead of an "M" printed on it, it read WINNER. The odds of finding the special candy were said to be 247 million to 1. But there were some flaws in the game. For one, the candies themselves were subject to certain anomalies of the manufacturing process. Small numbers of M&M's came off the line looking gray or white naturally. There was a process to weed these out before the candies were bagged, but the sheer number of the individual candies needing to be inspected almost guaranteed these "albino" pieces slipped through. The contestant who found a genuine piece—gray and printed with

WINNER—also had to have the bag it came in, and that bag had a small game piece attached to it as well as some special printing.

As the new game got underway, Robin noticed the freezer in the Colombo kitchen began to fill with unopened bags of M&M's. "Where did all the candy come from?" she asked her husband. There was even a very special M&M tightly wrapped in aluminum foil with a Post-it that read DO NOT EAT!

"Baby, these M&M's ain't for you. Don't touch 'em. Don't even look at 'em. These are off-limits. Don't monkey around with 'em."

"Okay, okay. Don't have a heart attack. I'll get my own candy if I want it. Sheesh." One night, after smoking a little weed before bed, Robin got the munchies and almost ate the foil-wrapped candy in the freezer before she realized what she was doing.

It was true that Robin had a sweet tooth. It was also true that she was naturally curious. It was even more true that she was persistent. Jerry Colombo soon informed his wife of his plans to "infiltrate" not only the M&M's contest but the biggest, most famous corporate contest in the world: the Publishers Clearing House sweepstakes. This would be the jewel in the crown, the Holy Grail. The future was wide open. Robin lit another cigarette. Was this something he was cooking up with Uncle Jerry? Did any of these other promotion scams come to fruition? If there was any evidence to suggest either, we never found it. But Robin was convinced it was true.

GLORIA BROWN:
A REAL NICE LADY. YOU'D LIKE HER

APRIL 2001...

Gloria Brown, Black, working class, and in her early forties, was up early making breakfast in her home in Jacksonville, Florida. A radio on the kitchen counter softly relayed the local news including a sound bite from Republican banker and attorney Alexander Mann "Ander" Crenshaw, the newly elected US representative for Florida's 4th congressional district, which included Jacksonville.

Gloria's sister had come over for breakfast and Gloria busied herself making scrambled eggs, home fries, and toast. The phone rang and Gloria nearly jumped out of her shoes. She answered and was greeted by a cheerful voice.

"Hi, Gloria! It's Amy from McDonald's. How are you doing this morning? Good?" Fresh off her successful debut as the lone civilian member of the FBI's Shamrock Productions undercover team at Michael Hoover's home in Westerly, Rhode Island, Amy was leaning into her role.

Gloria, caught off guard, tried to sound neutral and casual. "Uh . . . uh . . . Yes. Thank you for asking. I'm fine . . . uh . . . and you?"

"I'm doing great!" answered Amy, powering up to Full Perkiness. "We have some really exciting things going on right now and we want you to be involved!"

"Uh . . . sure . . . okay," answered Gloria, still not certain what was going on.

"We sent you a postcard inviting you to one of the biggest McDonald's Monopoly promotional events we've ever done. Not sure if you've seen it yet Gloria, but we'd love to get you locked in to be a part of it all."

Amy continued, selling the completely bogus event as a combination New Year's Eve blowout, three-ring circus, and Fourth of July all wrapped into one.

Four years earlier, in 1997, Gloria had been interviewed on camera—as required by the waiver she had signed to collect her winnings. It was the typical production: confetti, clapping, big smiles, Ronald McDonald, and, of course, an oversize cardboard check signed by the corporate clown in the amount of a cool million dollars. But a closer look revealed something in Gloria's eyes and posture. It was subtle, but there was an unease that was unexpected from a newly minted millionaire. Of course, Gloria was just regular everyday people and this kind of fuss was generally not in most average folks' day-to-day, so maybe it was understandable.

"Can I pencil you in?" asked Amy Murray at the end of the line.

"Uh . . . "

"It's going to be all-expenses-paid, Gloria. You'll have a blast. I promise. And who doesn't love a free trip to Las Vegas?" Amy coaxed.

"Uh . . . Okay, Amy. Yes. I'll go. Put me down on the list."

"That's awesome, Gloria! You're gonna have so much fun!"

Gloria breathed a sigh of relief. For all the years since her 1997 win, she'd followed every rule, granted each request, and had done everything that was asked of her as a winner. Gloria didn't want to do anything that might jeopardize her million dollars—or at least what she'd received so far from her win—but it was a stressful situation. Four years was a long time to live with the knowledge that you're a fraud and the hammer of consequence could fall at any moment. Still, nothing had ever happened. There had been no midnight knocks on her door and it appeared that she had gotten away clean as a phony million-dollar winner of McDonald's Monopoly.

And then Amy pulled a straight-up *Columbo* move.

Just as Gloria thought the phone call was ending, Amy added, "There's just one more thing. What we're doing, Gloria, is going to all the winners' homes and doing short interview segments there, too. Then we're going to cut it all together and make a whole thing out of it. I'll be there, of course, when we shoot—"

Gloria interrupted, "When are you planning to do this?"

"Real soon, Gloria. Is that okay?"

"Uh . . . it's just . . . it's just . . ."

Amy sensed that she might be losing Gloria and that it might have something to do with a video crew coming to her home address. Thinking on her feet, Amy changed tactics on the fly. "We don't have to come to your house, Gloria, if that's a problem. How about this? We shoot at some place near you, and then you won't have to worry about a video crew traipsing through your house and inconveniencing you. Would something like that work better for you?"

"Uh . . . Sure . . . Uh . . . I guess that'd be okay," said Gloria.

"We'll just book the conference room at the Marriott or the Hyatt or someplace. That sound good?"

"I guess that'd be alright," answered Gloria.

When she hung up the phone, her sister asked if everything was okay. Gloria just nodded and the topic wasn't pressed. The women enjoyed a nice breakfast while they visited with each other. Gloria's sister eventually left to go about her daily errands and Gloria found herself alone at the kitchen table sipping her coffee. She was committed now.

On the appointed day, the Shamrock Productions crew arrived early and set up in the conference room of a modestly priced chain hotel that was geared to meet the needs of the business traveler. They waited for Gloria's arrival. Director Doug Dewitt—played by FBI Special Agent Doug Mathews in his Adidas sneakers and polo shirt—paced around the room as they waited. Amy, the civilian, was settling into her role. She had been through this once already with Michael Hoover. She studied the notes on her ever-present clipboard. The rest of the undercover team fiddled with all the equipment they barely knew how to use. Among them was Special Agent Doug Astralaga. Astralaga had been assigned by Chris Graham to handle the paperwork on the case. It wasn't the most exciting job. To toss him a bone for doing this thankless task, Kneir and Graham allowed Astralaga to join the Shamrock Productions team as the lighting guy, something he knew absolutely nothing about.

When Gloria arrived, Amy did her best to make her feel comfortable. "Gloria! So great to see you in person! Hey, can we get you a water or some coffee or anything?"

"No thanks, Amy. I'm good."

Doug Mathews sensed her nervousness. It was palpable. He tried to calm her. "Hey, Gloria! I'm Doug Dewitt. I'll be your director today. You look great! That outfit's going to pop on camera. Awesome choice! Are you all ready to be a star . . . again?"

"Uh . . . Yes, Mr. Dewitt," she answered.

"Mr. Dewitt? I ain't that formal. You can just call me Doug. How about that?"

"Uh . . . sure. Uh . . . Okay, Doug," said Gloria.

"Hey, can we get a light reading on Gloria's face?" Agent Mathews asked.

Special Agent Doug Astralaga approached the reluctant interviewee and pointed a light meter at her. He didn't turn it on because he didn't know how. Gloria was too nervous to notice anyway. "What's that thing for?" she asked.

The agent just smiled reassuringly and said, "Just something that'll make you look even more gorgeous on camera." It seemed to work. Gloria smiled for the first time since her arrival.

Among the props the team had brought along with them was a large poster that had all the names of past individual winners surrounding a McDonald's Monopoly gameboard. It was pretty typical Microsoft Paint clip art. Mathews proudly dragged it into the frame. "Are we up? Ready to go?" asked Mathews as he clapped his hands loudly. "Let's do this thing, gang!"

Everyone took their places and prepared to operate their equipment. Doug Mathews showed Gloria and Amy where to stand and then dramatically called, "And . . . *action!*"

Amy started the interview. "We're here with million-dollar McDonald's Monopoly winner Gloria Brown of Jacksonville, Florida! How are you doing today, Gloria?" She pumped energy and excitement into her delivery.

Gloria was more low-key despite the team's best efforts to keep things peppy and upbeat.

Director Dewitt called, "Cut! Cut!" He addressed Gloria. "I know it's weird and a little uncomfortable being on camera, Gloria, but can we have you tell your story with some enthusiasm? Bring it up from in here," advised Mathews, who slapped his abs under his polo. "You look beautiful. Everyone's gonna love you. Let's see that sparkling personality of yours!"

"Okay, I'm sorry. I'm just not used to all this attention," said Gloria.

"No problemo, señorita," said Mathews. "We'll just try it again. Ready? Alright. *Action!*"

Gloria began her story with about as much energy as before. "Well, I'm from Jacksonville, but, at the time I won, I was staying with friends in Hilton Head, South Carolina, while I explored . . . uh . . . employment opportunities. I went into a McDonald's and found the winning game piece. That's basically it."

Amy tried to keep Gloria talking. "Hilton Head's great. I love that town. How long were you there looking for work?"

"Not long at all. I didn't really get a chance to explore anything there. I was just looking for work."

Amy changed tactics. "Gloria, a million dollars is a huge windfall. What kind of impact has the win had on your life over the past four years?"

Gloria seemed to sag under the weight of that question. Everyone in the room noticed it. That's when Special Agent Mathews called "Cut!" and began to improvise. He had an idea up his sleeve. He asked if she remembered the actual McDonald's she went to when she'd won.

As the camera was rolling he handed her a photo. "We brought a picture of it for you. That's it, right? They didn't grab the wrong one did they?"

Gloria confirmed, "Yes. That's exactly the one."

Amy knew right away it wasn't.

"Gloria, would you mind autographing it for us? Anyone got a Sharpie?" Mathews asked as Gloria looked at it more closely.

Unfortunately, the photo was of a Jacksonville McDonald's, not the Hilton Head location where Gloria claimed to have received her prize. Mathews had pulled it from an old FBI surveillance file of an unrelated case and had it blown up just for this purpose.

Gloria, felt-tip pen in hand, nervously mumbled, "Thanks a million, McDonald's."

Amy gushed, "That's good! Thanks a million. That's good."

As she was signing it for the camera, the questions continued. "Do you remember who you spoke with at the counter?" Mathews asked. She couldn't recall. It's one of those things one would expect to remember if they actually won a million dollars.

Amy was a naturally sympathetic person and felt a twinge of empathy. "You're doing great, we're almost done." Mathews felt he had enough, but he also knew it was important to keep up the appearances that they were having fun, like one would expect for a McDonald's commercial highlighting the Vegas reunion. "Let's just get a couple more shots to finish this out," he said with his youthful spunk. He continued, "Why don't you hold your signed picture and say something like, 'I got my McDonald's millions in Hilton Head in South Carolina' but then stand up, point to your star and say, 'And it made me a millionaire!'"

Gloria was relieved to hear this ordeal was almost over and her mood lightened a little. "I . . . I can do that, Doug."

"I know you can! Let's get this done . . . and *action!*"

Gloria stumbled through a few attempts. It was clunky and admittedly—if not intentionally—cheesy, but she had to acquiesce. Her fake smile poorly hid an uncomfortable and guilty pain. Mathews then handed her a small Ronald McDonald doll and guided her through the final take. Gloria stood up and smiled into the camera, "Ronald and I . . . Ugh . . ." She fumbled a bit before finally nailing it. "Ronald and I will see you in Vegas. Thank you, McDonald's!"

Amy was impressed how Doug Mathews was embracing his role as a director. But she was conflicted and a little troubled. Yes, it was a rush to have caught someone on camera in what was obviously a lie, but something about Gloria made it clear she was no sophisticated criminal. Amy couldn't help but wonder, *How in the world did this poor woman get herself into such a mess in the first place?*

– 9 –

JUST CALL ME BUDDY

Like Gloria Brown, William Fisher was just plain folks. If he were a Hamburglar, he wasn't a very good one. Approaching retirement age, William was paunchy, nearsighted, and suffering from an advanced case of male-pattern baldness. He wore glasses to correct his poor vision: an oversize pair of amber-tinted aviators he continuously pushed back into place when the bridge slid down his nose. He wasn't how you'd picture a guy who allegedly boosted a million bucks from one of the largest corporations in the world. He was just . . . average.

If there was one thing that stood out about William Fisher, it was that he was sweating profusely. Was it because he wasn't accustomed to the pressures of being on camera? Or was it from the anxiety of repeatedly telling Amy Murray and Doug Mathews a completely fabricated story about how he came to win a million dollars?

"Uh, you guys can just call me Buddy," he told Amy just before the camera started to roll.

"Why don't we go back to the moment you won in New Hampshire, and can you just describe the day for us? What were you doing in the morning and at work?" Amy asked, confidently, as if she was now a seasoned undercover.

Buddy began to tell the camera, "It was a Sunday, so . . . there wasn't a lot of . . . work . . . to do. I was browsing through the Sunday paper, as . . . I . . . am . . . wont to do." He fumbled. If one had to guess, his heart must have been racing as fast as his thoughts. He was clearly struggling and sweating profusely. As he continued to share how he found the insert and pull-off tab, the sweat just kept pouring off him.

"Cut!" yelled Doug Mathews. "Hey, Amy, I'm getting a lot of shine off that head."

"Let's take a little pause," suggested Amy. They grabbed one of the hotel towels from the bathroom. "Pat yourself down a little. Doug says you're glistening."

"Sorry, sorry," said Buddy as if he had some way of controlling an involuntary response.

"No worries, Buddy!" reassured Agent Mathews. The basic strategy had him and Amy hoping to catch these former winners incriminating themselves, telling obvious lies, and tripping up as they were asked to give the fake video crew the details of the fraudulent wins. He was finding his naturally ebullient personality was a perfect fit for this gig.

Buddy Fisher removed his glasses, hooked them onto his shirt pocket, and gave himself a thorough pat down with a neatly folded pad of absorbent paper towels. He blotted for a while, and the towels became damp and clammy. He finished up and asked Amy, "Better?"

She smiled. "That's great. Doug? What do you think?"

"I think he looks like . . . *a million bucks!*"

Buddy sheepishly smiled.

Doug Mathews sharply clapped his hands and said, "Alright! Let's get this thing going. Buddy, let's just do what we were doing before. I'd like you to tell Amy the story of how you came to find that million-dollar game piece . . . and remember, it's an exciting story. I mean, c'mon, you won a million dollars playing McDonald's Monopoly, man! That's not an ordinary story. That's an *incredible* story! Pump up that energy when you're telling Amy how it happened. Make us *feel* it!"

There was only one problem: Buddy was a terrible liar. If there were a Terrible Liars Hall of Fame, Buddy's portrait would have been there . . . above a plaque that read "William 'Buddy' Fisher: The worst goddamn liar in the entire history of lying—but he tried." It wasn't really Buddy's fault he was a lousy liar. There had never really been a reason for him to develop a talent for it.

Buddy's life was pretty much set on an honorable, if predictable, path. He was a hard worker and rose through the navy's enlisted ranks to become a master chief petty officer. It was an achievement. As any master chief will tell you, they are the top 1 percent of the navy, because only 1 percent of all recruits ever make it to that rank. It's not an easy rise; the master chief is an expert in various nautical subjects and skills and he's knowledgeable in many others. He's also an advocate for the sailors in his charge. A good master chief is the captain's most valuable tool; he is responsible for onboard morale and discipline.

Buddy had married at eighteen and was a father of three. His master chief skills carried over into his family life. Buddy ran a tight ship and he ran a tight home. He was by the book and disciplined and he expected his wife and two daughters and son to toe the line. So when his favorite child, a wild, rambunctious girl named Robin, brought home her fiancé—a refrigerator-size, balding mobster in a garishly printed silk sports shirt and a pinkie ring with a massive diamond—Buddy wasn't happy. He had Gennaro Colombo sized up in about three seconds. But there wasn't much he could do. Robin was an adult. She was also headstrong. Buddy knew that if he tried to intervene, it would just strengthen Robin's resolve. For all her wildness and stubbornness, she had a close relationship with her dad, much closer than the one she had with her mother.

Despite a master chief's prime directive to keep everything smoothly sailing along, nothing was going that way back in the hotel conference room. Buddy Fisher once again launched into an undramatic, unsure retelling of how he had come to find a winning McDonald's Monopoly game piece and became an overnight millionaire.

Doug Mathews tried his best to help Buddy. "Okay, just take a breath, Buddy. This isn't a big deal. We're all friends here. So you were telling us you found the winning game piece . . . and *action!*"

Buddy sat before the camera like a deer about to meet the front grille of a speeding Kenworth W990 semitruck.

"Did you go to the McDonald's in town to say that you won?" Amy asked.

Buddy took a deep breath before he found himself drowning again. "No, I went to a lawyer." Buddy, like many of the winners had attempted to remain anonymous. But when asked who his lawyer was, his mind went blank. Perhaps because he never had one. Another gush of sweat found its way to his forehead. He pounded a glass of water. His eyes darted around the room like a man at the tail end of a six-day cocaine binge. *What could be making him do that*, Doug Mathews wondered, *other than lying?* Mathews was no psychologist, but he had great insight into human behavior. He was convinced of Buddy's guilt . . . but profuse perspiration and shifty eyes weren't going to be enough to convict anyone in a court of law. But in the Court of Agent Doug Mathews's Mind, Buddy Fisher was as guilty as sin. Mathews hoped that by keeping Buddy talking, he'd nervously blab something incriminating and concrete. When asked if any of his family played or won anything before, he said, "Yes. A cheeseburger." At the end, just like Gloria, Buddy was asked to hug a little Ronald McDonald doll and give his line inviting everyone to Vegas.

It only takes one moment of weakness for a man to get himself into trouble. That's what Buddy Fischer told himself. His mind flashed back to how his trip down easy street began. It had seemed innocuous at the time. Robin had come over for a visit. He was still not on board with her husband. Robin and Jerry had been working overtime to get both sets of parents to approve of the marriage. They had seen great success when they changed the name of their son Gennaro to Francis in the Italian tradition as a show of respect and honor to Gennaro's father. Maybe a similar outreach to Robin's parents might be the key to bringing everyone in the family closer. It was worth a shot. Robin, who had always been closer to her father than her mother, used the occasion to present him with an opportunity.

Robin and Buddy were alone in the Fishers' small, quiet living room. Buddy was in his easy chair and Robin sat across from him on an American farmhouse-style couch, their knees almost touching. Robin reached out and took both of Buddy's hands. "Daddy? Can't you at least try to accept Jerry? I mean, you don't know him like I do. He's a good guy. He works hard. He's the father of your grandson," said Robin as she advocated for her husband.

Buddy, the navy master chief, scoffed, "He's a crook, baby girl. He's no good. All that work you talk about? It's not legitimate."

"Maybe you're right. Maybe you're right," agreed Robin. "But you've been in the navy your whole life. The navy's always taken care of you. Jerry doesn't have the navy. He has to make his own way. And, Daddy, he *always* manages to find a path. Most things he touches turn into gold."

"Robin . . . " Buddy sighed, exasperated that he didn't seem to be getting through to his daughter.

The visit didn't last much longer after that.

Not long after, Jerry Colombo paid Buddy a visit. He got right to the point with his father-in-law. "What if I could get you a million dollars?"

There was a pregnant pause.

"What?" Buddy was confused.

"What if I could get you a million dollars?" Jerry repeated.

"Who do I have to kill?"

"Very funny. It's nothing like that," Jerry assured him.

"Is it legal? Is it on the up-and-up?" asked Buddy.

"Of course it is," Jerry lied. "Completely legit." Buddy Fisher was a straitlaced, square guy who had followed the rules his whole life. He sensed something wasn't right. "I have a winning McDonald's Monopoly game piece. All you have to do is walk into any McDonald's and turn it in," Jerry assured Buddy.

"I don't know," said Buddy. "I gotta think about it." Jerry sensed that Buddy wasn't going for it.

"Well, you do that, Buddy. You've heard of the McDonald's Monopoly game, right? Well, I have an in. It's foolproof. I want you to have it. No strings attached." Buddy was unmoved.

Not long after, Robin was surprised to get a call from her dad. "Daddy! How are you?" asked Robin. "What's going on?"

There was a long pause. It was finally broken when Buddy said, "I want it. I want the big one. Tell Jerry I'm in."

Although Buddy never told his wife of fifty years the truth about how he came to acquire the winning game piece, it had the effect Robin desired. The families became closer, Jerry was accepted into the Fisher household, and although they never showed off with splashy purchases and nouveau riche ostentatiousness—it was crystal clear that the million-dollar windfall had brought a lot of joy to a family that needed it.

Seeing such great results, Jerry used a similar tactic with Jennifer, Robin's sixteen-year-old daughter from a previous relationship. The teenager—unsurprisingly—was sulky and annoyed whenever Jerry was around . . . and now that her mom and the mobster were married, he was *always* around. Jerry's feelings were a little hurt that he couldn't seem to bond with his wife's kid. "She's a high school girl, Jerry. They're difficult," cautioned Robin.

One day, out of the blue, Jerry offered Jennifer a million-dollar game piece when she turned eighteen. It'd be an easy win and untraceable to any scam because Jennifer had a different last name than her mother or her maternal grandparents. It was perfect. All the girl had to do was turn eighteen. Jennifer was thrilled and, strangely enough, the wall of ice between her and her stepfather began to melt.

But back in the present, in the hotel's conference room, Doug Mathews—as Shamrock Productions video director Doug Dewitt—was giving her grandfather, million-dollar McDonald's Monopoly winner Buddy Fisher, enough tape to hang himself.

– 10 –

THE TWO JERRYS

The FBI's Jacksonville field office hummed with activity. It was electric. Ever since Rick Dent and Doug Mathews had taken up the McDonald's fraud case, things had changed dramatically. Although Jacksonville closed a significant number of cases, the energy was always quiet and low-key, perhaps due to the bulk of cases involving healthcare fraud, but now Jacksonville was born-again hard. The place was like a popcorn machine: phones rang, keyboards clacked, typewriters—still in use—chugged, fax machines vomited reams of paper, printers connected to the computers steadily hummed, and agents and other employees rushed around the floor, pumped with raw energy. It was as if Jacksonville had, almost overnight, become the law enforcement equivalent of a telemarketing boiler room. An *aggressive* telemarketing boiler room.

Yet there were homey touches.

In the wire room three agents sat in their chairs, cut off from everything else in the world other than their headphones and what came through them. When Special Agent Rick Dent arrived with his daily Tupperware delivery of his wife's baked goods, they were happy for the interruption . . . and the treats.

"Agent Dent!" said FBI recruit Tim Adams.

"Daily rations, guys," said Dent, turning over the Tupperware. "Courtesy of the wife."

"Oh man. Please thank her for us," said Adams. "I have something for you, too." He handed the older agent a red metal box that looked like it was for tools or fishing tackle except for the heavy-duty combination lock that kept it sealed. The box also had a slot on the top through which the surveillance tapes could be dropped, but only Dent and Mathews had the combination to access the material inside. With a practiced hand, Dent dialed in the necessary numbers through rote muscle memory and popped the lid. He found three cassettes, all recorded the night before.

"Great job, guys. Enjoy the cookies. Try to stay sane," Dent advised.

Dent wasn't joking. He rarely joked. He was all business. With the clock ticking down to the end of this McDonald's Monopoly promotional period, they'd never have another chance to get to the bottom of what appeared to be a huge fraud case. The heart of the investigation was the wire room. It wasn't an easy assignment—despite Rick Dent's wife's baked goods. Agents had been brought in from other departments to handle the wire room. Three agents at a time would wear the headphones listening to calls. They worked in twelve-hour shifts, and the wires were monitored twenty-four hours a day, seven days a week.

Rick Dent's affidavit in support of application—the document he wrote to get the necessary judicial approval to put taps on individuals' phones—ran sixty-two pages long and sought wires on fourteen people, all with suspected connections to Jerry Jacobson. Among those named on the list were Robin Lisa Colombo—who, it was noted, was "also known as" Robin Colombo, Robin L. Etheridge, Robin L. Fisher, Catherine Sapp, and Stephanie Marks—William Fisher, Gloria Brown, and, of course, the suspected mastermind behind the scheme, Jerry Jacobson.

Besides the wires, the team had also assigned twenty-four-hour surveillance on Jerry Jacobson. This included the typical "follow car," but they also had air coverage—a plane or helicopter—if needed. But even with all this effort, the team had yet to discover any solid evidence that "Uncle Jerry" Jacobson was the brains behind the scheme.

More important, Rick Dent and Doug Mathews still had no idea how Jerry Jacobson—if, indeed, he was the ringleader—was managing to conduct the scheme. Despite all their efforts, Jerry Jacobson remained an enigma. *Who the fuck is this guy?* the team wondered. *Who the heck is this guy?* wondered Rick Dent.

When Doug Mathews made initial contact with the confidential informant—the person behind the number written on the "McDonald's Monopoly fraud?" Post-it Mathews found stuck to Rick Dent's computer—he had been given several names that were all related to one another in some respect. Despite that, not one had had a solid, undeniable connection to Jerry Jacobson. The information the team had collected so far showed flurries of phone calls just before and just after each million-dollar game piece was claimed . . . and then silence. The connections went cold. The FBI still had found no definitive, case-closed connection between Uncle Jerry and any of the winners.

In fact, other than the basics—like how he had been a cop for the Hollywood, Florida, police department for a hot minute before leaving due to a wrist injury—the team still didn't even have a full picture of their quarry. There was a whole lot about Jerry Jacobson they still didn't know.

While the FBI knew Jerry had been a police officer, what they didn't know was that Jacobson had long dreamed of a career in law enforcement, but it wasn't an easy path for him. He'd tried for years to find work with various departments in Florida but had trouble meeting the physical and health status requirements. He went "department shopping" throughout the state and was finally hired by the Hollywood Police Department.

Jerry Jacobson couldn't have been happier. He had finally gotten his dream job—one that he had lusted after ever since he was a kid—and was now a full-fledged law enforcement officer with a uniform, a badge, and a gun. More important, the job came with the kind of power that, say, an assistant floor manager at a big-box electronics store could only imagine.

Although Jerry was a cop, he showed he had no problem skirting the law. When his cousin Mark Swartz—another McDonald's Monopoly million-dollar "winner"—was dealing weed in South Florida, Jerry made Mark one of his main recruiters for the McDonald's scheme, although this arrangement eventually fell apart when Mark refused to give Jerry his kickback money. Then, while taking a dip in the ocean, Mark cut his foot on a piece of coral and developed an infection that eventually killed him.

But then everything came crashing down for Jerry. It started out as a twinge in the palm of his right hand. Not exactly painful, but not exactly comfortable either. Maybe he had strained it carrying groceries from the car to the kitchen?

Perhaps he had just gripped something too tightly for too long? It didn't matter. It was probably just one of those minor aches and pains that come and go. At least that's what Jerry thought at first. But the problem didn't go away. It hung around and grew worse until doing any kind of gripping with his right hand sent electric waves of pain shooting through his thumb, his wrist, and his forearm. It wasn't long before Jerry couldn't fire his service weapon. He couldn't even pull it from its holster. Physical therapy and home remedies didn't improve his mysteriously injured hand and Jerry eventually had to face the cruel reality that his time with the Hollywood Police Department was over. A cop who couldn't use his gun was useless . . . and a potential liability in the field.

Jerry had developed Guillain-Barré syndrome, a rare and serious nerve disorder. The disease was no joke, Jerry learned firsthand. It is characterized by its sudden onset, as the immune system begins to attack the nerves. A tingling weakness in the hands and feet is usually the first symptom. That's how it was with Jerry. According to his ex-wife, Marsha, the symptoms hit one day as he stood before the bathroom mirror to shave. He couldn't raise his hand to his face. Worried, he called Marsha, who helped get him to the hospital.

The symptoms spread quickly until the patient suffers paralysis and requires hospitalization. Worse, all treatment is symptomatic. There is no cure for Guillain-Barré syndrome. While most people eventually recover completely, some cases prove fatal. Recovery can take years, and weakness, fatigue, and numbness can linger on and become chronic conditions, but most victims of the syndrome can usually walk again after six months. Quality of life after a bout with Guillain-Barré syndrome can be significantly reduced. Marsha, despite having a job, basically became Jerry's nurse. She was a harsh taskmaster. "You're not going to sit here and have a pity party," she'd tell him. "Get up and walk."

Jerry Jacobson went through it all and by the time he came out of it, he found he needed a cane whenever he had flare-ups, but he could walk thanks, no doubt, to Marsha's constant pushing. However, with absolutely no chance of ever again working as a cop, Jerry Jacobson became depressed.

Back in the present, despite the buzz in the Jacksonville field office, despite all the wires, despite the hours of tape, despite Doug Mathews's Shamrock Productions undercover operation, the FBI still had not established a clear link between "Uncle Jerry" Jacobson and mobster Jerry Colombo. The team knew of the connection between Jerry Colombo, the "winner" of a Dodge Viper courtesy of McDonald's Monopoly, and his father-in-law Buddy Fisher, but they still had no undeniable proof that could link the two Jerrys in the ongoing scheme.

Jerry Colombo was suspicious, no doubt about it. He had contacts all over the Eastern Seaboard, most of it mob related. He supposedly ran a kind of "underground" security at Donald Trump's Taj Mahal in Atlantic City, as well as a supposed off-the-books, completely illegal casino there. It was through these connections that Jerry Colombo established a system to find fake winners for McDonald's Monopoly. None of the winners got their game pieces for free.

Robin Colombo, Jerry's wife, gave the rundown to us in our HBO documentary series. "Oh, you had to buy a winning piece," she explained. "And they weren't cheap." Robin continued, "For each million-dollar piece, Uncle Jerry Jacobson got a flat fee of fifty thousand. Jerry Colombo would get paid when McDonald's paid the 'winners.' And while the winners could claim a million dollars, the reality was that the company paid that out in increments of fifty thousand annually over twenty years. Half of that check, it was understood, would go to Jerry Colombo, every year, without fail. That was the deal."

Exceptions could be made, however. When Jerry Colombo's younger brother Frank was about to be married, Jerry promised him a million-dollar ticket as a wedding gift—no strings or processing fees attached. Jerry even showed Frank's fiancée, Heather, a game piece, encased like a prize in one of those clear plastic eggs that come out of gumball machines.

Frank had always been in awe of his older brother. Unlike Jerry—who'd grown up among friends and relatives in New York City, Frank was uprooted while he was still in high school and their parents moved the family to Florida. Frankie stood out for all the wrong reasons in the new environment: He dressed New York, he looked New York, and he talked New York. The kid was different—and American high schools are citadels devoted to conformity. Overnight, Frank became a target for bullies.

Isolated and unhappy, Frank was having lunch in the cafeteria—alone—when his brother Jerry, seven years older and a full-grown man, showed up with a crew in tow. He stepped his bulk up on a tabletop. "Listen up!" Jerry Colombo bellowed. With those two words, Jerry managed to command the attention of an unruly high school lunchroom. The place fell silent.

"See that guy over there?" Jerry huffed as he pointed at Frank. "That's my kid brother, Frank. He's a good kid. You'll like him if you get to know him."

Then Jerry's speech took a darker turn. "If any of you dopes tries to mess with my brother again, I'll be back. And I'll break your fuckin' legs. We clear? Good. I don't want to have to come back here, but I will. Okay. Thanks for your time and have a nice day."

Jerry climbed down from the table and walked out with his crew. Frank looked around and saw bugged-out eyes and dropped jaws. *What just happened?* the entire lunchroom wondered. The silence was deafening.

Frank would later point out, "Nobody ever messed with me again. Jerry was a tough guy. Jerry was dangerous. But if he was on your side, he was the most loyal, most protective guy you'd ever meet. Not only that, but Jerry was also full of good humor and charm. People were drawn to him. He had a big personality. He had plans."

Also possessed of a big personality and full of her own plans, Jerry's wife, Robin,s was, by now, familiar with the mechanics of the McDonald's Monopoly scam. "Jerry would meet Uncle Jerry at highway rest stops where they'd exchange money and game pieces," she explained. Sometimes Frank would even accompany his brother to these exchanges. There, among the truck drivers, lot lizards, and hustlers involved in illicit sexual commerce, the two Jerrys took care of business unnoticed. "You might not have noticed Uncle Jerry under any circumstance," said Frank. "He was completely average. A nice guy."

"He was a fucking gangster," Robin would later say of Uncle Jerry Jacobson. Whenever Robin and Jerry Colombo would have one of their epic spats, it was Uncle Jerry who would get on the phone and explain to Robin why she had to patch things up with Jerry: "He really loves you and Little Frankie. Robin, you can't leave him. You can't divorce him. It'd kill him. Look, maybe I can sweeten the deal. How about I get you that new car you've been wanting? Need some cash?

Whatever. Just patch things up with Jerry. This is silly. I know you love him, too."

Uncle Jerry had Robin there. She did love Jerry despite all the attendant aggravations he brought to the table. And, she had to admit, Jerry Colombo was an outstanding and devoted father and a great provider for her and the baby.

If there was one thing she worried about, it was getting caught. Robin generally trusted her husband's game plans, but this McDonald's Monopoly thing had what she saw as a fatal flaw. "It was so dumb. All the people Jerry recruited to be winners were white guys—shady white guys—and Italians. Duh. Someone was going to figure out what was going on eventually. I told him, 'You need to start bringing in some women.' I told him a little diversity couldn't hurt either. Get a woman of color to be a winner. I mean, c'mon!"

– 11 –

GLORIA BROWN BECOMES A MILLIONAIRE

1997...

Gloria Brown and Robin Fisher had known each other for years and considered themselves good friends. Gloria first met Robin through a tenant who lived in Gloria's rental property. Robin, who still lived at home with her folks, would stay at the rental property whenever she was having problems or needed a break from Mom and Dad. Gloria, always the caretaker, would listen to Robin's problems and offer guidance. Occasionally, Gloria would lend Robin what little money Gloria could spare. Over time, they became close. Robin eventually started working at the optical store where she would meet Jerry Colombo, marry him, and pull up stakes for the relative luxury of a big, fancy house in South Carolina.

Gloria's life took a turn, too. She went into social work. It was a spiritually fulfilling gig, but Gloria was never going to get rich by helping people. She was barely breaking even. Meanwhile, she was raising a son as a single mom and doing her best to put food on the table and provide for him. Both were full-time jobs. In what little free time she had, Gloria could be found at church, praying for a miracle, asking God for a little relief from her increasingly difficult circumstances.

Gloria's prayers were seemingly answered when she entered a church raffle and won a house. Gloria was grateful. It was a big windfall, but it wasn't an ideal situation. The house was tiny and cramped, and although Gloria maintained it as best as she could, the repairs and expenses never stopped.

Worse, the house was in one of Jacksonville's worst neighborhoods. The nighttime quiet was often ripped by gunfire and the mechanical churn of police helicopters—"ghetto birds" was the term at the time—which would light up the streets as bright as day as they hovered and searched. *This is no place to raise a kid*, Gloria thought.

Pulling up stakes and moving to a picket-fence suburb was a great idea, but it was far beyond Gloria's financial ability. She was stuck, for now, in less-than-ideal circumstances. So, Gloria did what working-class people have always done: she started saving. She saved hard. It took a few years, but all the scrimping, all the sacrifices, all the budget meals finally paid off and Gloria was able to put a down payment on a "fixer-upper" in a better neighborhood.

Of course, that left Gloria Brown with the raffle house in a bad part of town at a time when the real estate market was weak. A recession had hit in 1990 and while it was officially over within the year, home prices continued to decline until they finally bottomed out in 1997, 14 percent lower than what they had been in 1989.

Gloria did the only thing she could think to do: she rented out the raffle house. It was a solid plan on paper. She would apply the rent money she received toward the expenses of making the necessary repairs to the fixer-upper. Unfortunately, the new house had a lot more problems than she had been led to believe. Those she did address cost far more than the initial estimates she had received from the contractors. Bills began to mount, and Gloria began to stress. She worked as much overtime as she could get and still carve out time for her son. She wanted to be a good mom. She didn't want her son to be a latchkey kid because she was constantly at work, constantly hustling. She juggled the financial responsibilities between the two money pits, "robbing Peter to pay Paul."

It wasn't sustainable, financially, physically, or emotionally. Gloria Brown was in a real fix. She did what she had always done in difficult situations: she put her faith in the Lord and prayed with all her might for a break, for some relief.

In 1997, the Lord seemed to answer her prayers once again.

Sitting at her kitchen table, arranging her bills into two piles, one "to be paid" and the other "to be paid later," the phone rang. She thought for a moment to just let it ring. She hadn't received a good phone call in months. It was all telemarketers and bill collectors. By the fourteenth ring, Gloria realized the caller wasn't going to stop, so Gloria picked up the receiver and hesitantly said hello.

Her mood brightened instantly when she heard a familiar voice. It was her old friend Robin Fisher—now in South Carolina, married and going by Robin Colombo. She invited Gloria to come visit her. "It's been too long."

"I don't know if I can. It's not an ideal time right now," said Gloria.

"I think you'll want to come," said Robin. "I have an opportunity for you, but I can't really talk about it over the phone."

Gloria remained noncommittal, but Robin's offer, however vague, intrigued her. Besides, she was desperate and willing to grab hold of anything that might help her out of her current financial situation.

The next morning, Gloria called her sister and asked if she could watch the boy for a few days while Gloria went out of town. "South Carolina? Why you goin' there?" Gloria's sister wanted to know.

The next day, Gloria walked her son to her sister's front door. "I still don't know why you have to go out of town," her sister said.

Gloria stammered something about "business," hugged and kissed her son, thanked her sister once again for watching the boy, and said, "I'll see y'all in a couple of days." She got in her car and hit the road.

Many hours—and several rest stops—later, Gloria pulled up in front of the Colombos' house in a Charleston suburb. Gloria felt almost embarrassed to park her car—heavily used, dusty and dirty from the trip—in such a fine neighborhood. In the Colombos' driveway was a pair of shiny new his-and-hers Ford Explorers. Before she could drive off to find a less conspicuous place to park, she heard Robin's distinctive Rebel-Yell-and-Marlboro voice: "Girl! Get in here!" She looked up and saw her standing on the front porch, waving. Next to her was, she assumed, Jerry Colombo. Black slacks, wild print shirt, and big as a mountain. He seemed friendly though, grinning broadly and waving along with his wife. He came to the car and helped Gloria with her bags. "How was your trip?" he asked her.

"It was good," said Gloria.

"We're going to have such a great weekend," he told her.

Gloria thought it was a strange thing to say. She didn't know Jerry. She had come to visit Robin. Gloria had to drop the thought when Robin, shrieking with joy, embraced her friend with all the force and passion of a spider monkey locking on to a banana. Gloria, long operating under difficult circumstances, was nevertheless happy to see her friend doing so well.

After a brief tour of the Colombo house, Robin and Jerry suggested a trip to the mall. "I can't really do any shopping, Robin. I'm just a working mom these days," she pleaded.

"Don't worry about anything," Jerry Colombo said, inserting himself into the situation once again. "You're our guest. Let's go, ladies."

At the mall, Gloria and Robin caught up with each other, but Jerry was never more than a few paces ahead or behind the two women. It was the same when the trio returned to the house. Jerry did not, would not, leave them alone. He sat in the kitchen while Robin put together a meal, chatted nonstop, and smoked like a chimney.

"Dinner is served!" crowed Robin. She brought a big bowl filled with a green mixed salad and put it on the table. Gloria marveled how gracefully she did it while managing to have a lit cigarette dangling from her lips. The ash must have been half the length of the ol' coffin nail and yet Robin was so adept a smoker that it never fell into the food. Not that it would have mattered to Jerry, Gloria thought as the big man dug into the salad with a pair of tongs. He plopped a big portion of salad on his plate and then dressed it with a little olive oil and red wine vinegar. Gloria had to stifle a laugh. Jerry looked ridiculous with his big, bear-like paws handling a pair of tiny cut-crystal cruets.

"Pasta up soon!" announced Robin, joining them at the table for the salad course. *So elegant*, thought Gloria. She couldn't help but notice a look that passed between Robin and Jerry. It was subtle, but Gloria saw it anyway. There was something unusual about the dynamics at the table and Gloria couldn't figure out what it was.

Later, as they all hung out and relaxed in the TV room, Robin suddenly asked Gloria, "Honey, you ever hear of the McDonald's Monopoly game?"

"Well, yeah. Who hasn't?" As a single mom on a budget, Gloria was well familiar with the game and McDonald's itself. Its menu was a godsend to working moms like Gloria: stopping for a Happy Meal could save at least an hour during a hectic day and it was easy on the wallet.

"Well, Jerry runs the whole thing," said Robin proudly. Jerry Colombo leaned back in his chair as if to say, "That's right. I'm the *man!*" Gloria was skeptical.

"How'd you like to be the next big winner?" Jerry wanted to know.

"He can totally make it happen," assured Robin. "Jerry controls who wins the prize."

"Well, that'd be great," said Gloria, trying to remain non-committal. She thought the whole thing sounded too good to be true. Besides, was she really supposed to believe that a big outfit like McDonald's was letting some goombah like Jerry Colombo pick the winners of its big-ticket prizes in a popular nationwide promotion? It didn't seem likely.

Robin sensed Gloria's apprehension. "It's totally legit, girl," she told Gloria. "Jerry works directly with McDonald's."

"So all the winners are selected beforehand? That sounds . . . weird," said Gloria.

"That's just the way the world works, honey," said Jerry like it was no big thing. "There's too many variables when random people win the big prizes. McDonald's doesn't like variables and the unexpected. I mean, what happens if the million-dollar winner turns out to be a convicted child molester or something. What then, huh? What then? So the guy I work with, we make sure that kind of thing never happens."

Gloria remained indifferent. *Was this really on the up-and-up?* she wondered.

"Girl, you don't have to make up your mind right now. Let's enjoy our dinner. Think about it, though," urged Robin.

For the rest of her stay, it was the only thing on Gloria's mind . . . but she remained noncommittal. Robin was her good friend, but Gloria still wasn't comfortable with Jerry Colombo. She didn't like the way he hovered constantly and how he tried to steer everything to his advantage. Gloria felt like she was being hustled by the guy. She could tell he was a control freak, and that worried her. *There's just something off about this guy,* Gloria thought.

On her drive home to Jacksonville, Gloria continued to chew on the Colombos' offer. After all, she was getting deeper and deeper into a difficult financial situation with no way out. A million dollars—however it was acquired—would fix everything. She was just everyday ordinary folks. She didn't have a lot of options. It could be the solution to all the problems she was facing.

She had been home in Jacksonville only a few hours when she picked up the phone and punched in a number. A man's voice answered. "Yo!"

"Uh, is this Jerry? It's Gloria."

"Gloria! I take it you finally smartened up?"

Gloria didn't like Jerry Colombo's tone or attitude. *Who does this guy think he is?* she thought. But she played along. She had made up her mind that she would do what was necessary to get that million dollars.

Jerry rattled off a lot of details that left Gloria overwhelmed and a little confused, but she didn't really care about it anyway. Her focus was on the million-dollar grand prize and all the positive things it could bring about for Gloria and her son. It could be a game changer. As a churchgoing woman, Gloria also thought that God was answering her prayers through Jerry Colombo, as unlikely as that may seem.

And then Jerry hit her with the catch.

"And, look, Gloria, I'm gonna need a hundred and twenty-five grand up front before we can start to move forward," he told her.

"Wait. What?" Gloria was stunned.

"Hey, I'm givin' you a break here. Nothin' is free in this world, honey. I thought you knew that," said Jerry.

"But Jerry, I'm barely making ends meet. I don't have that kind of money," she pleaded, seeing her million dollars slip away.

Jerry was reassuring. "Sure you do, Gloria. Sure you do." Then Jerry went through a list of her assets, including her two homes. *How does he know all that?* Gloria wondered. Had Robin told him? She wanted to speak with her friend.

"Can I talk to Robin?" she asked Jerry.

"She's not here," Jerry said curtly. "Let's get back to business here. Now, I have a mortgage broker—a good buddy of mine—who can help. You meet with him tomorrow. It's all set up. And after you meet with him and go to the bank—where you will get cash, not a cashier's check, not a money order—you'll meet me."

"Where will I meet you?" asked Gloria.

"I'll let you know later. Don't worry about it."

Once again, Gloria couldn't escape the feeling she was being railroaded, but the promise of a million dollars loomed large. She was also afraid to back out at this point. She was dealing with a known mobster and knew how the scheme worked. She was worried that she "knew too much." She was locked into this thing now.

She met with the broker who talked fast and steered her into taking out mortgages on both houses. Unfortunately, she was only able to get $25,000. Her heart sank and she asked if she could use the broker's phone. She called Jerry Colombo.

"Jerry, I'm here with the broker but all I can get is twenty-five thousand."

"Take it. Go to the bank and get cash. It's good enough for now," Jerry ordered. "We'll work out a payment schedule. Like five yearly payments of twenty-five grand until I get my total. Something like that."

"And then?"

"And then you'll meet me at the St. Johns County Rest Area northbound on I-95 at four this afternoon. Don't be late, huh?" Jerry said and abruptly ended the call. Gloria finished up her paperwork, received a check, and headed to the bank to get cash. As soon as she had it in a canvas deposit bag with a zipper, her anxiety went into hyperdrive. It was the most money she had ever held in her hands. She worried the bank might report her for suspicious activity. Maybe they thought she was involved in drugs or something else illegal. *Oh Lord, this is bad,* she thought. It was too late to back out now. She had to meet Jerry soon.

Gloria met Jerry at the highway rest stop and gave him $25,000. He took it with a grunt and before she could even say anything, Jerry was speeding down the road to merge back onto the interstate. Gloria intuitively knew she had just made a huge mistake.

A few restless days later—was she ever going to hear from Jerry Colombo again?—Jerry called. "Hey, Gloria. I got your new address and phone all set up and we're ready to move ahead."

"What? What new address? What's going on?"

"Gloria, you gotta relax, honey. It's no big deal. I've just got too many winners based out of Jacksonville. We're gonna say you're from Hilton Head, South Carolina. Let's get together and we can go over everything. See you then." Click.

The next day, Gloria found herself at her kitchen table facing an answering machine while Jerry loomed behind her. She could smell his cologne in the enclosed space and wondered if that was the cause of her growing nausea. "Here," Jerry said as he thrust a slip of paper at her. "Memorize this. You need to know this address and phone number backwards, forwards, and in your sleep. And once you know it, get rid of that piece of paper. Now, I need you to leave a greeting on the answering machine."

"What do you want me to say?" asked Gloria.

"Just say it's you and tell 'em to leave a message," ordered Jerry.

Gloria took the phone and said, "Hi, this is Gloria. Leave a message at the beep."

Jerry sighed. "Do it again," he ordered.

"Hi, this is Gloria. Leave a message at the beep."

Jerry muttered a curse. "Again."

"What's wrong?" Gloria wanted to know.

"Sound happy, for cryin' out loud."

Gloria tried again. "Hi, this—"

"Happier!" demanded Jerry. By what seemed like the seventy-fifth take, he was satisfied. Gloria was not. She knew

Jerry wasn't playing. She knew his family's reputation. She was locked in now. If she backed out, what then? Gloria didn't need the Mafia threatening her or her son. It was game on, and she'd just have to see how it all played out.

When it was all over, Jerry asked if he could use the phone. Gloria watched as he punched in a number on the keypad. When he got an answer, Colombo's mood changed visibly. Where he had been curt with Gloria, he was now all smiles and sunshine. "Uncle Jerry! Hey, we're all set."

Gloria wondered who this Uncle Jerry might be, but she had read Jerry Colombo's mood and didn't want to cause any commotion.

A few days later, Gloria was in Hilton Head, South Carolina, in the back seat of Jerry Colombo's Explorer sandwiched between two beefy, intimidating meatsicles wearing sunglasses. "Oh, these two jagoffs are my cousins. Can you believe such a thing?" The two men never said a word.

Jerry Colombo parked the Explorer on a side street. "The McDonald's is just around the corner. You're going to ask for the manager and then turn over the game piece. And then you're going to jump up and down, scream, cry, laugh, and *be happy!*" He reached into his shirt pocket and handed her a game piece in a Ziploc bag.

"Jerry, I don't know if I can go through with this," Gloria said on the verge of tears.

The goon on Gloria's right stepped out of the car and held the door open for her. Again, silence. There was no arguing with this crew. Gloria got out on shaky legs and walked in a trance to McDonald's. A few steps away, she turned back only to see Jerry glaring at her as if to say, "Knock off the shit and get this done!"

Inside the McDonald's, standing in line, Gloria's knees felt like they were filled with jelly. When she finally reached the counter and handed over her game piece to the manager, the place exploded. All the staffers shrieked and clapped. This was huge. This was an event. A real million-dollar winner in their restaurant. Gloria tried to feign joy and mirror the excitement of the McDonald's staff. Inside, though, she felt like a condemned prisoner being led to the gas chamber.

Then a snag.

"Ma'am, I need to verify the game piece. I'll be right back," the McDonald's manager told her. "Somebody get the lady a drink," he ordered the workers. Somebody handed Gloria a supersize Coke and she took a seat at one of the tables. Minutes turned to an hour. Eventually the manager emerged from the back office. "Congratulations, Miss Brown," he said.

Shakily, Gloria made it back to Jerry Colombo's Explorer. Her relief that the worst was now over disappeared quickly. Jerry was fuming. "What the fuck took you so fucking long? Did you fuck things up? Fuck, fuck, fuck! What did you tell them in there? Huh? What the hell did you tell them?"

Gloria was terrified. "That's just how long it took, Jerry. I can't control that." Jerry huffed and dropped the matter. They went back to Jacksonville and dropped off Gloria. Alone, she had time to think. She was now a registered million-dollar winner, she told herself. The hard part was over. Now, all she had to do was sit back and start collecting her annual checks from the McDonald's Corporation.

But as the first Black woman to ever win the million-dollar prize, McDonald's wanted to hype it. So did the local Hilton Head press. She got the call from McDonald's publicity department requesting an interview. She tried to brush them off but was reminded that as part of her win, she was obligated to participate. The calls kept coming. She called Jerry Colombo. "Jerry, what am I supposed to do?"

Jerry sighed as if it were the dumbest question he ever heard. "You do the press."

It was a whirlwind. Gloria was videotaped and photographed receiving a giant cardboard check from Ronald McDonald while McDonald's employees cheered. Local Hilton Head TV stations did stories about Gloria's win. Local newspapers covered the event, too. Even radio stations talked about it. Gloria was famous. McDonald's even decided to fly Gloria to company headquarters in Chicago where she was picked up in a stretch limo and greeted personally by actor and celebrity Sherman "George Jefferson" Hemsley.

Gloria was learning her new millionaire lifestyle wasn't all she'd thought it would be. For one thing, every relative, every friend, every casual acquaintance thought she was now rolling in cash and wanted short-term loans, long-term loans, "a little help," or something. Everyone she knew had a hand out. Gloria had to explain to them that she would receive $50,000 a year from the corporation over the next twenty years . . . and that was before taxes. She was hardly rich.

The win put Gloria even further behind than she was before. Jerry Colombo—who'd already received $25,000 tax-free from Gloria—was still relentlessly after the rest he felt he was owed. When the first check from McDonald's arrived, Gloria handed it directly over to Jerry Colombo, who, once again, left Gloria on the hook for paying the government its cut. With every subsequent check, she was told, half of the money belonged to Jerry. She was now further behind the eight ball than ever and sinking faster every day.

Gloria Brown briefly considered calling the authorities, but was that the right move? Things were already bad. Gloria didn't need vengeful mobsters coming after her and her son. She felt trapped and could see no way out.

- 12 -

LEE CASSANO AND THE $100,000 SHAKE

1997...

L ee Cassano was living her best life. At twenty-nine, she was
a former beauty queen and naturally drew attention from
most guys.

She was employed at Jacksonville International Airport as a
ticket agent for Trans World Airlines (better known as TWA),
which was still a major player in the travel game despite bank-
ruptcies in 1992 and 1995. It was a good gig. JAX was the fastest
growing airport in Florida. The travel hub handled a hundred
departures and arrivals every day, seven days a week, 365 days a
year, and was used by sixteen airlines that served 4.5 million
passengers annually. That meant action and Lee was down for it.

Lee loved to party. If it all went away tomorrow, it wouldn't
have really mattered to Lee. She knew that with a flirtatious
toss of her hair and big smile, she could land a new job—in
almost any field she desired—anywhere in the country. Lee
lived a carefree life.

One of the perks that TWA employees enjoyed really
appealed to a free-spirited woman like Lee: free travel. On a

weekend whim, Lee would learn of an unsold seat from her circle of flight attendant friends and use the "employees fly for free on unsold seats" policy to go anywhere in the world. Lee was determined to see as much of the planet as time and good looks would allow. Everywhere Lee went became a grand adventure, mainly because of Lee.

One day at JAX, as Lee helmed the TWA ticket desk, she was interrupted. "Hey, gorgeous. That's a *byooteeful* scrunchie. Did you bedazzle it yourself?" He was big, balding, and wore a billowing printed shirt that may have been silk but was more likely polyester and did nothing to hide his bulk. *Is this goof for real?* Lee wondered. Did he not see she was out of his league?

Jerry Colombo was persistent. Lee's disdain was merely a challenge to him. *He's confident, I'll give him that*, thought Lee. He kept at it. "My name's Jerry. What's yours?"

Lee decided to play along. She was bored. Maybe this little game could provide some distraction during a rare slow moment at work. "Lee Cassano," she answered truthfully.

"Cassano? What is that, Irish?" Jerry teased.

Lee giggled. This guy was a real joker. "It's Italian," she told him.

"Italian! *Mamma mia!* Me, too!" Jerry said. *No shit*, thought Lee.

"Yep. One hundred percent. My name's Jerry Colombo if you can believe such a thing. Hey, you know any good places to eat around here?" asked Jerry.

"What? Like a pizza joint?" Lee teased.

"Nah. I was thinking more of some surf 'n' turf. Steak and lobster. Something classy. They got anything like that around here?"

"Big spender," said Lee.

"You have no idea," said Jerry. "Look, I hate to eat alone and I'm starvin'. Why don't we blow this pop stand and go grab a bite?"

Lee giggled. "Are you crazy? I'm working. I can't just leave and go off with some dude I just met."

"I get it. I get it," said Jerry. "Maybe some other time." Jerry pulled out a money clip decorated with a Morgan silver dollar and peeled off a couple Ben Franklins. "But here, you go get yourself a nice meal somewhere."

"I can't just take your money," said Lee, intrigued.

"Sure ya can," Jerry said with a smile. "You can also give me your phone number if you don't like taking money for nothing."

Lee couldn't believe Jerry's boldness. He may not have been an Adonis, but he was witty and quick, and she liked his smile. She gave him her number—and took Jerry's money. "And here, this is for you." Jerry gave her a business card with just his name and phone number printed on it. "Use it anytime," Jerry told her before he disappeared into the swirl of humanity on the airport concourse to board his flight.

What the fuck just happened? Lee wondered as she watched Jerry walk-waddle into the crowd. It didn't take too long before she and Jerry became phone pals. From there, over the next few months, the relationship became what some might describe as "complicated." Jerry squired Lee to fancy dinners, to parties, and on weekend getaways all on his dime. He was a big spender—and Lee liked that.

She also knew he was married. And although she claimed nothing happened between them, Lee really didn't care too much about Jerry's home situation. They were just enjoying each other's company and having fun.

One day, on another adventure, Lee found herself in Jerry's Corvette—he had told her it once belonged to a famous R & B singer. "This fuckin' guy!" Jerry's story began about the entertainer. "He's got problems. So many problems. And he don't know about how to handle money, either. Typical. Anywho, he goes and gets himself into a situation where he can't pay what he owes, and next thing you know, I got his car." Lee could absolutely believe it. Then Jerry popped the question: "Speaking of money, how'd you like to make some easy dough?"

Lee stammered, caught unaware, "Sure. That'd be awesome."

Jerry pulled the Corvette off the road. He parked and reached into the console. He produced an embroidered purple velvet bag that read CROWN ROYAL in gold embroidery. Lee suppressed a snicker. Crown Royal, in her estimation, was midshelf booze at best and the velvet bag was a cheap attempt at "class." Of course, Jerry would carry valuables in one.

The big man fished around in the bag and handed her a small piece of cardboard that had a number printed on it. It was a $100,000 McDonald's Monopoly game piece. "That's a lot of money, honey. It's all yours. And all you have to do is take that into any McDonald's and collect your winnings. Cool, huh?"

"You're just going to give me a hundred thousand dollars?" Lee asked, skeptical.

"Well, I thought we could split it. After all, fair's fair," Jerry told her.

"Jerry . . . " Lee sighed. Something seemed off about this.

"No, no, no. I can sense some apprehension here. Trust me. This is how the game works. It's no problem. All you gotta do is claim it," Jerry assured her.

"Why don't you do it yourself?" Lee asked.

"What? And deny you the thrill of being a big winner? Baby, please . . . "

Lee, for all her bravado and party lifestyle, was still unsophisticated about some things, so, of course, she agreed to cash in the game piece and collect the winnings. Why not? What could possibly go wrong? She had Jerry wrapped around her little finger . . . or so she thought.

"Let's go cash this thing in now," Lee urged Jerry.

Jerry took back the game piece. "Not so fast, little girl."

"What's the problem?"

"Nothing big, but this ain't the first time I've done this and I've about worn out Florida as a place to cash in winning game pieces. It'd look weird for another Florida win," he explained. "What I suggest is we cash it in someplace else. Philadelphia, for example."

"Why Philly?"

"Hey! Can you quit askin' fuckin' questions and just listen?" Lee was a little thrown by Jerry's shift in tone. "We're gonna do it in Philadelphia. Now are you in or not?"

"What do I have to do?"

"You'll set up a Philadelphia address and phone number and then you'll cash in. Easy peasy. No problemo," Jerry soothed Lee.

"Well, okay. I'm friends with a couple flight attendants based out of Philadelphia. Let me make some phone calls. I don't see them saying no. We should be golden," Lee said.

"Well, let's get on it then," said Jerry, wheeling the 'Vette back onto the highway.

Lee put out a few feelers to friends in Philadelphia and had no trouble being given permission to use an address and a phone number. She called Jerry. "We're all set," she told him.

"Meet me in Philadelphia," he said.

A simple day trip was easy for Lee to arrange. She met Jerry at Philadelphia International Airport. He was waiting for her when she arrived and they went immediately to the nearest McDonald's. Before Jerry gave her the winning game piece, he coached her the same way he did Gloria Brown.

"Now, you're going to walk in there, ask for the manager, and give him this game piece. The manager will verify the piece is real and you'll give him the Philadelphia address and phone number. When he verifies the piece, act happy. I mean, really sell it. Don't just smile and say thanks. Scream, laugh, cry, jump up and down, do whatever the fuck you gotta do and make it real. Don't fuck it up," he demanded.

Lee wasn't happy with Jerry's tone, but maybe he was just as excited as she was to get this latest adventure going. "That won't be a problem, Jerry. I am happy."

"Now, go get that money. I'm going to make a phone call to my uncle Jerry while you're inside."

"Uncle Jerry? Is he here in Philadelphia? Are we going to visit with him later?" She had heard Colombo talk about Uncle Jerry, and she assumed he was an important figure in his life. Beyond that, she didn't know much. She was curious about him.

"No. Don't worry about it. Family business. Just go turn in the game piece, okay?"

"Alright, alright. I'm going," Lee said.

Jerry watched Lee walk to the entrance of the McDonald's. He liked the bounce of her ponytail and the swing of her hips. *Now that's a good-lookin' broad*, he thought.

It wasn't too long before Lee exited the McDonald's, sipping a large drink through a straw and with an extra bounce to her step. She slid into the front seat. Success. She stickily kissed Jerry on the cheek and it felt cold. "They even threw in a free vanilla shake!" she said. "Want some?"

Business in Philadelphia concluded, Lee went back to Florida. A few days later, she called her friend in Philly. "Hey, did that letter I've been expecting arrive yet?"

"Nothing yet, but I'll let you know as soon as it does," said Lee's friend.

"No rush. I'm going to go to Hawaii for a few days. Talk to you when I get back," Lee told her, once again using her TWA connections for more free travel and fun. At the end of her stay, she returned home to find the message light on her answering machine blinking like a Christmas tree. She punched a button and heard a mechanical voice say, "You have twenty-five new messages."

Lee was a popular girl, but that seemed like an unusual number of messages even for her. She sat down to go through them. The first was from Jerry Colombo. "Hey, baby. It's Jer. Call me back. Thanks."

The next message was from Jerry, too. "Lee, call me back, huh?"

The next, Jerry again. But now a tone started to creep into Jerry's voice. "Hey, what the fuck? Call. Me. Back."

By the twenty-fifth call, Jerry sounded pissed off and threatening, "Look, you better call me back. What's up with our check? I hope for your sake that you haven't gotten any funny ideas in your head."

Lee was exhausted—and a little scared—by Jerry's messages and his barely concealed rage. But she still had enough confidence to control and cool out guys like Jerry Colombo. She dialed him up. He answered on the third ring. "Jerry, it's

Lee. I went to Hawaii. Just walked in the door. Got *all* your messages."

"I don't give a fuck where you've been. Get on the horn to Philly and find out if you got mail."

Lee did as she was told and got word that an envelope with a McDonald's corporate logo had arrived. She relayed the message to Jerry and they agreed to meet once again in Philadelphia where they would cash the check for the whole amount with nothing set aside for savings or checking accounts. Cash on the barrelhead.

When Jerry met Lee at Philadelphia International, Lee noticed the change in Jerry's demeanor almost immediately. Gone were the smiles, the jokes, the goombah charm. "Let's go to the bank," he ordered. Lee followed him to the car.

Jerry barely said two words on the short drive to a Bank of America branch. As they walked to the entrance, Jerry said, "Don't say a fuckin' thing other than you want to cash this check. If they want anything beyond two pieces of ID, you let me handle that, okay? Got it?"

Lee got it.

At the cashier's window, Lee's apprehension lightened as the teller laid ten packs of Franklins, each totaling $10,000 and held together with paper currency straps, and placed them on the counter. "Would you like an envelope for all that?" the teller asked. She was an older woman in a gray sweater with a pair of eyeglasses dangling from a chain around her neck.

Before Lee could answer, Jerry snatched up the bills with his fat, bearlike hands and stuffed them into his pockets. "We got it, thanks," he told the teller, who took an immediate dislike to him. As soon as he stuffed the last bundle into his pocket, Jerry turned and waddled out. Lee went to follow, but the teller told her, "You be sure to put aside half of that for taxes," she warned. Lee nodded and split to catch up with Jerry.

In the car, expecting her split, Lee finally met the real Jerry Colombo. As Jerry fumbled with the cash, stuffing it into a large manila envelope, she said, "Half of that belongs to me, you know."

Wrong thing to say.

Jerry glared. "Look, you'll get your money when you get it. We're not making any split here in Philly. Now, please, just listen to the radio or something. I got a lot of things on my mind and you're giving me a fuckin' headache."

Okay, sorry I asked, thought Lee suddenly worried about ever seeing her money.

Back home in Jacksonville, Lee found Jerry suddenly hard to reach. The few times she did manage to catch him, the mobster was noncommittal about paying her split, but eventually agreed to the original deal. Tax time was approaching and Lee couldn't help but remember the bank teller's advice.

"So when can we meet?" Lee asked now that Jerry had agreed to honor the deal.

Once again, he was a jerk. "Christ, Lee. Stop being so fuckin' annoying. 'When do I get my money? When do I get my money?' You're like a broken record. I'll be down in Jacksonville next week. Is that soon enough for ya, your majesty?" *Click.*

– 13 –

THE CHURCH OF FUZZY BUNNY'S

1998...

n 1998, in a well-appointed kitchen in a South Carolina
suburb, a toddler sat on a linoleum-tiled floor beating a
stainless-steel pot with a wooden spoon. Jerry Colombo, a
proud papa, watched his little son Frankie bang out a solo.
Robin Colombo prepared dinner and smoked a cigarette. It was
the picture of domestic bliss, but with a uniquely Colombo tint.

"Will ya just get a look at this little *gaguzz*'? He's gonna be
the next Dino Danelli!" the big man said, the affection undeniable in his voice.

"Who's Dino Danelli?" Robin wanted to know.

"You mean to tell me that you don't know Dino Danelli?
He's the drummer for the Young Rascals, for cryin' out loud."

"Okay, real current reference, but what's 'guh-goots'
mean?" asked Robin through a cloud of bluish gray cigarette
smoke.

"*Gaguzz*'. It's a term of endearment. From *cucuzza*. It's a
type of squash Italians like," explained Jerry as little Frankie

bashed the pot and accented the rhythm with the occasional yawp. "See? See?" Jerry said as Frankie really put some soul into the routine. Jerry couldn't help but laugh. Frankie was cute as hell. "It's like he's short and squat . . . just like a little fuckin' *gaguzz'* out in the garden."

"No. Don't call him that. I don't like it. It sounds dumb. And we speak *American* in this household," Robin said.

"Look, it don't fuckin' matter, okay? It's just a word."

Robin scoffed. "Okay, okay. Don't get so fucking touchy."

A possible beef cooled out, Jerry continued, "As I was sayin', look at him scootin' and bangin' around—"

Just then, Frankie dropped the spoon and ran on his short little legs to his father. He hugged Jerry's legs and said, "Daddy."

Jerry's heart melted and he picked up Frankie and sat the kid in his lap. "He's such a good boy." He gave the kid a kiss on the top of the head. Then Jerry got serious. "You know, I been thinkin'. The casino's getting to be too much of a risk. I mean, what if something happens? Can you imagine?"

Robin could. For years, Jerry had managed an off-the-books gambling joint in South Carolina and had done well with it. But with all criminal enterprises, no matter how many county officials have been greased, busts were a regular part of the game. The last thing Jerry wanted now that he was a family man was to do a bit behind bars. Robin had felt that way ever since she gave birth to Frankie.

"So now what?" asked Robin.

"I been thinking it's time to go legit. Completely legit. Totally on the up-and-up."

Jerry's plan: a strip club.

To be technical, it wasn't a strip club as would be imagined anywhere outside of the Bible Belt. Jerry had to improvise to fit the local regulations. That meant no nudity. Like a Hooters or a Tilted Kilt, the place would serve food and beverages and the dancers and waitresses would wear tiny "Daisy Duke" cutoff jeans, cowboy boots, and snap-front shirts tied and lifted to expose the midriff. Not only that, there'd be a sandy pit for a beach volleyball court—Jerry believed it would provide a tropical feel to the place—and maybe a bocce court and a place to toss horseshoes. As he laid it all out for Robin, he emphasized the family nature of such a venture.

Jerry had secured a location in nearby Ladson, South Carolina. It was in Charleston County just off State Highway 78 near where Von Ohsen Road cut through. It was perfect.

Jerry even had a name for it: Fuzzy Bunny's.

"'Fuzzy Bunny's'? Who's Fuzzy Bunny?" asked Robin.

"It's not a who, it's a what," explained Jerry. "It's a reference to a lady's, uh, you know . . . uh, *parts.*"

"Well, then it should be spelled B-U-N-N-I-E-S. You use an apostrophe, it's possessive. Like, you know, the owner is someone named Fuzzy Bunny. Are you a fuzzy bunny? I don't think so."

"Yeah, well, nobody's going to overthink it like that. Besides, I already had the signs made," said Jerry.

Robin didn't like Jerry's idea at all. Putting Jerry in the middle of a gaggle of scantily clad "dancers" would be like hiring a drug addict to supervise a pharmacy. There would just be too much temptation—and opportunity—for Jerry to cheat. Robin was well aware of Jerry's after-hours proclivities. Jerry had even carried on with the personal trainer he had hired to help Robin shed the baby weight she had gained during her pregnancy with Frankie.

Robin, Jerry could handle. Charleston County was a different story.

This was a place where Fox News was considered to be a little on the liberal side. It didn't matter if there was nudity or not. Fuzzy Bunny's was *titillating* and even that was a no-go in deeply conservative Charleston County. Jerry had a fight on his hands. The county was not going to allow him to open.

Jerry decided to fight the battle in the court of public opinion and went to the media. The press and television were all too happy to cover such a colorful story. All of a sudden, Jerry was on every local news broadcast pleading his case. "I mean, let's be reasonable here," he said. "I'm not doing anything illegal. I'm just a working guy trying to earn an honest living for me and my family. I got a little toddler at home, for cryin' out loud. I don't know what's up with Charleston County. Fuzzy Bunny's is gonna be a classy joint—fully clothed, by the way—with some dancing girls. It's more like art than anything. Plus, we'll have some great food, some great drinks, and even a volleyball court where you can leave the kids. I'm tellin' ya, it's a place the whole family can enjoy!"

The county remained unmoved and denied Jerry a business license. It claimed that Jerry's location wasn't zoned for the type of place Jerry wanted to open—despite the fact it had been a bar before Jerry acquired it. To take it even further, Charleston County now claimed the site was only zoned for a church.

Jerry Colombo was persistent. Did these hillbillies really think they were going to stop a sophisticated New Yorker such as himself? He knew exactly what to do. Jerry rented a portable illuminated billboard and parked it in front of the location right on State Highway 78. Motorists couldn't miss it. It was surrounded with flashing lights and read:

THE CHURCH OF FUZZY BUNNY'S
MASS 7 NIGHTS A WEEK
PREACHER WANTED

The local news had a field day. There hadn't been this much excitement in Charleston County since anyone could remember. On one of the network affiliates, a serious-looking reporter stared into the camera and said, "Jerry Colombo's plan to become the Church of Fuzzy Bunny's is actually causing more issues with the county and outrage among religious leaders. Bibles, a bar, and strippers—those aren't things that seem to go together." Jerry Colombo didn't care what the squares and conservatives of Charleston County thought. He reveled in "stickin' it to the Man."

To Uncle Jerry Jacobson, Jerry Colombo's need for attention was becoming a real problem. The Fuzzy Bunny's story had managed to grow beyond the local news. It was the perfect combination of silly and sexy, and while it wasn't front-page news, the story had gone national. Jerry Colombo's face and name and mob connections were intractably linked to it. Uncle Jerry called Robin.

"What's he doing?" Jacobson wanted to know. "This is no good."

"I know, I know," she said. "I keep telling him, but he won't listen."

"You gotta do what you can to fix this. He doesn't listen to me, either."

One night, while Jerry was in New York "on business," Robin decided to treat herself and little Frankie to a nice sit-down meal at a local restaurant. To get to town, Robin's route took her directly past the Church of Fuzzy Bunny's. As she drove along with Frankie safely strapped into his car seat, she tapped a finger in time to an Allman Brothers tune coming over the radio. As Robin drove by Fuzzy Bunny's, she had to do a double take. There, bold as daylight, was her husband—who was supposed to be in New York—his goons, and a group of "dancers" walking out the door. Catching her husband in a lie, Robin lost it.

She cut the wheel of her Ford Explorer and bounced over the curb and drove straight at her husband and his crew. At the last moment, she slammed on the brakes and screeched to a stop in a spray of gravel. Before Jerry could figure out what was going on, Robin exploded from the driver's seat, a tiny tornado of fury, lacquered nails, and big hair. "The fuck, Jerry? New York, huh?"

"But, baby, I can explain!"

"You can always explain. Fuck you," hissed Robin. "I want a fuckin' divorce!" Then she addressed Jerry's goons, "And I'm goin' to the FBI to report each and every one of you assholes."

Jerry grabbed his wife by her arm and dragged her back into the club. "What the fuck? Are you nuts? You can't talk like that. That's how people get disappeared. Boom! You never hear from them again. We're not gettin' no divorce. Believe it. Now get your ass home and put Frankie to bed."

Robin left in a huff, but she didn't go home. She took Frankie and went to stay with her parents. After getting settled, she called Uncle Jerry Jacobson. "Jerry, I left him. I left Jerry. We're done."

According to Robin, Jacobson didn't like what he heard. Did the Colombos have no ability to keep things quiet and low-key? It was constant drama with these two. He tried his best to cool down the situation. "I know, Robin. He's volatile. He's wild. He goes his own way. But let's be realistic. You aren't getting divorced. Stay with the folks for a few days, let things calm down a little. I know Jerry as well as you do, he'll settle down and be sorry about everything in a day or two. Then you two get back together and work things out. Frankie needs his parents."

Robin sighed and lit a cigarette while she talked. "Yeah, you're right. I just don't know what to do with the guy sometimes. He drives me crazy."

"Well, it's just too bad you didn't marry a better Jerry. Me, for example." He was joking, of course, but who knows. He still saw himself as a good guy, a former cop. In his mind, he wasn't really hurting anyone besides a faceless corporation that was going to award the prize money anyway. What harm did it do to steer things a little? He saw Jerry Colombo—rightly—as a mobster. He still didn't see himself that way, but he had started the drift to the dark side after his bout with Guillain-Barré syndrome. It had changed him whether he fully recognized it or not.

"Oh, c'mon, Uncle Jerry." She knew she couldn't get divorced. For better or worse, she was stuck with Jerry. And while things at home were tense and fucked up, she still loved him. He was the father of her child. She went back home.

Things remained tense, but the Colombos tried to work things out. One day, on the road in Robin's Explorer, with Jerry in the passenger seat and little Frankie asleep in his car seat in the back, they fell into their usual default state of bickering.

"Hey! Hey! Hey! You missed the fuckin' turn!" said Jerry.

"No, I didn't. What the fuck are you talking about?" answered Robin.

"Damn. You cannot drive. Pull over here. I'm gonna drive," said Jerry.

Robin had enough of Jerry's shit. She slammed both hands against the wheel. "Goddamn it, Jerry! I know where I'm going! Shut up!"

"Shut up? Shut up? Don't you fuckin' talk to me like that. Who puts the food on the table? Who bought this car? If I throw you out on the street, you got nothin' without me!"

As the fight geared up, Frankie woke up and started to cry. "Now look at what you did," said Jerry.

"Me? You're the one yelling and screaming like a maniac," yelled Robin like a maniac.

Jerry turned to calm Frankie. He unbuckled the straps of the car seat and took the kid out and placed him on the big bench seat. Robin punched him in his fleshy side as he turned. "Ow! Quit hittin' me, ya bitch!"

"Don't take him out of that seat! It's not safe!" She punched Jerry again for emphasis.

"Jeez! Stop! He'll be fine. Just let me—"

BOOM!

The world went sideways in an explosion of glass, metal, and plastic as the shiny chrome grille of an eighteen-wheeler slammed into the passenger side of Robin Colombo's Ford Explorer.

Frankie's wails brought Robin around. Groggily, she assessed the situation. The Explorer was pancaked between a big rig and the concrete abutment of an overpass. She was covered in blood. Checking herself as best she could, she wondered where it all came from. There was no blood on Jerry. He looked a little disheveled, but he didn't seem to be bleeding.

She frantically looked after Frankie, who appeared dazed but was sucking on a lollipop he must have found somewhere

inside the vehicle. One of his arms hung limply, possibly broken, but, overall, he seemed okay and calm.

Everything else was a mess. They were all banged up and
injured, and the arrival of EMT vehicles and cop cars, lights
flashing, cast a hellish blue hue over the scene. The car was
totaled. "Jesus, it's a wonder anyone walked away from that,"
said an officer. A recently arrived wrecker winched the totaled
Explorer onto his flatbed and took off for the junkyard.

At the hospital, the whole family was there. Robin's parents,
Jerry's parents, Jerry's brother Frank. *The news traveled fast,*
Robin thought. The room was filled with splashy get-well bou-
quets of flowers and everybody seemed to believe that Jerry,
although injured, would recover. Everybody was concerned, but
there was also a palpable sense of relief. After being checked out
and patched up, Robin and Frankie were okayed to go home.

Jerry Colombo, from his hospital bed, conscious and
hooked up to various monitors and drips, motioned for his
brother Frank. "I need a favor," Jerry whispered to him.
"There's fifteen thousand in cash in my glove box. Go to where
they towed the car and grab it. There's also two hundred thousand in a suitcase at Robin's dad's house. I need that, too. Go
get it." Frank, not wanting to let his big brother down, excused
himself and took off.

His first stop was the local impound lot. "Hey, you got a
smashed-up Ford Explorer in here?"

A highway patrol officer in a straw "Smokey" hat looked
up from a clipboard. "Yeah. We do. Holy smokes. That was
some accident."

"Yeah, yeah, yeah. Look, I need to get something from the
glove compartment," said Frank. He still had to get over to
Robin's parents' house to get that suitcase.

The officer led him to a heap of metal that had once been a Ford Explorer and said, "There ya go. See what I mean?"

Frank nodded. When the officer left him alone, he opened the glove box. It was empty.

He raced over to Robin's parents' house next. He banged on the door, and Robin's dad, Buddy, opened it. He was surprised as Frank bulled past him and made a beeline for the closet where he had been told the money was. "Hey! What do you think you're doing? What's going on?" Buddy demanded. Frank ignored him. He flung open the closet door and saw the case that was supposed to contain $200,000. Opening it up, he was shocked to find it empty. "Where's the money?" he demanded.

"Money? What money?" asked a confused Buddy. "There was never any money in there," he assured Frank. Later Frank would say, "Everybody said the money was never there, but why would Jerry tell me it was?"

Frank—who knew a thing or two about how Jerry earned a living—had one more thing he needed to do: he had to get over to Robin and Jerry's place and do a sweep. Specifically, he wanted to clear the Colombo freezer of McDonald's Monopoly winning game pieces and those unopened bags of M&M's candies he knew about. It was a quick stop. He found everything he needed, grabbed it, and took off to return to his brother's bedside in time to hear Jerry mutter "Happy Mother's Day" to their mom.

Hopeful for a recovery, the family stayed by Jerry's side, but he seemed to get worse with each passing day. It was a jolt for Frank to see his big brother, a guy he always saw as unbreakable and invincible, lying in a hospital bed hooked up to machines and barely conscious. This was serious. He stayed and held Jerry's hand. He wasn't leaving. On the fourth day, a

doctor came in and told the family Jerry was bleeding inter-
nally and that things didn't look hopeful. He advised the family
to consider taking Jerry off life support.

Frank wasn't involved in those decisions, leaving it to his
parents. It was a sad time. When Jerry's folks made the decision to let nature take its course, they went into the waiting
room and cried, but Frank stayed. He wouldn't leave until Jerry
took his last breath.

With the do-not-resuscitate order in place and life support
removed, it took a few hours for Jerry to pass. It seemed like a
lifetime to the family. It was too painful for the parents to stay
in the room, but Frank had vowed to stay with his brother to
the very end. He held his brother's hand until the moment
came. Robin, recovering at home and looking after Frankie,
was notified by phone. Everyone was in shock. It was hard to
believe that Jerry Colombo, such a force of nature, had been
taken from them so suddenly.

More than a week had passed since Jerry Colombo had
died. Frank had gone back to double-check to see if any other
cleanup duties needed to be addressed. When he got to Robin
and Jerry's house he saw that somebody else had gotten there
first. The place was ransacked. Drawers were open, the con-
tents spilled on the floors. Cushions overturned. Pillows had
been disemboweled, spewing cotton batting. A real mess.
Frank wasn't a wiseguy like his brother, but he knew enough to
understand it was suspiciously coincidental that his brother
gets in a serious accident and then has his house robbed.

Robin, meanwhile, was a mess. She knew Jerry's parents
blamed her for the accident . . . because they told her as much.
Mourning the loss of her husband, seeing a bleak future, Robin
succumbed to bad impulses and tried to commit suicide by

stabbing herself in the neck. It wasn't a great attempt. As she said later, "It didn't work. They put me in the nut hut."

After her release, Robin turned to narcotics and began a long downward spiral. She was arrested for fraud and incarcerated. Without a caregiver, Frankie was sent to live with Jerry's parents, who did their best to poison the child against his mother. "You know what else she did? After your dad—God rest his soul—passed away, she took all his money. All *your* money. She's a real tramp. But don't worry, Nana and Nano love you very much."

The mysteries surrounding the accident—the missing $15,000 from the Explorer, the $200,000 from Robin's parents' house—were never solved. Frankie was never convinced that William "Buddy" Fisher hadn't snagged it for himself. To this day, Robin Colombo disputes that, believing it could have been taken by anyone. "Look, Jerry didn't hang out with the most honest, upright people, you know," she'll say through a cloud of cigarette smoke. "And how do we know the accident wasn't a mob hit? You want me to prove that it was? How about you prove to me that it wasn't. How about that, huh?"

– 14 –

LEE CASSANO SPILLS HER SECRET

L ee Cassano was not a happy girl. Jerry Colombo had been a real dick ever since they had cashed the check the McDonald's Corporation had issued to Lee at a bank in Philadelphia. Lee would be glad to be rid of the guy once she got her cash. It was time to move on to her next adventure.

Lee primped in front of her bathroom mirror. She put her hair up in a ponytail, gave herself a spritz of hairspray and a couple pumps of one of her favorite fragrances. She moved to the bedroom where there was a full-length mirror and gave herself a final once-over. Nice. But something still bugged her. Where was her money? She couldn't get the thought out of her mind. Lee Cassano sat in a booth in a nondescript coffee shop and sipped her increasingly cool coffee. *What the fuck, fat boy? Whatever happened to my money?* wondered Lee.

A server interrupted Lee's thoughts. "Warm-up?"

"Huh?"

"More coffee?"

"Yeah, sure. Thanks."

Lee went back to obsessing. She got several more refills from the waitress. On the twelfth visit, the waitress—who had witnessed innumerable breakups, kiss-offs, bust-ups, and sad partings on the job—poured out some concern along with the coffee. "Anything wrong, honey?"

"No. I just have a lot on my mind," she answered. It was true. Her tax preparer had been on her about filing her taxes on time and kept reminding her that she would have to pay on her McDonald's winnings. She had been desperately trying to reach Jerry Colombo, but he had seemingly vanished.

Lee had no idea about the accident. When she finally learned that Jerry Colombo was dead, she knew she'd never see her dough. It was over. What could she do? Dead men pay no debts.

Worse than not getting her cut, she was still on the hook to the taxman. Lee's financial life was a lot like the rest of her existence: it was not concerned with tomorrow. Faced with all this, the weight of the world was on Lee's delicate shoulders. Despite the advice from the bank teller when Lee and Jerry collected the win, Lee hadn't put aside anything to pay the hefty cut the Department of the Treasury demanded from her because Jerry had never handed over her share of the money.

As April 15 approached, Lee filed her taxes but didn't pay what she owed. She couldn't. She didn't have it. While Lee enjoyed the perks of working for TWA—like the travel and the fun—she didn't make a lot of money. The taxes she owed on her winnings were going to be around $50,000 according to her preparer. Lee was really up against it. It was a huge bill she had no way of paying. The debt was like a big black vulture that had perched on her bedpost. It was the first thing she thought about when she got up in the morning and the last thing that crossed her mind when she drifted off to sleep. It even haunted her dreams. She was beyond stressed.

Over the course of the next year, she received several letters from the IRS. The amount she owed was accruing interest and grew a little bigger with each subsequent letter. After a couple years and increasingly serious-sounding letters from the IRS that warned of garnishments and liens and other terrible things, Lee decided to throw herself upon the mercy of the agency.

She called the local IRS office. On hold for hours, she was relieved to finally speak to an agent. She had never told her story to anyone, but here she was pouring it all out for a complete stranger.

"So I met this guy . . . He had a winning game piece . . . I cashed it in for him . . . We were supposed to split it . . . I never got my cut . . . He got killed before he could give it to me . . . I can't pay the taxes on it . . . I don't really see this as my responsibility, do you? . . . How is that fair?"

The IRS employee on the line couldn't have sounded less interested. Lee's secrets spilled. She ended the call and didn't know what to expect or what would come next. Weeks went by and turned into months. Had they forgotten about her?

Lee started to breathe a little easier. No news is good news. Then there was a knock at Lee's door. She answered and was shocked to find an FBI agent there.

The agent was unfailingly polite and all business. Lee appreciated that he didn't try to flirt with her. "Miss Cassano, you did call the IRS to make a report, didn't you?"

Lee's knees went weak. Problems with the IRS are one thing. Problems with the FBI are a whole different ball game. "I did. I did," Lee answered.

The agent had a clipboard with an 8" x 10" black-and-white photo that he showed to Lee. "Do you know this man?" he asked.

Lee looked at the photo. The man was white, middle-aged, and completely average. There was nothing about him that stood out in Lee's mind. She handed the picture back. "I've never seen this guy in my life," she answered truthfully.

"How about a name? Have you ever heard the name Uncle Jerry?"

Lee had heard the name before. Jerry had mentioned having to call him when she was in Philly cashing the check from McDonald's. She had also heard the name whenever she asked Jerry Colombo for her cut. "You'll get it when you get it. Everything goes through Uncle Jerry first." She even remembered how Jerry Colombo once introduced her to Robin as "Uncle Jerry's girlfriend."

"Okay. Thanks for your time, Miss Cassano. We'll be in touch."

The agent left and Lee stood with hands and knees quivering. *What just happened? The FBI? Really? What now?*

– 15 –

A.J. GLOMB CAN'T REFUSE

1998...

A ndrew "A.J." Glomb was in his late fifties and trying to find his next adventure in life. Due to a few missteps, he had a bit more free time on his hands than he wanted. Years earlier he had been enjoying a blue-collar lifestyle. He had worked his way up to general manager of a trucking company after years of driving and middle management. It helped get him out of Pittsburgh and move to Miami: the perfect place to drive around his vintage red Ferrari 328. With his salt-and-pepper hair, matching mustache, tinted eyeglasses, and snazzy South Florida threads, A.J. was easygoing and laid-back. His longtime friends would say that A.J. had always been the kind of guy people were drawn to. A.J. had something that made folks want to be around him. It was hard to describe other than to say that A.J. Glomb was cool.

His phone rang one day. It was his good friend Don Hart. They had connections from back when A.J. was in the trucking business but bonded on both being from Pittsburgh and both owning similar Corvettes. Don was even there the day A.J. bought his Ferrari from a state trooper. They spoke almost daily, and their friendship had grown over the last twenty years. A.J. looked up to Don as a bit of a mentor, given his success in business.

"A.J.! I got something you might be interested in. Write down this number and go to a phone booth and call me."

"Oh no, no, no. I had enough of that in my life. Sorry Don, I don't even want to hear about it. Just got off probation two years ago. Not interested."

A few days later, curiosity got the better of him and A.J. called him back. They spoke briefly by phone but planned to get together a few hours away at a car auction in Orlando, Florida. After selling his most recent trucking company, Don had a very successful car dealership in Atlanta. This was business for him, but they both enjoyed the cars as much as the company. While sitting together, Don explained that he'd been helping find winners for the McDonald's Monopoly game and handed A.J. a plastic bag with a winning game piece worth $1 million. A.J. immediately quipped, "Now I'm a millionaire just like you." At first A.J. didn't understand why Don was even involved. He didn't need the money. Don told him that he was friends with the guy who could get them, and that guy didn't have to worry about him running off with the money. Made sense. With a million dollars in his hand, A.J. was intrigued. The plan was A.J. would cash it and he and Don would just split it after his guy got his cut. A.J. always had a taste for adventure and excitement . . . and was ready to assume some risk because, to put it simply, he was bored.

A.J. loved to have a good time. In the late seventies, being a part of the Miami scene had brought him into contact with lots of people—some shady, some even shadier, and some were celebrities. Hedonism was the rule and travel, drugs, sex, and rock and roll were the daily vibe. In 1979, A.J. met Harold Robbins, the famous author of such wildly popular potboiler novels as *The Carpetbaggers*, *The Betsy*, and *The Lonely Lady*, at a club in Monte Carlo, a place A.J. frequently visited. Robbins, who'd sold more books over the course of his career than J. K. Rowling, was dedicated to pleasure. Naturally, A.J. and the novelist ended up chatting.

A.J., who had never even tried marijuana, was intrigued by something he had read in one of Robbins's novels. "Harold, in your books you make a reference to poppers and how they really make sex so much more intense—"

"Oh, yeah. Amazing," said Robbins.

"Uh, what exactly is a popper?"

"It's amyl nitrite. They use it to treat heart conditions like angina. But what it really does is intensify things—especially if you're buzzed on coke and weed. It comes in these little inhaler packs. You crush the container inside the pack and then inhale the fumes. If you time it so that you do a dose right as you orgasm, it's superintense."

A.J., already buzzed, surveyed the scene on the floor of the club. There were beautiful European women and everybody was dancing. He was ready to get down. "Got any? Think I could try some?"

"Got you covered," said the author. Robbins took out a little cotton packet, no bigger than a couple inches, that contained a crushable vial with a single dose of amyl nitrite. Robbins handed it to a woman who had joined them at their table. She crushed the capsule inside and then shoved the cotton pack under A.J.'s nose. "Inhale deep, baby!"

A.J. did as instructed and immediately felt the effects of the drug. There was a sudden drop in blood pressure and the whole world seemed to spin. A.J. suddenly felt like an accordion, squeezed one moment and pulled apart the next. Robbins was right. This was intense . . . and A.J. hadn't even gotten to the sex part yet. In fact, it was too intense, and A.J. panicked. His eyes darted around and his throat tightened. The popper had thrown A.J. into a genuine freak-out. He found a phone and called a reliable friend. "Drop what you're doing *and get me the fuck outta here!*"

Not long after, back in Florida, a cousin who knew A.J. as the kind of guy who could acquire almost anything gave him a call. "A.J.! What's up, dude? How you been? Hey, do you know where I could get some . . . 'ludes?"

A.J. was hip to a lot of things, but he was still a babe in the woods when it came to drugs. He had to ask, "Sure. But what are 'ludes?"

His cousin laughed. "Quaaludes, dude. Pills. Drugs."

"Not a problem," A.J. assured him. "Let me make some calls." A.J. figured someone among his many contacts could hook him up. He put in a phone call to the friend who had rescued him from his Monte Carlo casino freak-out. "Hey, man. Do you know where I could get something called 'quaalude'?"

Of course, he did. "How many do you need?"

"I'm not sure. My cousin asked for some and I'm just trying to help him out," A.J. explained.

"How much money do you want to make?" his friend asked.

A.J. hadn't really considered selling drugs, especially to his cousin, but being a natural-born hustler, he said, "Might as well get me a thousand."

"You got it."

A.J. completed the deal with his cousin and ended up with a nice little profit in his pocket, despite not having a clue about drugs or selling them. When another friend called and asked about getting some cocaine, he was all in. A.J. was officially in the drug business.

Things went well for a few years. A.J. made money and had all the intrigue, excitement, and adventure he could ever want. This was the era of the "cocaine cowboy" in South Florida in the 1980s. It was probably the most notorious time and place to be a drug dealer in the long history of the trade. It was decadent and flash and A.J. was smack-dab in the middle of it all.

Unfortunately, everything eventually comes to a close and on September 10, 1982, the party was over: A.J. was grabbed by the DEA and Organized Crime Drug Enforcement Task Force (OCDETF) Strike Force while meeting a connection outside the Pan American gate at Dallas Fort Worth International Airport. This was one of the first cases by the OCDETF, so they wanted to make a big deal of it. But as they arrested him and his friend, a pat-down revealed they had nothing on them. They were clean. Glomb had wisely decided to ship the cocaine via air freight on the same flight. They were about to get away with it until his contact on the ground showed up and was searched. Extremely overweight, his pants fell down during the search revealing the air freight bill in his pocket.

They had him dead to rights, but there was some irony to it. A.J. had been moving major weight without a problem. To be popped with such a small amount was almost . . . embarrassing. On December 6, at his hearing, the judge said, "Mr. Glomb, you're accused of conspiracy to possess cocaine with the intent to distribute. How do you plead?"

"Guilty, your honor," answered A.J., standing tall like a genuine outlaw.

In February 1984, A.J. received his sentence: twelve years behind bars plus a $15,000 fine. The judge's gavel fell like the hammer of doom. A.J. had a little time to get his affairs in order before he was to report to Federal Prison Camp (FPC) Montgomery on March 20. The camp was minimum security and located on the grounds of Maxwell Air Force Base in Montgomery, Alabama.

It had hosted a couple of figures from the Watergate scandal. Charles Colson, special counsel to United States president Richard Milhous Nixon from 1969 to 1973, did seven months after he pleaded to a charge of obstruction of justice. Former US attorney general John Mitchell served nineteen months for obstruction and lying to a jury.

A.J. was told by everyone that FPC Montgomery was "a country club." The reality was that no matter how comfortable and relaxed the place was, it was still a federal prison. A.J. would have to follow orders, toe the line, and be restricted twenty-four hours a day for twelve long years. It sounded like the worst country club in the country.

A.J. decided Europe sounded better, so he booked it. Nowadays, A.J. looks back on this time where he lived every day as if it was his last. He was a fugitive, constantly looking over his shoulder, but there was travel and intrigue. It was exciting. There was action. He was like a character from a spy movie. He had several fake identities and occupations as he lived his life on the run.

But he couldn't stay away forever. The next year, after shipping a Ferrari to California, A.J. was nabbed in a San Diego doughnut shop. The court remanded him to custody and A.J.

Glomb, outlaw, went behind bars. While there, being a well-rounded, knowledgeable guy, he got involved with an educational program inside where he taught other inmates and helped many get their GED. For his service, A.J. got a good behavior reduction of his sentence.

Honestly, a whole book could be written about A.J. Glomb. And probably should be. From his son tragically dying at nineteen in a car accident to the time he comically failed at being a hit man by hiding the gun in a bologna sandwich, he's up there as one of the most interesting and likable people we've ever met. One of the many surprising things we learned about A.J. was he wanted to be a policeman, and was, before his gun went off at a party. The irony.

So now holding the McDonald's million-dollar game piece, Don told him how it would work. A.J. would need to head up to Aliquippa, Pennsylvania, to claim it since too many winners had been showing up in South Florida and that piece was supposed to land in the area. Aliquippa had been home for A.J. for many years. His parents still lived there, as did his older brother, younger sister, and some extended family.

A.J.'s interest was tickled. The best part was, A.J. didn't have to put up any money. The risk felt super low. As he would later say with a shrug, "If someone offers you a million dollars, you're gonna take it . . . unless you've got to kill somebody. Then, you might not be interested." A.J. was positively, absolutely interested.

"I'm in," A.J. told Don Hart.

He flew into Aliquippa and was picked up by his cousin. On the way from the airport his cousin apologized for needing to make a pit stop. "Sorry, A.J., I gotta stop at McDonald's for the kids, they're obsessed with this Monopoly game they got going right now." A.J. couldn't help but laugh. "Don't bother," he told him. "I got the million-dollar game piece already." His cousin just laughed it off as A.J.'s typical sense of humor.

As the night went on, and the million-dollar game piece started burning a hole in A.J.'s pocket, he began having second thoughts. A.J. called Don Hart. "Don? Look, I've been thinking I might not be the best guy to cash in any million-dollar game piece no matter how legit the piece might be. A million dollars attracts too much attention and I don't need my name popping up on anyone's radar, or my face on the local news. They'd have a field day with my history and it might not end well for me. Also, my folks are elderly and it's a small town. I can't risk everyone coming up and bugging them about me winning a million dollars." Don wasn't worried, because A.J. already had a solution in mind.

A.J. decided the safest route would be to give the winning game piece to a trusted friend from San Diego. The next day he was on a plane. The plan was simple. The friend would cash in the winning game piece, get his winnings, and he, A.J., and Don would then make a three-way split. It was easy. They did a couple more of these deals, with A.J. acting as the recruiter. He knew a *lot* of people.

However, Don Hart began to feel uncomfortable with the whole thing and wanted out. So Don connected A.J. to Jerry at a party he was hosting. "You guys talk amongst yourselves; I don't want to know anything about it," he said, before walking away from his involvement altogether.

Ever since Jerry Colombo had died in a tragic traffic accident, Uncle Jerry Jacobson had been in a bind. Colombo had been his recruiter to find McDonald's Monopoly "winners" and now Don Hart, who he'd known and trusted, was backing out. But Don vouched for A.J. After all, Don was middleman to the middleman. A.J. was the person who was making all the connections anyway.

After a sit-down with A.J., Jerry Jacobson brought him on board. Why wouldn't he? Unlike Jerry Colombo, A.J. wouldn't be a constant worry. A.J.—even when he was running dope— knew how to keep a low profile. He didn't crave the spotlight. In fact, he did his level best to avoid it. More important, A.J. was smart. He had worked in legitimate businesses and knew how to handle himself. He also was funny, likable, had a calm demeanor and had a vast network of contacts, colleagues, and acquaintances across the country from which to recruit "winners." He'd proven it already with a handful of winners he'd done with Don. Glomb also brought a level of sophistication to the enterprise that Jerry Colombo could have never done. A.J. was the first to come up with the idea of using an annuity broker he knew and trusted to facilitate the two men's efforts to buy out the annual McDonald's payments to the "winners." This allowed them to bypass waiting years to collect all the winnings. Sure, it meant that the take-home was far less for the actual winner, but who wanted to wait twenty years to get all their money? Eventually, almost all games like the lotto started offering the lump-sum options. A.J. was just smart like that. There was no up-front money that had to be paid to Uncle Jerry. Everyone got their cut at the same time.

For A.J. Glomb, it was all gravy. Easy money, fun, excitement . . . it may not have been legal, but A.J. didn't see it as a serious crime. At most, A.J. surmised, he was guilty of possessing stolen property—hardly a crime at all in his mind. If he did have the misfortune of catching another bust—it'd be a slap on the wrist. According to Don, Jerry told him that once a

McDonald's employee had tried to take a winning game piece from inside the store and he was just fired. For A.J., this McDonald's Monopoly thing was a fun little caper, a side hustle, where he could help some of his friends and put a little play money in his pocket.

And so, from 1998 to 2000, A.J. Glomb worked to recruit ten winners for Uncle Jerry. The McDonald's Monopoly scam lived on. After Jerry Colombo's death and Don Hart's exit, Uncle Jerry was in great hands with A.J. Glomb.

You Deserve a Break Today:
HOW'S HE DOING IT? PART I

Throughout the 1990s, Jerry Jacobson stole high-value game pieces used in McDonald's Monopoly promotional game. Exactly how he did it was a mystery, though. Despite their best efforts, the FBI remained in the dark as to Jacobson's method. It wasn't until Jacobson was arrested and deposed that his scheme came fully to light. It didn't vary and it didn't change. This was Jerry Jacobson's system.

It was like a scene from a Cold War thriller: deep inside a concrete missile launch facility, two airmen receive a code that is refreshed every twelve hours. From a safe with double combination dials they extract a top-secret book that looks a lot like the three-ring binder with laminated pages Mom uses to keep her recipes. The book contains the meaning of the code. Each lock of the safe requires a different combination, and each man only knows the digits to open one of them. If the codebook indicates they have a go, two special keys, each worn from a chain around the neck of each man, were inserted into two steel latches. Under each latch was a cartoonish red button controlling the circuitry that would launch a nuclear missile and trigger Armageddon. The repetition was to prevent sabotage, chain-of-command breakdowns, accidental launches . . . and to give everyone something to do until the mushroom clouds bloomed.

Nobody was going to die in today's similar ritual at Dittler Brothers, the secure facility that made the game pieces for McDonald's Monopoly, but there was still a lot on the line. The process was to ensure the unassailable integrity of McDonald's popular promotional game. If you asked anyone at Dittler Brothers why the company went to such lengths for a silly game, most workers would answer, "Because it's McDonald's, man!" The company was an institution, a pop culture phenomenon, and as such practically demanded this kind of attention to detail and to security. Besides, McDonald's provided almost 75 percent of the printing company's yearly revenue. Dittler Brothers also made tickets for scratch-off games, raffles, and various state lotteries, but the McDonald's Monopoly game pieces were the cherry on top of the printing facility's sundae. McDonald's Monopoly kept the lights on at Dittler Brothers, Inc.

So, now, deep inside the secured building, the Simon Marketing security chief—the architect of this very process—and Hilda Bennett, the third-party accountant from PricewaterhouseCoopers who provided an additional layer of security, similar to how her firm controlled the ballots for the Academy of Motion Picture Arts and Sciences annual Oscar Awards—stood before a cabal of Dittler Brothers executives and solemnly began the ceremony.

In a Western-cut jacket, dress shirt, slacks, and pol-
ished black cowboy boots, Jerry gave off a country squire
vibe. Hilda Bennett wore a Lord & Taylor pantsuit, the
businesswoman's go-to. On the dais, Jerry made a show
of inspecting a sealed manila envelope. It was almost as
if he were a magician putting on a show for the executives. "As you can see," he said, "the holographic seal is
intact and has not been tampered with." He held up the
envelope for inspection: David Blaine without the showmanship. Hilda Bennett glanced at her watch and noted
the time in the official-looking notebook she carried. Jerry
then initialed the envelope over the sealed flap and
passed it to Hilda, who did the same.

Now witnessed and marked, Jerry once again held up
the envelope so the Dittler Brothers execs could get a
good look and see that everything was on the up-and-up.
Hilda once again looked at her watch and made a note in
her book.

Jerry then gravely placed the single manila envelope
bearing his and Hilda's signatures and the holographic
seal into an unremarkable black briefcase with a combination barrel on each side of the case's handle. He closed
the lid like an undertaker shutting a coffin. Then, as the
executives and Hilda respectively looked away, Jerry set
the combination for one of the locks. Hilda then under-
took the same procedure for the other lock. Once again,
the executives looked away, as did Jerry Jacobson.

A Dittler Brothers representative then made a show of
attaching the briefcase to Jerry's wrist with a handcuff. It
was as if the security chief was a government courier

carrying top-secret intelligence. Business concluded, Jerry and Hilda headed to the airport. There they boarded a Delta flight to Des Moines, Iowa. They sat side by side.

As the seat belt light came on, a flight attendant approached Jerry. "Sir, I have to ask you to either place your case beneath a seat or in one of the overhead bins."

Jerry smiled at her, raised his eyebrows, and subtly showed his wrist so that the attendant could see the situation. The woman nodded and brought a blanket for Jerry to conceal the case and its hardware. Jerry settled back into his seat and closed his eyes to catch some winks before they landed. So far, everything was proceeding according to plan . . .

– 16 –

THE TALE OF A LARCENOUS HEART

SPRING 2000

Out on I-85 just past the Georgia state line in Oconee County, South Carolina, is the town of Fair Play. It's near Lake Hartwell, which isn't a lake at all. As the locals will tell you, "It's a big-ass reservoir." If you're passing through and traveling faster than thirty-five miles per hour, you might miss Fair Play, which is to say it's small. It's also rural. And religious. It's a place where neighbors help neighbors. It's got six churches on 6.7 square miles of ground, and that's in a town whose population has never cracked seven hundred residents.

Established in 1833, legend says Fair Play got its name when two drunken no-accounts, now more politely described by historians as "settlers," met on a muddy street and went hand to hand following some unknown dispute. Eye-gouging, choking, biting, testicle-twisting . . . these pioneers were not exactly engaging in Marquis of Queensberry rules. The fight grew progressively ugly. That was when a bystander witnessing the savagery cautioned, "Play fair, boys. Play fair." Nobody remembers the interloper's name these days—his advice was ignored at the time anyway—but his ineffectual words echo through history as the basis for the town's name.

The fight might have remained the most exciting thing to ever happen in Fair Play—until the year 2000 when twenty-eight-year-old resident George Chandler claimed his million-dollar prize at the McDonald's in Walhalla, eighteen miles away. It was a big enough story that news crews descended upon the Golden Arches as George, accompanied by his nine-year-old son, stood grinning and almost dazed as he received his giant cardboard check from Ronald McDonald.

If anyone deserved to be a million-dollar McDonald's Monopoly winner, it was George Chandler. He had paid his dues and then some over the course of his short life. George had grown up in grinding poverty. It was the kind of hard-scrabble existence almost unheard of in the developed world. It was surreal, like a mash-up of Erskine Caldwell's *Tobacco Road* and the *Book of Mormon*. He was a likable kid: helpful, cheerful, hardworking, and blessed with a charming, outgoing personality. Unfortunately, those tools didn't do much to ease the deprivation the boy endured. The large Chandler family's home didn't even have running water . . . in 1980s America.

Times may have been tough, but the Chandlers managed to keep on keeping on through faith. They belonged to the local ward of the Church of Latter-day Saints (LDS) and were active congregants. It made the family outsiders in a region that was primarily Baptist, but the LDS community, despite being small, was tight-knit and close. It was at temple that George met an older, successful elder in the church, Dwight Baker. Initially, George had been a friend of Dwight's son, but Dwight soon took a shine to the kid. The older man had made his bones as a real estate developer, and was one of those rural sharpies who was always elbows deep in various deals and projects. Baker saw something in George. The kid had hustle. He was no whiner, either. Despite the grim circumstances at home, George met the day at a run and with a smile on his face. Dwight Baker was impressed. He started to keep an eye on the boy.

When he was fifteen, one of George's sisters decided to escape her family's poverty and get married. Her mother didn't approve of the plan. When George, helpful by nature, aided his sister's elopement, his mother threw him out. To underscore her disapproval, she dragged George's few belongings and clothes into the yard and lit a match.

With no place else to go and literally just the clothes on his back, George showed up at Dwight Baker's front door. Dwight and his wife, Linda, had five children of their own, and their house had just burned down. They were living in temporary housing but still took George in. He needed long-term care. Eventually the Bakers went through the steps required by the state of South Carolina and officially took George in as a foster son.

The kid followed Dwight around in awe of his success. He had never known anyone who owned a BMW at that point. For the first time in his life, George had something resembling stability and he thrived. He had a mind like a sponge when it came to business, and Dwight was astounded by the kid's instincts. *Is he a savant?* wondered Dwight. It certainly seemed so.

When George told his foster dad he planned to drop out of the ninth grade, Dwight had no objections. The kid went to work and did well. By the time George hit his early twenties, he owned his own injection-molding business and had scored a million-dollar contract to make parts and equipment. In addition to that, Dwight had brought George in on several property development opportunities. Both men made money. A deep trust had developed between George and Dwight. George not only saw Dwight as his mentor but also as a father. To George, his relationship with the Bakers was as strong, if not stronger, than any blood ties he had to his own biological parents.

One morning, George and Dwight met up for breakfast at a nearby diner. Biscuits, gravy, grits, eggs, and bacon . . . but no coffee, in accordance with both men's LDS beliefs.

"You gonna eat that toast?" asked Dwight.

George smiled and pushed two slices of toasted, buttered white bread across the red-and-white checkered tablecloth. Dwight snatched a diagonally cut piece and used it to sop up the yolky remains of a couple of sunny-side ups. "I gotta ask you something," Dwight said between bites.

George nodded. Dwight often brought up proposals like this. Casual but pointed, nonetheless.

"Sure," said George.

Dwight began the pitch. "Now this is sensitive material," he cautioned. "What I say doesn't leave this table or go any farther than you and me."

"Always," said George. "You know that."

"Well, I'm just saying because this is confidential," said Dwight. George thought the older man was being unusually serious.

"I'm listening," George told him.

"I have a good friend," Dwight began. "Luckiest guy in three counties. Well, almost the luckiest guy in three counties."

"Define 'lucky,'" George requested.

"He just won the million-dollar grand prize in the McDonald's Monopoly game," Dwight told him.

"That's pretty lucky," George agreed.

"Well, maybe not as lucky as you think," Dwight said.

"Why's that?" George was truly curious. Winning a million bucks just by randomly finding a token seemed lucky to George. What were the odds of that happening?

Dwight continued. "Poor guy's going through a divorce and it's getting ugly. He doesn't want to give half his winnings to his soon-to-be ex over the next twenty years," he explained.

"Understandable," admitted George. "There's nothing pretty about divorce. What's he going to do?"

"Well, I'm glad you asked. He's so determined that the wife doesn't get her hands on his winnings, he'd sell that game piece for a hundred thousand dollars. I'd buy it myself but I've got all my cash tied up at the moment. Was thinking you should buy it," advised Dwight. "It's a great opportunity."

George pushed the grits around his plate and contemplated the situation. "I don't know, Dwight. Is that even allowed?"

"I honestly don't think anyone cares," answered Dwight. "McDonald's is paying out that money one way or another."

George had some doubts, but he had seen people selling tickets and prizes on eBay, so Dwight's proposal didn't seem *that* odd to him. Besides, George knew all about the ugliness of separations. He had just finalized divorce proceedings with his own ex-wife. It was quite the bitter ending. He'd lost nearly half his property and was left a single father. He sympathized with Dwight's friend. Besides, this wasn't some stranger bringing him this opportunity. It was Dwight Baker. George owed everything to Dwight. What would have become of George if Dwight hadn't been there when George was tossed out by his own mother? Dwight had no reason to lie to George or lead him astray. Besides, Dwight was a pillar of the community and an elder in their local LDS ward.

"Of course I'll do it," said George.

Dwight reached across the table and patted George's hand in a fatherly manner. "Oh, man. That's great news. You're a good kid."

George's agreement was testament to Dwight's skill as a salesman. For as long as anyone could remember, Dwight was a natural huckster, a real-life pitchman seemingly pulled from a late-night infomercial. George was aware of Dwight's nature, but he always saw him as a mentor and someone who would never hustle his foster son.

In business, Dwight was affable, avuncular, and always engaged with his clients. Sometimes he even became friends with them. Such was the case when Dwight was selling lake-front plots he was developing over at Lake Hartwell.

The client obviously had money, Dwight surmised from his clothes and luxury car. The client was gregarious—almost as much as Dwight was—and seemed to have a good head for business, too. They started palling around and became close friends.

That client was from Atlanta and his name was Jerry Jacobson, head of security for Simon Marketing. As the friendship grew and deepened, the men's wives—both named Linda—also became friends. It wasn't unusual for the couples to take trips and have dinner together.

After a couple years of this, the fun was temporarily interrupted when Dwight was seriously injured in a motor grader accident. As a property developer, Dwight often did some of the labor needed to improve a plot of land. This time, doing a bit of leveling like he had done countless times before, the grader lost its grip on a soft and muddy incline and rolled.

Dwight was unable to jump clear and his body took the full weight of the machine. Had he been on hard ground, he would have been crushed like a bug. The mud saved him.

It was a long recovery. Dwight was bedridden for months. He grew depressed. Even out of bed and recovering with the help of a cane did nothing to lighten his mood. One day, his wife brought him the phone, a big smile on her face. Dwight took the call and heard Jerry Jacobson's voice. "Hey, buddy! How you feelin'?"

"I'm okay," lied Dwight. Jerry could hear it in Dwight's voice, and he was concerned. Dwight was always a bolt of lightning. Constantly on the sell. The person he spoke to now sounded so meek and defeated.

"Hey, did I ever tell you about the time I got laid up with Guillain-Barré syndrome? In bed and paralyzed. My greatest enemy? Depression. It did a number on my head. I'll be there soon. We gotta get you out of the house for a little while."

Before Dwight could beg off or make an excuse, Jerry ended the call. The next day, he was at Dwight's door. "Let's go for a drive, huh?" Dwight, who currently needed a walker to get around, was not very mobile. When Jerry arrived, he pulled up next to the side door of Dwight's house and helped his injured friend into the car. Dwight was appreciative that Jerry came to get him out of the house.

In the car, Dwight was quiet for the first few miles. The sunlight, the smell of the fields, the brisk air that blew through the slightly opened passenger window with a whistle, all of it demanded his attention. *I have been inside too much*, thought Dwight. He turned to Jerry. "This ride is just what I needed," he said. "Thanks, buddy."

"I told you: I know what you've been going through. It's good to get out. Move around a little bit. Loosen up. You don't want to sit around the house all day. You're not built for that," said Uncle Jerry.

The miles began to add up. The country music station played softly over the car's stereo system. Jerry could see that Dwight was starting to enjoy himself. The oppressive mood in the car began to lighten and lift. The two men chatted and made conversation. Things got interesting when Jerry asked, "If I could put you on to a surefire way to collect a million dollars, would you be willing to put up a hundred thousand in order to get it?"

Dwight assumed it was a hypothetical along the lines of "If you had to party with a ghost, would it be Casper or Boo Berry?" He bit. "Yeah, of course I would. Heck yeah."

"Well, let's do it," said Jerry.

"Wait. You're serious?" asked Dwight.

"Serious as can be, my friend."

Realizing Jerry wasn't joking, Dwight had a confession to make. "Well, I'm awfully grateful you thought of me, Jerry. I just can't do it right now. The accident put me back and I'm overextended on the lake project. I just don't have the cash right now." He suspected the whole thing was shady, but the idea of putting up $100,000 and getting back $1 million was intriguing and not easily dismissed. Besides, what was business if not risk?

"C'mon, Dwight. You're a business guy. You don't have to put up your own money. Find somebody and maybe get a cut from them as a finder's fee or whatever. You're creative. I know you won't have trouble finding someone to throw in on this," Jerry said.

"What do I say?" wondered Dwight. "'Say, friend, I can't give you any details, but if you give me a hundred grand, I can get you a million dollars'?"

"Dwight, c'mon. Find somebody and make up a story about how a friend of yours—who will remain nameless because he doesn't exist—is going through a nasty divorce and wants to keep his winnings away from his greedy wife. It's bulletproof." They drove along in silence for a few more miles when Jerry said, "Wanna go get a burger or something?"

"No. Linda'll have something at home. I'm watching the ol' figure. I put on a few pounds when I was laid up. Trying to slim down," Dwight answered untruthfully. A hamburger would kind of hit the spot, but he had some thinking to do.

Jerry took a turn and then another and began the long drive back to Dwight's home, never mentioning the million dollars again. When he dropped Dwight back home—once again helping him out of the car, wrangling the walker, and getting him back in the house—he told his friend, "Think about what I told you."

Dwight thought about Jerry's proposition for several days. Maybe it was the boredom of being cooped up inside the house or maybe it was the pain medication, but Dwight eventually decided he would get on board with Jerry's plan. He knew that his foster son, George Chandler, had just scored big with his injection-molding contract and had cash on hand. George was a good kid.

They met for breakfast the next morning and after the last of the egg yolk was sopped off the plates, they went straight to George's warehouse where George wrote two checks for $50,000—one for Dwight and one for Uncle Jerry—and handed them to Dwight. George received the winning game piece—in a Ziploc bag that wasn't even sealed—just as Dwight Baker had promised—and he had no trouble cashing it in at the McDonald's in nearby Walhalla.

It was easy. George may have been on the hook now for the taxes on a million-dollar windfall, but he was a smart kid, and he'd figure out something. Despite knowing it would take a few years to break even on the deal, it still seemed like a good long-term investment.

When Jerry explained to Dwight that their arrangement could be ongoing, Dwight hesitated. His LDS faith held him back . . . for about a hot second. Dwight Baker, Mormon elder and respected local business leader, was faced with the fact that he had "a little larceny" in his heart.

– 17 –

WHO WANTS TO BE A MILLIONAIRE?

n Fort Lauderdale, A.J. Glomb had finished dinner with his longtime girlfriend Judy, poured a glass of top-shelf booze, and plopped down in front of the TV. Like a huge slice of the country, they were tuned in to the popular game show *Who Wants to Be a Millionaire*. Host Regis Philbin posed the show's million-dollar question to contestant Kevin Olmstead, an environmental engineer from Ann Arbor, Michigan. Game show history was about to be made. Regis, perched on a swivel chair on the dramatically dark set, leaned forward to ask the million-dollar question: "Okay, Kevin, this is the big one. Who is credited with inventing the first mass-produced helicopter?" As Regis asked the question, it appeared on-screen with four possible answers: *A) Igor Sikorsky; B) Elmer Sperry; C) Ferdinand Von Zeppelin; D) Gottlieb Daimler.*

It wasn't a question that most viewers would know the answer to off the top of their heads. It wasn't even a question that most contestants—steeped in trivia and obscure factoids—would know the answer to. *Who Wants to Be a Millionaire* had been in a bit of a doldrums over the previous months. July was the last time the show boasted a million-dollar winner. Since then, only eight contestants had even made it to the million-dollar round.

To goose up the excitement of a show that didn't seem to produce winners anymore, the show added a bonus pool. Each time a contestant choked and failed to reach the final round, $100,000 went into the pool. By the time Kevin Olmstead found himself opposite Regis Philbin, the amount of the pool totaled $1,180,000.

"Okay, Kevin. It's time. Final answer," prompted Regis.

Without a moment's hesitation, Olmstead leaned in to the mic and said, "I know this. It was the Sikorsky helicopter, so I'm going to make Sikorsky my final answer."

Regis Philbin's tenor almost went up a whole octave. "You just won two million!" The audience erupted in applause, Kevin and Regis rose from their chairs and embraced, the camera panned over the ecstatic faces of Kevin's family, and confetti rained down upon the set.

America loves a winner, and A.J. was about to help manufacture one. Jerry had just given A.J. the *People* magazine winning game piece and told him it needed to be a winner near Rhode Island. A.J. knew exactly who to call. He walked down to the local pay phone, a habit from his drug days when doing a deal. He picked up the phone, dropped in a few quarters for long distance, punched in a number, and waited.

"Hello?" a male voice answered on the other end.

"Michael! Michael Hoover!"

Michael recognized the voice immediately. "A.J.! You get my birthday card I sent you?"

A.J. didn't miss a beat to reply, "Yeah, always so thought-ful. Listen I got something for you."

A.J. knew Michael Hoover from back in the day when A.J. was still running drugs and living the high life. They had met at a Las Vegas casino when A.J. took a seat at a blackjack table to play a quick hand. Michael Hoover, in vest and tie, was the dealer. A.J. ran into some luck and before too long, he had tipped Michael well and had struck up a conversation. A.J. was gregarious. So was Michael Hoover. They became friends and remained so. When A.J. was in prison, Michael Hoover sent him cards to mark every birthday and Christmas. He had also helped A.J. get a fake ID when he went on the run.

A.J. played it cool. "Nothing we need to discuss right now, but I was thinking of making a little trip up that way. You gonna be around?" he asked.

"Where am I going to go other than to work at Foxwoods and back? Money's a little tight as you know. I'm working nights, but I'm around," said Hoover.

Though McDonald's Monopoly business wasn't discussed here, Hoover pulled out at least one complaint from his catalog of bad trips, bummers, misfortunes, and bad luck. There had been an auto accident, a broken leg, a girlfriend leaving, and the loss of a job. As A.J. would note later, "Michael's life kind of fell apart." But Glomb was sympathetic. His quarters ran out, but the trip was set.

After a three-day drive up north, stopping to see friends and family along the way, A.J. arrived at Michael's house in a Jaguar he'd recently purchased from Don. Up until now A.J. made a point of telling a made-up story to most of the friends that he gave a piece to. But with Hoover he told him the truth.

After all, Hoover was one of his best customers when he was in the drug business; they'd even gone to a few orgies together back in the day. Apparently that bonds you.

A.J. showed Michael the winning game piece and walked him through everything to expect. "It's like taking candy from a baby," said Glomb. Michael was all in. The plan was A.J. would stay with him for the next couple days to help him walk it into a McDonald's, fill out all the proper forms, and see they were mailed off.

"You should expect a call in a couple weeks. Sometimes it takes a little less, sometimes a little more," A.J. told him as he was getting in his car for the long drive home.

"What should I tell them when they ask how I got it?" asked Michael.

A.J. just laughed. "I don't care. Just don't tell them you got it from me. Where do you see *People* magazines? Keep it simple. Nothing to it."

Jerry Jacobson had provided some deep intel to A.J. Through a computer program at Simon Marketing, Jerry was able to learn which product—like a magazine insert—held a winning game piece. The program also revealed which region of the country this game piece would be found. It was crucial information. If the winning game piece was destined for New England but was acquired and redeemed in Phoenix, it would raise alarms. Knowing the who, what, when, and where of the winning game piece would be necessary for the story Hoover would eventually tell the FBI undercover team operating as Shamrock Productions under the direction of Special Agent Doug Mathews and McDonald's young PR guru, Amy Murray, civilian. Now as for why Hoover came up with such a complicated story, that we'll never know. Perhaps he thought it sounded more believable than, "I was just grocery shopping and saw the magazine there at the checkout, so I bought it along with a pack of gum."

More McDonald's Monopoly winners had started to pop up. Dwight Baker, after putting his foster son, George Chandler, onto a million-dollar win in South Carolina, found another recruit, an acquaintance named Ronnie Hughey. Together, they came up with their own story. Aware of the need to avoid clusters of winners all from the same area, Hughey went so far as to get a Tennessee driver's license and to establish a fake address in that state.

Uncle Jerry's scheme grew under A.J. Glomb and Dwight Baker in ways that never could have happened when the late Jerry Colombo was involved. Neither man knew of the other, and they each had different deals with Jerry. Dwight assumed Jerry was handling the other game pieces and just ran out of people he knew. Was Jerry hedging, not wanting to rely on just one middleman? Was the volume of winners getting too large? Was it something else? Whatever it was, Dwight and A.J. independently knew a lot of people and were effective at selling the idea to them. It didn't hurt that McDonald's—given the success of the game—began running the contest several times a year. Uncle Jerry's operation was expanding quickly. The people brought into the scam by A.J. and Dwight began to recruit others. After Hughey claimed his million-dollar prize, he brought in a friend of his from Texas, John Davis . . . who would be the last "winner" of the McDonald's Monopoly promotion.

Davis's involvement proceeded according to the usual pattern from Dwight: Davis handed off the $100,000 up-front money to Ronnie Hughey who then handed it off to Dwight Baker. Dwight Baker, cash in hand, called Jerry Jacobson. "We are a go," said Dwight.

Unfortunately, that call did not go unnoticed.

In the FBI wire room in the Jacksonville field office, Tim Adams, the rookie agent, was doing everything he could to stay alert monitoring the lines when he caught a call that made him sit up and take notice. "Get Mathews and Dent in here now," he told one of the other rookies in the room. "They're gonna wanna hear this. Get Chris Graham, too."

Mathews, Dent, and Graham came down to the room and Mathews excitedly asked, "What do we have?"

"You need to hear this now," said Adams. He punched a button and replayed the recorded call. They listened to Dwight Baker lay out how things were going and that he "got it" from "his guy."

"Let's meet now," suggested Jerry Jacobson.

"Now?" said Dwight. He sounded a little put out.

Jerry Jacobson had a window. "Yes, Dwight, now."

Capitulating, Dwight asked, "Where?"

"Same place off I-85," said Jerry.

Dwight took a beat to answer. "I'll try. Might take me a little longer with traffic." The call ended and Adams switched off the recorder.

"That's it? They don't give a location?" said Mathews.

"Somebody get a map," said Rick Dent, as always calm under fire. He was the guy you wanted in your foxhole when the shit came down.

A map was brought in and Dent spread it out on a table. "So if you were in their shoes . . . "

Mathews crowded in. "We should be careful. We want to catch these guys. Let's not arrest them too early."

"If I wanted to meet with you and I asked you to come to me, what would you tell me?" asked Dent.

"I'd tell you to get bent. If I gotta drive, so do you. We meet halfway. That's fair," said Mathews.

Somebody got a map. There were exactly 110 miles between the two men's homes. At a midway point a bit closer to Jerry was the popular Château Élan golf resort. Could this be the meeting place? Chris Graham had a hunch it was. He decided to act.

"Call Atlanta," said Chris Graham, the special agent in charge. "Get a surveillance team out there now."

A call was made, the Atlanta office was looped in, and a surveillance team rushed to the location. It was all seat of the pants. There was no time to finesse this thing. The van from Atlanta screeched into a space where they could observe discreetly. They set up the cameras.

Back in Jacksonville, the team fretted they didn't have the right location. The Atlanta team wondered the same thing as they sat observing nothing.

And then a silver Lincoln Navigator pulled into a spot next to a red minivan.

There, in front of the FBI's surveillance camera, "Uncle" Jerry Jacobson exited the minivan and slipped into the passenger seat of the big Lincoln Navigator. They didn't have to wait long for an answer. Jerry Jacobson stepped out of the Navigator holding a thick envelope. "I don't know, but, man, you couldn't ask for a better camera angle. We got it *all*. Tell Jacksonville."

– 18 –

CHERCHEZ LA FEMME

MAY 2001...

Dwight Baker had been a busy man. He was grateful for meeting Jerry, becoming friends, being brought into the scheme, successfully recruiting others . . . It all seemed to be foolproof. Of course, he was aided by his self-described larcenous heart. With his greed guiding him, Dwight Baker decided it was time to collect his reward.

Dwight Baker, despite steering recruits into Jerry Jacobson's feeder system and getting his cut for his efforts, was still facing a mountain of medical bills and had limited access to cash thanks to the failure of his latest property development deal. He also found himself in possession of a winning McDonald's Monopoly game piece worth $500,000 that would be paid out as a lump sum rather than $50,000 a year like the million-dollar prizes. He wanted to claim it for himself but couldn't risk questions from the community about how he and George had both won. Dwight needed to bring in someone close enough they wouldn't run off with the money. He thought he had found the perfect recruit.

Brenda Phenis was Dwight's sister-in-law.

She had just gone through a divorce and moved from South Carolina to Indiana. Dwight, originally being from Indiana, found time to meet with her to bring up his $500,000 game piece.

"So, Brenda, you know the McDonald's Monopoly game that George won a while back? Do you ever play?"

"A few times."

Dwight tossed her a smile. "Well, what I'm about to tell you must remain confidential. Linda and George don't even know. Turns out McDonald's picks the winners in advance. And I know they guy who does it."

"Why are you telling me this, Dwight?"

"Well, I just so happen to have the $500,000 winning game piece that will pay out all at once, you don't have to wait twenty years to get it all. I can't turn it in myself because of my connection to George but you can. It's gotta be split a few ways after taxes, but it's free money for you. I just need someone I can trust with this, and you're family."

"Why don't you tell Linda? What makes you think I won't tell her?" she asked.

"The less people that know about this the better. What good would telling her do?" Dwight really only wanted her to answer if she was in or not. He had to take the risk if she could keep it a secret.

Brenda, fifty, had been around long enough to know nothing was ever really "free." But she needed the money. "What do I need to do?" she asked, affirming her interest.

The first thing Dwight said was, "We can't do it here." Then he explained the scheme and how they would have to play it.

After an address in Asheville, North Carolina, was established for her, Brenda walked into a McDonald's in the Land of the Sky, as the city was nicknamed, and claimed her prize. It took longer than expected for Brenda to receive the check. Dwight could only wonder why. He had no idea that the FBI weren't ready to make any arrests and were trying to stall as long as possible. It was a lot of money to ask McDonald's to pay out in order to maintain the appearance everything was normal. The deal Brenda had made with Dwight had her kicking back $90,000 to Dwight and another $70,000 to Dwight's unnamed "guy," Jerry Jacobson. However, when the check finally arrived, a thought crossed Brenda's mind: *I'm keeping the dough.* Stronger people than Brenda Phenis have succumbed to their own greed when suddenly confronted with money. Was it because she wasn't strong enough or that she knew Dwight would have to tell Linda, which he wasn't going to do? Or was it something else entirely?

Brenda went dark, much to Dwight's alarm. He rushed over to the Asheville apartment he had rented for her. Letting himself in with his key, he saw an empty FedEx envelope from the McDonald's Corporation. If he had been concerned before, he was absolutely freaking out now. He also didn't have $70,000 to give Jerry his cut. Jerry had been good to him, but Dwight feared him enough not to screw him over. He made it clear on several occasions that he wasn't just doing this out of the goodness of his heart. Dwight raced back home to Linda.

"What happened to Brenda?" Dwight asked his wife. "Have you heard from her?"

"No. Why?"

Dwight spilled his guts to Linda and brought her up to speed. He didn't know what else to do. She was shocked. She hadn't a clue about what her husband was telling her. Instead of targeting her anger at Dwight, to his surprise, it was aimed at her sister Brenda. Had he misjudged Brenda's trustworthiness? Clearly.

Dwight had already laid out a plan for Brenda: after she received her winnings, they would go to California to get a cashier's check for the money. She opted instead to do it solo, making a pit stop in Vegas.

Dwight began making phone calls and eventually reached someone who knew Brenda had just left for California.

"When is she coming back?" Dwight demanded.

"Relax, dude. She'll be home tomorrow," said the contact.

Dwight ended the call. "Linda! We gotta get to Indiana! Now!"

There was no time to analyze the situation now. They had to get to the airport and stop Brenda before she did anything with the money and disappeared for good. It would be a long, mad ride.

"You're driving too fast!" Linda said to Dwight. He was. It was almost a ten-hour drive from South Carolina to Indiana. Dwight wanted to make it in six. His right foot was glued to the floorboard.

"Stop trying to call her. Stay off the phone." Linda ignored Dwight's pleas for caution and punched in Brenda's number on a cell phone. She put it on speaker. It rang. It rang again. And then he and Linda heard Brenda's voice.

There was much angry crosstalk.

Brenda laid out what was up. "We had a deal, I'm changing it. I'm keeping the money. Go ahead and sue me. Call the cops."

Linda made it clear Brenda needed to be on that flight to Indianapolis and she and Dwight would be waiting for her. A few more unpleasantries were exchanged before Brenda hung up Dwight's cell.

Dwight and Linda were both upset. The very idea! How dare Brenda try to rip them off? "My own sister!" said Linda.

"We'll stop her," Dwight assured her. "I'm gonna kill her when I see her!" he shouted.

People were listening. When Brenda hung up the phone, she hadn't ended the call. Did she forget to hit cancel or press the wrong button? No one knows for sure, but because the FBI had gotten permission to tap Dwight's phone, they not only heard the entire conversation between Linda and Brenda but now had a live wire, essentially, in the car. When Dwight mentioned "killing" Brenda, it was just a figure of speech. Dwight may have been a lot of things, but killer wasn't one of them. He was just venting out of frustration. Still, the FBI didn't know that with certainty and had to take it seriously. Did Dwight Baker, LDS elder, successful businessman, and local real estate developer just threaten to murder his sister-in-law? People have been killed for a lot less than half a million bucks.

The normal situation when surveilling a subject is to hang back, be cool, and stay out of sight. Just gather the evidence electronically and let the suspects incriminate themselves with their own words. The only time the FBI would go in hot was if someone's life was in danger.

Given the way Dwight and Linda were raving and sputtering, the FBI wasn't taking a chance. "Get the US Marshals out there now!" was the order and a plainclothes team was scrambled. Marshals spread out through Indianapolis International Airport to keep eyes on the concourse. In the airport's surveillance room, another team of marshals had eyes on Brenda Phenis, looking as if she didn't have a worry in the world besides wrangling her suitcase through the milling crowd of travelers.

"What's the woman's name?" asked a marshal.

"Phenis."

"Is that French?"

"Don't know. Hey, hey! There's our male suspect."

They watched Dwight Baker hustle around the floor, desperate to find Brenda. Like Dwight, Linda Baker was also on the hunt for her sister, cruising the concourse like a shark gliding over a coral reef. Brenda appeared unfazed . . . until she spotted an angry Linda Baker striding her way. She froze. Turning around, she looked for an exit, but saw her route blocked by a determined Dwight. *Oh shit!*

None of the three noticed the teams of US Marshals surrounding them.

Back at the FBI field office in Jacksonville, squad chief Chris Graham fretted to Rick Dent and Doug Mathews. "This is a delicate situation. I wish we had eyes on this thing. If those marshals move too fast and scoop up Phenis and pals, it could compromise the operation." He hoped that by keeping back a bit, there was less chance of things spinning out of control. The last thing they needed was someone to panic, bolt, and kick off a potentially dangerous situation in a public place.

"Gonna be worse if they act too late," added Dent.

Back at Indianapolis International, the marshals hung back as Dwight and Linda confronted Brenda.

"What the heck, Brenda?" hissed Linda. "We were trying to be good to you."

"Where's the money?" demanded Dwight.

"Y'all need to step off," cautioned Brenda, holding up an open hand.

The argument continued as the throng of travelers flowed around them. All of it under the unblinking eye of the US Marshals.

- 19 -

FINAL WINNER

JUNE 2001...

Remnants of Tropical Storm Allison swept the Southeast with heavy rain and flooding. Powered by the warm waters of the western Gulf, the storm never quite reached hurricane status, but it definitely made itself known. It remained stuck over Texas for several days before it drifted east along the Gulf Coast into southern Louisiana. The rain fell in buckets, up to seven inches in some areas. Alabama and northern Florida, both of which had been under a moderate drought before the storm, experienced localized flooding. While Jacksonville was mostly spared the worst of it, another kind of storm was brewing in the FBI's field office as Rick Dent and Doug Mathews's investigation came to a head.

On the muddy grounds of one of his properties, Dwight Baker met with his pal Ronnie Hughey. As they walked the plot, the thick South Carolina mud sucked at their boots. Dwight had sold him a million-dollar Monopoly piece and Ronnie had cashed it in. Now, Hughey was fully invested in the scheme and ready to collect his own finder's fee. He told Dwight he knew "the perfect guy" to be the next winner.

Dwight handed off a winning game piece to Ronnie. "For our next winner, John Davis of Granbury, Texas! Come on down!" he crowed. The two men shook hands, kicked the mud off their boots, and got back into their cars. They went their separate ways believing everything was A-OK.

It wasn't. The FBI's wire room had been monitoring Dwight closely. He was gregarious and gave them a lot to work with. They learned more every day. There were maps with pushpins. There were cards with names written on them and notes upon notes of how each was connected to the other. The wire room hummed. When Rick Dent entered with yet another Tupperware container of decadently delicious chocolate and macadamia cookies and handed them off to Tim Adams, the rookie agent gave him the tapes from the night before in exchange. "More cookies, guys. You're gonna love these." As Dent signed for the latest batch of tapes, Adams smiled. "We know the next winner."

They sat down to listen to what was on the tapes and learned that John Davis, of Granbury, Texas, would collect his winnings soon. Mathews gave a heads-up to Amy Murray. "We know the next winner! Guy from Texas. John Davis. I'd guess he'll claim it any day now, so stay on your toes."

When Amy got the call from the McDonald's Redemption Center alerting her that a man named John Davis had just presented a million-dollar game piece at a Texas McDonald's she acted like it was just another day at the office. The excited supervisor in the Redemption Center was much more amped, "Amy! Amy! We have a winner! A million-dollar winner!"

"Okay, calm down, calm down. That's great though. Who is it?"

The excitement surrounding the presentation of a winning game piece was always contagious and the supervisor in the Redemption Center was not immune to it. "It's a fella named John Davis. He's local. From Granbury. Jeez! A million bucks. Can you believe it?"

"I can. I can," said Amy. She remained professional and handled the call just as she did previous ones when she wasn't looped in with the FBI. When she got off the phone with the Redemption Center, she immediately placed a call to Doug Mathews to inform him the stolen game piece had been claimed. "Davis just presented his token at McDonald's," she said. "Are we going to pay him a visit?"

"You know we are . . . but I have an idea," said Mathews. "Let's really make it a big deal this time. What do you say?"

Amy, used to Doug Mathews's ideas at this point, knew it was always good to get some clarification first. "What do you have in mind?"

"Well, we're celebrating this guy's win, right? What's at every big celebration?" he asked.

"Uh, balloons?"

"Not unless you're celebrating a kid's birthday or something. I'm talking something that'll really attract some attention . . . and will look great on camera!"

"Doug, we're not shooting a real video, remember?"

"Yeah, yeah, yeah, but *he* won't know that," Mathews reminded her. "Something loud and flashy is what Shamrock Productions needs."

Uh-oh, thought Amy. "What are you thinking, Doug?"

"Do you know where we can get a confetti cannon? That would be so cool, don't you think?"

Amy had to agree that if they wanted to sell the subterfuge to John Davis, going big might be just the thing. "That would be cool, Doug. Not sure what a confetti 'cannon' is, but I'm sure I can find one."

The Shamrock Productions van navigated a course through a humid, new, upper-middle-class suburb in Granbury, Texas. "Damn. These are some cheesy-looking houses," said one of the agents on the team.

"They're called 'McMansions,'" corrected Mathews.

The team had really come together as Shamrock Productions and now operated and acted like the real thing . . . although none of their skills involving lights, sound equipment, or camera had progressed beyond the rudimentary. Doug Mathews couldn't have told anyone how to turn on the camera, but he didn't really care. He had a confetti cannon. It sat on the floor of the van like an equal member of the team. Mathews patted the squat black device that resembled a mortar launcher with a keg-size bore. "And there will be noise when you fire it, right?" he asked Amy.

"I assume," she said. "I guess we'll find out."

The van turned down an oak-lined street, passed the battered brown Extreme Plumbing panel truck that housed the team's backup, and pulled up into John Davis's driveway. Immediately, the latest fraudulent winner in the McDonald's Monopoly promotional game came striding out of his front door. "Charging out" may have been more accurate.

Mathews went into high alert. The agent behind the wheel nodded and smiled at Davis. "You guys sit tight," Mathews ordered as he sprang out of the van and matched John Davis stride for stride. Their target's dark energy was unsettling. Davis, forty-four, barreled toward them chest-first, arms pumping. He was a man on an unknown mission. Doug Mathews's experience told him that guys who walk up like that on complete strangers almost always have trouble in mind. Did he have a weapon? Had their cover been blown? They weren't going to know until Doug talked to the guy. Or the bullets started flying.

"Hey, guy! How ya doin'? You're John, right? I'm Doug Dewitt, your video director. I'm here to make you a star! Put 'er there, man!" said Mathews. He was chest to chest with Davis and was already pumping the hand of the million-dollar winner. It slowed Davis's roll.

Temporarily taken aback by Mathews's almost aggressive display of friendliness, Davis stammered, "Hey, hey, yeah. Good to meet you. Yeah, I'm John. Can I please ask y'all something before you come in?" There was a pleading look in his eyes.

Mathews quickly sensed this wasn't the threat he initially suspected. He softened a bit. Davis explained, "My wife's something of a neat freak. She gets upset by things like this. She's already a dang nervous wreck worrying about you guys coming in and moving things around and making a mess—"

Doug Mathews sized up the front of the house. Not a thing out of place. It was clinically neat. Even the doormat looked brand-new. No stray dried leaves. The more he looked, the more he saw an exhibit, not a home. "You want us to take our shoes off before we come in, don't you? I mean, that's cool. Not a problem."

John Davis sagged with relief. "Aw, man. That's so great. Thank you. Thank you. Why don't you bring your people in?"

Mathews returned to the team waiting at the van. "We're good to go. Everything's cool. Let's make some magic!" Distracted by the operation, he may have neglected to tell them about Mrs. Davis's concerns.

Inside the house, the Shamrock Productions crew were amazed by how unlived-in the place looked. It was like a museum exhibit for "Life in Suburban America, 2001," but without a trace of human activity. When John Davis introduced everyone, the missus smiled and nodded—she did not shake hands or hug. When one of the crew stepped on the carpet, Mrs. Davis whipped out a handheld vacuum cleaner from somewhere and gave a quick once-over. She smiled sheepishly. "Sorry. You guys go ahead and do what you need to do. Don't mind me."

Director Doug Dewitt put everyone in place and set up his camera angles and lights. As the agents that made up the Shamrock crew followed his instructions, still mostly unclear about how to operate the equipment, Mrs. Davis shadowed them. A water bottle casually placed on an end table? Gone. Strips of gaffer tape placed at the ready on the back of the couch? Removed. A granola bar wrapper tossed in a decorative-use-only waste basket? Disappeared. By the time Amy had finished her interview with John Davis, the missus was emitting little yelps as she raced around and tried to keep everything just so.

As Amy wrapped up her interview with John Davis, Mathews prepped for "the big finish"—the presentation of a giant cardboard check for one million dollars made out to Davis and signed by Ronald McDonald, spokesclown. It had come straight from the printer and was still wrapped in a thin cellophane skin. Mathews peeled it off. The strips were small, hard to see, and carried a strong electrostatic charge. They stuck to everything. Mrs. Davis once again sprang into action, grabbing the most visible pieces with forefinger and thumb.

"Okay, John, ready for the big finish? Come over here and we'll get you receiving your check. Sound good? Okay, guys, we got one shot at getting this right. Amy? Ready?"

Amy positioned the confetti cannon. "Ready," she said.

Doug Mathews began the countdown, "Three . . . two . . . " He nodded at Amy. That was her cue to fire the cannon. She had never used one. In fact, there were several she could have picked in the McDonald's Promotions Department storage room when Doug Mathews made his suggestion. She was unsure which to take. She called Mathews who told her, "Just get the biggest one you have."

Unfortunately, Amy had missed the small-print warning sticker that cautioned the device was for outdoor use only.

When she pressed the red button on the Party Boss 8000 there was a deafening *BOOM* in the living room. The explosion of confetti reduced visibility to about a half inch. Even Doug Mathews, always cool in the field, was taken aback. "Whoa!" He blew confetti out of his mouth and tried to brush it off his lips and tongue.

Amy Murray was so startled by the blast that she lost her balance and fell back into one of Mrs. Davis's not-for-sitting chairs. Mrs. Davis shrieked. Confetti fell for what felt like a full three minutes. When it finally stopped, it covered every square inch of the living room. Everything was buried under deep drifts of bits of pastel-colored paper.

Mrs. Davis looked aghast. So did the rest of the room. This was a confetti apocalypse.

"Got it! That was great!" gushed Mathews, still spitting out tiny pieces of paper. "Now let's clear out of here!" He felt sorry for upsetting Mrs. Davis and leaving her with such a mess, but there wasn't much he could do about it now.

With the Davises still in shock from the intensity of the blast, the FBI team packed up in record time and were out the door and back on the road before the couple could completely recover.

In the days after Shamrock Productions' visit, the wire room monitored all incoming and outgoing phone calls on John Davis's phone. Every recording contained a weird mechanical whine. Tim Adams and the rest of the guys couldn't figure it out. "What the fuck is that noise?" he asked.

"Is something shorting out somewhere?" another agent asked.

"Damn, there it goes again. What the hell is that?"

When Doug Mathews came down to the room to sign out the tapes, Adams was apologetic. "Hey, Doug. I don't know what's up with these tapes."

"What's the problem?" asked Rick Dent's rookie.

"I don't know. There's some kind of noise on all the calls."

"Lemme hear," Mathews asked.

Adams played back a sample. Sure enough, Mathews heard the whine. Unlike the rest of the wire room, he knew exactly what it was.

"Oh, *that*? That's a vacuum cleaner."

You Deserve a Break Today:
HOW'S HE DOING IT? PART 2

When Simon Marketing security chief Jerry Jacobson and company accountant Hilda Bennett touched down in Des Moines, Iowa, they wasted no time—other than a quick bathroom break for Jerry—before they got into a chauffeured vehicle and were whisked away to another secure printing facility.

There were printers in different regions throughout the country. If the Simon Marketing computer indicated the next million-dollar game piece would turn up in the New England area, a printer from outside Boston did the job, distributing one or two game pieces in that locality. When they arrived, they were led into the facility through a huge vault door made of hardened steel. On each side of the door was an electronic keypad that required two Dittler Brothers employees to enter the correct codes to unlock. When the door swung open with a whoosh of air, Jerry and Hilda were escorted onto the floor.

The printing area was kept kitchen clean and hummed with activity. Countless medium-size red fries boxes lay flat along a steel conveyor track. McDonald's fries were almost as iconic as its Big Macs. The recipe came about through a happy accident. Originally, the spuds were deep-fried in hydrogenated vegetable oil—the industry standard—but it was expensive and the firm McDonald's contracted to supply the oil was too small to provide for the growing restaurant's needs. The solution was a blend of 7 percent hydrogenated vegetable oil and 93 percent beef tallow—rendered cattle fat. The blend was known within the company as "Formula 47," a number that came from the total cost—in cents—of a hamburger, a shake, and fries at the time.

Then, in 1966, a self-made millionaire with terrible dietary habits named Phil Sokolof suffered a heart attack at the age of forty-three. Recovering, Sokolof blamed the high amounts of cholesterol and fat he consumed as the cause of his near-fatal episode and in response formed the National Heart Savers Association. Sokolof used his fortune to launch a multimillion-dollar campaign of newspaper and radio ads that accused McDonald's and other fast-food companies of killing Americans with high-calorie, high-cholesterol, high-fat menu items. He kept it up for years. In 1990, McDonald's finally caved to growing pressure and negative publicity and dropped the beef tallow in favor of 100 percent vegetable oil. The new fries had 0 percent cholesterol and 45 percent less fat than the old Formula 47 fries . . . and customers universally hated them. They complained the new fries lacked flavor. Sales fell through the floor. In response, McDonald's added "natural beef flavoring" derived from milk and wheat by-products. Fries sales recovered. A medium-size order of McDonald's fries now carried 340 calories, 42 percent fat, and 53 percent carbohydrates. Packed tightly into the company's signature red-and-gold cardboard boxes and served up hot and salty, the fries were also 100 percent comfort food and a guilty pleasure.

As the red fries boxes began to move along the conveyor track, Jerry and Hilda saw the process of how McDonald's Monopoly game pieces were attached to the boxes. Gears whirred and there was a dreadful mechanical chug as workers supervised the line of flat cardboard boxes moving along the assembly line. First, the game pieces were affixed to the flat boxes by a robotic device as they moved along their course. As they continued their journey down the line, the boxes were stacked and sealed in shrink-wrap before they were put into boxes. These were sealed, placed onto pallets, and loaded onto a truck for distribution.

It was an efficient system. As the last of the fries boxes completed its journey, a Klaxon went off and yellow lights flashed on the manufacturing floor in preparation for the winning game piece ceremony. Ten flat fries boxes without game pieces were removed from the line and set aside. Most of the employees on the floor had left for the day but a handful remained. The ceremony was about to begin.

Standing next to the steel conveyor track, the remaining employees saw Jerry and Hilda step onto the floor accompanied by the printing facility's security officer. Standing in an area where their actions could be clearly witnessed, the Simon Marketing executive made a show of unlocking the handcuff that held Jerry's briefcase to his wrist. Freed, Jerry leaned over the case and dialed in the combination known only to him. Hilda did the same with hers. The lid to the case was popped open and both Hilda and Jerry inspected the envelope sealed with a hologram

sticker. It was intact with no sign of tampering. The hologram sticker was yet another level of security. The ones
Simon Marketing used were made in China and had all the
bells and whistles: fluorescent ink, hidden images and
microtext, and hidden inks that could only be read under an
ultraviolet light. For little adhesive-backed stickers that
came on a roll of plain old paper, they were very high-tech.

Jerry took the envelope and dramatically raised it high
for all to see. He looked like a priest celebrating Mass. "In
my hand, I hold the winning game pieces," he said solemnly. "We will change people's lives for the better. We
should all feel lucky to be a part of making this happen."
Then, under the watchful eyes of the gathered employees,
Jerry Jacobson broke the hologram seal on the envelope
and removed a "seed pack" that held ten game pieces,
only one of which was a winner, a security protocol put in
place so no one knew exactly which one it was.

Somebody started the assembly line again and it
hummed back to life.

Taking the ten "naked" fries boxes that had been
removed from the line, Jerry affixed the winning game
pieces to the boxes by hand. Like a magician performing
a well-rehearsed trick, he went along the running assembly line and randomly took a fries box affixed with what
was termed a "common" game piece: one that read BETTER
LUCK NEXT TIME or FREE FRIES. In its place, Jerry swapped it
with one of the potential big-ticket boxes. He repeated the
process until all the possible winning fries boxes were
mixed in among thousands of common boxes, sealed,
and placed on trucks to be distributed.

– 20 –

JUST THE FAX

Even with its undercover operation, the surveillance, and the wiretaps, the FBI still didn't know *how* Jerry Jacobson was getting his hands on the legitimate winning game pieces. But it had more than enough evidence to make arrests.

It was go time.

Assistant US Attorney Mark Devereaux and the Jacksonville FBI field office were faced with the logistics of coordinating the simultaneous arrests of eight suspects and an additional dozen people wanted for questioning. It was more complicated than just going out and breaking down doors. The targets were scattered across the country and the arrests had to take place at the same time to avoid any tip-offs or have any of the suspects go on the run.

Taking the lead, Devereaux and the core Jacksonville team briefed the various regional FBI offices they'd be working with on all the details of the case and coordinated surveillance of the targets' schedules, routines, and residences. Travel arrangements were made for the Jacksonville agents who would assist the various regional offices for the takedown. It would all go down on Sunday, August 19, 2001.

"Damn, this is really complicated when you see it all laid out like this," said Doug Mathews. He looked through a hefty, thirty-page report that contained all the details of what was about to happen with the McDonald's Monopoly case. It was highly sensitive material. The report—in FBI parlance an EC or "electronic communication"—held names, addresses, the locations where the arrests would take place, the time and date of the plan, and other sensitive details. Top secret and highly classified, the report was faxed to all the regional FBI offices that would be involved in the operation. Satisfied, everybody went home for the weekend.

On Monday, six days before the scheduled busts, the Jacksonville office received a phone call: "Hi, this is John Boyanoski from the *Greenville News* in Greenville, South Carolina. We think you might have faxed us something by mistake."

Uh-oh.

Mark Devereaux and agents Graham and Dent immediately took the call via speakerphone. As Boyanoski went into more details about the fax, Devereaux mouthed, "Holy shit!" Rick Dent mouthed, "Holy smokes!" and Chris Graham looked like he was about to get sick.

"Hey, John. Thanks for the call," said Chris Graham. "Can you describe the front page of the document?"

"No problem. I got it right here. It starts out with . . . " and Boyanoski began reading. All three men blanched. How did this happen? Who fucked up? This was beyond the pale, a total and complete screwup. An unforced error. The entire top-secret EC that contained every little detail of the upcoming operation had somehow been faxed to a regional newspaper.

John Boyanoski was a cub reporter. The real-life equivalent of Superman's pal Jimmy Olsen at the *Daily Planet*, enthused and engaged with the whole idea of being a journalist. The fax had come through on Friday evening after Boyanoski had left the office. One of the weekend staffers took the fax, assumed it was for Boyanoski, and plopped the whole thing on the young reporter's chair without even looking at it.

At his desk with a Styrofoam cup of lousy coffee he had bought at a convenience store during a pit stop on the way to work, John Boyanoski began to read the document. His first thought was that this was a standard police report. He received them all the time. He was a beat reporter. Mostly they were boring and didn't rise to "scoop" level. As he read the EC, he was struck by its level of detail. This was big. A major bust across several states was about to go down and it involved a scheme to defraud one of America's most iconic brands: McDonald's.

John Boyanoski may have been young, but he wasn't stupid. This was the kind of story that makes a reporter's career. John leaned back in his chair and took a sip of cold convenience store coffee. He was disappointed. He assumed the EC had been sent to other newspapers as well. If the fax came through on Friday night, the story had likely already been well covered by competing papers. It had "Big Story" written all over it. *Ya snooze, ya lose*, John Boyanoski thought. He checked the *New York Times*, interested in how the Gray Lady covered the story. Oddly, there was nothing. He checked the *Washington Post*. Again, nothing. The *Wall Street Journal*, too, had no mention of a story involving McDonald's being defrauded of millions of dollars. Very strange.

In the tiny newsroom, Boyanoski swiveled his chair and asked his editor, "Hey, Chief, did you read this?" as he held up the EC.

"That? Yeah. Of course," before getting back to important editorial work.

"Oh, bullshit! You never even looked at it. You know what this is? The FBI just sent us all the details of an impending nationwide raid," Boyanoski cried.

The editor was suddenly interested. He snatched the EC and began flipping pages. Each was punctuated by a "Wow," or a "Damn," or a "Shit!" The kid was right. This *was* big. Now that the thirty-page document was officially deemed important within the newsroom, it acquired a power of its own. It intimidated the staff. They seemed almost reluctant to touch it. Who knew what could result from breaking such a big story? Did you want to get your balls squashed by the FBI or McDonald's? Because that was a definite possibility if you broke this scoop carelessly.

Boyanoski wasn't intimidated. "Let's kick this upstairs," he suggested. They took the EC to Chris Jacobs, the editor in chief of the *Greenville News*. He leaned back in his chair and began flipping through the pages. "Jesus." "What the fuck?" "Hey, this George Chandler is a local guy! He's from Fair Play." When he finished, Boyanoski was fired up. He was ready to head back to his desk and start writing the biggest story of his career.

Chris Jacobs had a different idea: "Why don't you call the FBI and see what's up?" Boyanoski's heart sank. This was his scoop. His big break. And now he was watching it grow wings and fly away from him. It was the story of a lifetime, and he speculated he had just lost it. Jacob's instincts were correct though. They conformed to what Boyanoski had learned about ethics during his undergraduate years studying journalism at Syracuse University. It was still frustrating. He kicked his chair and muttered under his breath, "Goddamn it." Then he sat down and made the call.

Back in Jacksonville, fingers started pointing. "How could this have happened?"

"Which one of you idiots sent that fax?"

"Maybe it was the rookie."

"It was probably the rookie."

"It was definitely the rookie."

"It was Doug Mathews."

Doug Mathews: "Wait. What?"

Despite all his undercover work, some on the team still had doubts about Mathews. Had the rookie, in a showboat moment or just through plain old sloppiness, somehow sent the fax? It wouldn't be the first time a newbie made a mistake, but was it Doug Mathews or something else?

A little FBI elbow grease soon revealed the problem: a glitch with the speed-dial setup on the fax machine. The weight of suspicion was lifted off Doug Mathews. The FBI needed to get the *Greenville News* to hold off publishing the story until the bust went down the coming Sunday. While that seemed reasonable to the FBI, would it make sense to the newspaper? Chris Graham was in full crisis-management mode. "Devereaux, you need to get up there and talk to those guys. Convince them to hold that story."

"How do you suggest I do that?"

"You're the US attorney, for cryin' out loud. Scare the fuck out of them. Paint them a picture. I've already arranged your flight."

"The FBI's plane?" asked Devereaux, a note of concern in his voice.

"The plane's fine. Man up. And take Mathews with you."

Hearing his name, Mathews had an opinion: "Fuck that! I'm not getting up in that tiny little lawn mower with wings squeezed in between Devereaux and some pilot. Did you know they make you piss into an old Tide container if you have to go? It's gross."

"Look," said Graham. "We already have two South Carolina agents going to Greenville, but you two guys know this case and what it means. You have to impress upon the paper that they *have* to wait on this thing."

"I'll go," said Rick Dent.

"What?" Doug Mathews was surprised. "No. No. I'll go. I was just complaining. You know me," said Mathews.

"I can tell you're not comfortable with it. I'll go," said Rick Dent.

"Fine," said Mathews. "Enjoy pissing into a bottle."

"The flight's only an hour. I can hold it."

Before Mathews could come up with a witty rejoinder, Devereaux and Dent found themselves on the tarmac waiting for the FBI's plane to fuel up. "How long does this usually take?" asked Dent.

An aircrew serviceman walked by with the hose. "Not long."

"Looks like the plane only carries about five gallons of fuel anyway," said Devereaux.

With the plane fueled, they were ready for takeoff. Devereaux got in first, squeezing in behind the pilot. Rick Dent followed, forcing himself into the impossibly tight space. *Maybe the wife's baked goods are catching up with me*, he thought.

The pilot twisted around in his seat. "Here. You guys might need this," he said as he handed Devereaux a wide-mouthed orange plastic jug with big blue letters that read TIDE. "Just be sure to be accurate. No splishing, no splashing, and definitely *no* pissing in my plane. Enjoy your flight."

The tiny plane fired up its engine. It sounded like a mosquito. The prop spun. The pilot took instructions from air traffic control and maneuvered the plane to the runway. "Here we go!" said the pilot and the insect-like little plane took off.

A few hours later the plane returned from Greenville. If Deveraux and Dent were exhausted, no one could tell. Deveraux, always enjoying a little theatrics, kept Mathews, Kneir, and Graham in suspense. Dent had a constant poker face. "Give me a minute, gotta hit the head," said Deveraux. A few minutes later he exited the men's room, towel in hand. "Crisis averted." Mathews and Graham gave a sigh of relief. "Are you talking about the *Greenville News* or what you just did in there?" asked Mathews. "They're not running the story," clarified Deveraux. "You could have called to tell us that," said Mathews. Deveraux responded with a smile, "I like seeing you sweat. It's what you get for skipping out on the trip."

"How did you talk them out of running it?" asked Graham.

"All we had to do to get them to keep quiet was to make a gentleman's agreement. They won't run the story until after we've made the bust. In exchange we grant the paper—and that reporter Boyanoski—an exclusive on the story. They get all the insider stuff," explained Devereaux. "Oh, they did want to know what idiot accidently faxed it to them. Don't worry Mathews, we just said it was actually our best undercover agent and we couldn't reveal his identity."

"You know that wasn't me! Next time you hop in that plane you might want to double-check no one poked any holes in that Tide bottle," joked Mathews.

Devereaux, prepared to go toe to toe, went for the finish, "Whoever said you were the best undercover agent?"

– 21 –

SCENES FROM BEFORE A BUST...

SUNDAY, AUGUST 19, 2001...

H ell was coming for breakfast.

John Boyanoski found himself embedded with an FBI team. A black SUV with agents, their eyes hidden behind shades, had picked him up at his home in the predawn hours. At the FBI office, he watched as agents darted around, coordinated team locations, and marked the checklists written on a giant whiteboard. An agent approached and handed Boyanoski a set of official FBI headphones that would allow the reporter to hear everything happening on the ground. He tried to act like this was no big deal, that he'd done this type of thing a thousand times, but that was just bravado. He'd never seen anything like this. It was intense.

It wasn't just Boyanoski. Rookie agent Doug Mathews, too, was in awe of the sheer scale of the operation. McDonald's Corporation knew arrests were imminent . . . but it didn't know who, where, or when.

They weren't the only ones unaware of what was about to go down.

Down in Fort Lauderdale, the sun was coming up. A.J. Glomb poured a cup of coffee while his girlfriend went outside to grab the Sunday paper. At six a.m., the humidity was already thick and clammy. It was 82 degrees and climbing. Typical for South Florida at this time of year: hot, humid, and miserable.

Later that morning, A.J. stepped outside and blinked into the rising sun. It was eerily still on the street, but it was early in the morning. The only thing that seemed out of the ordinary was a county worker checking the sewage system via a manhole in front of A.J.'s house. *Why the fuck is this dude out so early?* Glomb wondered. He was also curious about the guy's uniform. He was the cleanest-looking sewer worker A.J. had ever seen. With his pressed jeans, mirrored shades, yellow hard hat, and well-trimmed mustache, the stranger looked like the misplaced winner of a Village People lookalike contest. *Must be an emergency*, A.J. thought. He nodded at the worker. The guy nodded back. A.J. continued to watch him.

"Can I help you with something, sir?" asked the worker, sounding a little testy.

"Nah. Just getting a start on the day," A.J. answered. "Are you guys gonna have to shut off the water?"

"No. Just checking the line," the guy answered.

"Can I get you a cup of coffee?" asked A.J.

"No thanks. I'm on duty." The worker went back to doing a whole lot of nothing.

A.J. Glomb shrugged and went back inside. *Well, that was weird*, he thought.

In Jacksonville, Gloria Brown was up early, making breakfast for her son. The kitchen smelled of frying bacon. Gloria pulled the crisp slices out of the pan and put them onto a couple of folded paper towels on a plate to let them drain. She cracked a couple of eggs into the pan to let them fry in the remaining bacon grease. *That's where your flavor is,* she thought. She poured a glass of orange juice for the boy. She began setting the kitchen table, laying everything out on a clean red-and-white checkered tablecloth. She moved the stack of bills she had been poring over earlier with a sigh. Times were still tight thanks to the taxes she owed on her million-dollar win. She went to wake up her son.

Agents had eyes on a gray two-story house along a country road in Westminster, South Carolina. The sun was rising overhead and the local songbirds were warming up. Comical cardinals, foraging and clowning along the ground, emitted their metallic chirps as they fussed and feuded among themselves.

Meanwhile, a light came on in an upper window. It was Dwight Baker, LDS elder and McDonald's Monopoly scammer, drawing a shower. While he let the water run to get it up to the right temperature, Dwight turned on the radio for the local weather report. Instead, he got a tune: Blake Shelton's "Austin." *I'm headed out to the lake and I'll be gone all weekend long . . .*

Dwight had plans to visit one of his properties at Hartwell Lake later that day. He was going to be gone . . . just not in the way he thought.

Michael Hoover was wrapped in a fluffy white bathrobe and flipping channels on the hotel's cable system. A heavy knock on the door startled him. It was Hoover's brother. "Mikey, you're not even dressed! We gotta take that picture." The Hoover clan had gathered for a family reunion in Milwaukee.

"I have an appointment for a massage," said Michael. "This hotel has everything!"

"Okay, okay. Look, as soon as you're done with that, we'll be down in the lobby. Find us so we can take the picture."

"Don't worry. I'll be there."

He would not be.

In a Dallas suburb, John Davis was in his driveway doing a little maintenance on his pickup truck. Inside the house, a vacuum cleaner was running.

Near Atlanta, Georgia, mastermind Jerry Jacobson sat in his kitchen with a cup of coffee and the Sunday paper . . . oblivious to the four black unmarked Ford Crown Victorias slowly gliding down his street from opposite directions like circling sharks . . .

Greenville News reporter John Boyanoski sat inside the FBI's field office in downtown Greenville. He observed the hum of activity unfolding all around him as he quietly sipped cold coffee from a Styrofoam cup. He was ready to document the story of his life.

– 22 –

NOBODY EXPECTS THE FBI!

SUNDAY, AUGUST 19, 2001...

Everything and everyone were now in position for the big
bust . . .

- Doug Mathews was stationed down the block from A.J.
  Glomb's house. He checked his watch for the fiftieth time
  and waited for the go-ahead from Central Command.
  With him were a pair of FBI agents from the Miami field
  office as well as a couple of US Marshals, one of them
  disguised as a worker doing routine maintenance in front
  of Glomb's house. He checked his watch again.
- Agent Janet Pellicciotti was in Indianapolis for the arrest
  of Brenda Phenis.
- Agent Doug Astralaga, who had been the lighting guy on
  the Shamrock Productions crew, was in South Carolina
  for the takedown of Dwight Baker.
- Agent Tim Adams, finally freed from listening to calls in
  the wire room, was in Jacksonville to grab Gloria Brown.
- Agent Rick Dent and US Attorney Mark Devereaux were
  in Atlanta for the grand prize: Uncle Jerry Jacobson.

They were all jacked on anticipation and adrenaline. And then the word came down from Chris Graham who was running Central Command: "We are a go."

———————————

Back in his house, A.J. Glomb read his Sunday paper and sipped his coffee. He was interrupted by someone ringing the bell at the entrance to his gated property.

A.J. sighed and went outside. Standing outside the gate were two polite cops from the Broward County Sheriff's Office. *What the fuck?* A.J. wondered.

They were friendly. Earnest. "Good morning, sir. Sorry to bother you . . . "

A.J.'s years as an outlaw had taught him one thing: how to be cool under pressure. Nothing could blow things quicker for a dope smuggler than twitchy eyes, fumbling, stuttering sentences, and fear. Especially fear. Cops sensed it the same way vicious dogs did. If you showed fear, it was your ass. A.J., with his cup of coffee in hand, casually leaned against the gate, took a sip of coffee, and said, "What's up, guys?"

"We've had lots of burglaries in this neighborhood. We have a suspect. Would you mind coming with us to get a look at him? Maybe you've seen him around," said one of the cops.

The other officer said reassuringly, "We have him in a prowler down the street. It won't take long."

"Nah. That's okay. I never had a problem with burglars or burglaries around here. Never seen anyone suspicious. I don't think I'd be any help," said A.J.

"This'll only take a moment of your time," said the other officer.

"We could really use your help on this," said the first cop. "Guy says he lives around here. Maybe you've seen him before and you can tell us we got the wrong guy and we can kick him loose."

Feeling there was no getting rid of these guys, he gave in. "Yeah, sure," offered A.J. "Let's go."

A.J. followed the cops to their squad car and got in the back seat. They drove down the block to a knot of police cars and black SUVs. Doug Mathews and his team were waiting for him. *Shit*, thought A.J. He had fallen for the oldest trick in the book.

At the Fort Lauderdale Police Department station, A.J. went through processing. He let out a bitter little chuckle when he noticed the officer who fingerprinted him was the Village People impersonator he had encountered earlier that morning.

Dwight Baker stepped out of the shower and wrapped himself in a towel. He gave the steamed-up mirror over the sink a swipe with his hand and shaved. On the radio, the DJ gave his audience the local weather forecast and introduced Tim McGraw's current hit "Grown Men Don't Cry." Dwight sang along as he dried off and pulled on a pair of plaid boxer shorts: *All mornin' I'd been thinkin' my life's so hard . . .*

Dwight was about to find out it was going to get a lot harder.

Dwight grabbed a comb and started to arrange his hair when he thought he heard the doorbell. He lowered the volume on the radio. Ding-dong. *Who the heck is coming over here this early?* Dwight wondered. Pulling on a pair of chinos, Dwight padded down the stairs in his bare feet. Out of habit, before he opened the door, Dwight took a quick peek out the front window . . . and saw two men with walkie-talkies and navy-blue nylon windbreakers branded with three big letters: FBI. *Uh-oh,* thought Dwight. *They've come to collect their due.*

He raced into the kitchen where his wife, Linda, and their kids were having pancakes at the table. "Hey, guys. Hey, guys. Something's about to happen and I just want to say that I'm sorry." His wild-eyed terror was infectious. When the doorbell rang a second time, Linda just about leaped out of her skin. "We're screwed!"

They were. The FBI slapped on the cuffs and marched them out to the front yard one at a time.

By a strange coincidence, not long before his arrest, Dwight had flown to Utah for his daughter's wedding . . . and was seated next to Special Agent Doug Astralaga. When the arrest happened, Astralaga asked, "Hi, Dwight. Remember me?" Dwight didn't.

George Chandler was behind the wheel of his pickup bouncing down a picturesque country lane on a hot summer day. He was feeling good and had the oldies radio station cranked. Creedence Clearwater Revival's "Bad Moon Rising" came on and George started to sing along, *There's a bad moon on the rise.* George tapped the steering wheel in time to the tune, not knowing how prophetic those words were. He was interrupted when his cell phone rang.

"Hello?" George answered.

"Mr. Chandler . . . ," said George's secretary, "the FBI is here at the office and would like to speak with you."

"Put 'em on the phone then," he replied.

"Is this George Chandler?" asked a male voice.

"Who's this?" George asked.

"This is Special Agent Astralaga from the FBI, George. I'm calling to let you know that we just picked up your foster parents, Dwight and Linda Baker. I'd like to come in to ask you a few questions."

George struggled to process. Why was the FBI calling about Dwight and Linda? He was positive there was some kind of a mix-up.

"You must have got the wrong people," said George.

"No, George. This is very real. But maybe you can help clear some things up. That's why I'm calling. We really need to talk," advised the agent.

"I'll meet you at my office," George said.

"Wonderful."

"Be there soon," said George. He cut the wheel on his pickup truck and headed for the unknown.

Michael Hoover was lying on a massage table in his hotel room. He imagined himself a heftier version of Alex Rocco as Moe Greene in *The Godfather*. Michael let his cares drift away as the attendant—a blond, sturdily built middle-aged Russian woman in a white jumper—slathered him in massage oil and worked out his knots. He was halfway between being fully consciousness and the dream state.

Until the phone rang.

Michael grunted but ignored it. He hoped the caller would give up after a few rings and he could go back to being pampered. The massage therapist shook Hoover's shoulders. "Hey, you need to answer your phone."

Annoyed, Michael wrapped himself in his "privacy" towel and got up from the table. He picked up the receiver; it was the front desk. "Sorry to bother you, sir," the caller said. "We have an urgent message for you at the front desk."

"Can't you just tell me the message over the phone?" Michael asked.

"We need to verify it's you, sir," said the front desk.

Michael sighed. He wrapped himself in his fluffy, hotel bathrobe. "Hey, I'm sorry," he told the therapist. "I gotta take care of this. Can you just hold on until I get back?"

She was already lighting a cigarette. "*Da, da.* I can watch the television?"

"Sure. I'll be right back."

Michael Hoover, shiny with massage oil and wrapped in a big white terry-cloth robe, padded up to the front desk in his slippers. He was immediately taken into custody by FBI agents. As they slapped the cuffs on him, Michael thought back to *The Godfather* and Moe Greene. *At least I didn't catch a bullet in the eye.*

In Jacksonville, Gloria Brown got a phone call from her sister.

"Oh my goodness, Glo, turn on the news right now!"

"I'm making breakfa—"

"Do it NOW!"

Gloria turned on the small countertop TV she kept in the kitchen and tuned in to the local news. There was her picture along with a big banner that showed her name and the words "McDonald's Fraud." There was even an exclamation point.

Gloria went limp and sank to her knees right there in the kitchen. "Oh Lord!"

Then came the knock at the door.

Gloria shakily rose to her feet and almost as if she was in a dream, she opened the door. Standing there were FBI agents, Tim Adams, and a local female agent. Their badges, FBI windbreakers, and parked SUV could only mean one thing: it's over. "We're not talking about whether you did it or not 'cause we know you did it. Right now it's about how much prison time you're gonna serve. So you can either cooperate now or pretend you have no idea what we are here for," stated Agent Adams clear as day. Gloria's eyes welled up. Her son had stopped playing with his toys, curious to see who was at the door. As tears rolled down Gloria's cheeks, she came clean. She decided to cooperate, then and there, and was rewarded for it. After sharing details of how Jerry Colombo gave her the backstory and she had invested a small amount of money into a pager company (despite cell phones just starting to blow up), Agent Adams took a statement and spared her the cuffs.

Brenda Phenis sat in the back of a black Crown Victoria. Handcuffed, she was a blubbering mess. Special Agent Janet Pellicciotti handled the arrest and was doing the best to calm her.

In the Atlanta suburb where Jerry Jacobson lived, everyone who lived on the block was out to see the show. In their quiet part of town this was the biggest excitement anyone could ever remember, and they didn't want to miss a thing. Still, they were surprised at who was being taken down.

"Jerry?"

"It's always the quiet ones, isn't it?"

"What did he do? Does anyone know?"

"I knew there was something sketchy about that guy."

"No, you didn't. You told me last week he was a nice guy."

"Well, I guess I was wrong, wasn't I?"

"Guess so."

The neighbors watched as Jerry was driven away.

Robin Colombo sat in the gray confines of a small jail cell. It had been her home for several months, but she could see the end of her sentence for credit card fraud just peeking over the horizon. She had even taken to crossing off the days that remained on her sentence with a red marker on a calendar she had taped to one of the walls.

A corrections officer stopped in front of the bars and said, "Colombo, warden wants to see you."

"What's going on?" Robin wanted to know.

"I'm not a messenger service," said the officer. "Get your ass up. I'm taking you there now."

In the warden's office, which was full of pictures of the warden with local state officials and sports memorabilia, sat two stone-faced FBI agents in dark, somber suits and sunglasses. The warden made introductions.

"Miss Colombo, as we speak, multiple arrests are taking place across the country in connection with Jerry Jacobson's scheme to defraud McDonald's of millions of dollars in cash and prizes."

Ever the outlaw, Robin sniffed, "I don't know what you're talking about. I've been in here for the whole time."

"We have you on tape talking to Jerry Jacobson—and calling him 'Uncle Jerry.'"

"I talk to a lot of people," Robin said. "You can't expect me to remember all of them."

"Ma'am, this would be so much better if you cooperated," advised one of the agents.

"How about this," Robin said. "What if you give me a card and I'll call you if I remember anything?"

"Fine," said the other agent who handed her a card. "There you go. Ready?" he asked his partner.

"Yep. Let's go. She doesn't want to talk."

They stood up and turned to leave. Robin was triumphant. *I know how to handle these dopes*, she thought.

One of the agents turned back as he reached the door. "Robin, I need to add that this might be your only chance to cut a deal and regain custody of your son." Little Frankie had been under the care of the late Jerry Colombo's parents, who did not speak kindly of their former daughter-in-law.

As the agents took a few steps away from the warden's office, the deputies who ran the jail came for her with shackles and cuffs. "What's this all about?" Robin asked.

"Oh, your security status has been changed. Face the wall, please."

Robin gasped, "Aw, hell no!" With a quick step, she was at the door. She kicked it open and shouted down the hall. The

FBI heard her yell in her raspy voice, "Get back in here! I'll play ball! I'll cooperate!"

The takedown finished, *Greenville News* reporter John Boyanoski enjoyed the perks of having an exclusive story. He was taken to the courthouse where he got first access to the arresting officers, the FBI agents, and Dwight and Linda Baker. He got lots of photos, too. It was the story of a lifetime and it was exciting for a young reporter. When pictures of Dwight and Linda hit the front page of the *Greenville News*, they were excommunicated from the Church of Jesus Christ of Latter-day Saints.

Jerry Jacobson, having once been a cop himself, knew the intake process. He was fingerprinted and stood for his mug shots. Once that was completed, he was taken away to a conference room where he was met by Rick Dent, Mark Devereaux, and his lawyer.

Again, Jerry knew the score. He was caught. Defense attorneys Ed Garland and Janice Singer took on his case. After many tense sessions, a press conference, and combative negotiations with Mark Deveraux, he agreed to make a deal. There were enough lingering questions about the conspiracy and how it all worked that would finally be revealed.

Following the bust, United States attorney general and com-
poser of the patriotic song "Let the Eagle Soar" John Ashcroft
soberly addressed the television cameras. He praised the FBI
for breaking open a criminal enterprise that had operated for
years and defrauded McDonald's—and its customers—of millions of dollars and high-ticket prizes. He praised McDonald's
Corporation for its close work and cooperation with the FBI.

He cautioned the country: "Breaking the law is not a game."

– 23 –

AFTERMATH

AUGUST 2001...

The fallout from the arrests was swift. High in the board-room of the McDonald's Corporation, meetings were called, points were made, and passions ran high.

"This is going to be bad. Who signed off on this?"

"We did."

"Well, we need to do something! Ideas! Now!"

"It was an inside job. Head of security at Simon Marketing."

"At Simon?"

"Yes, sir. A man named Jerry Jacobson. Ran their security for years."

"And that's the guy, you say?"

"That is the shape of it, sir."

"And Simon never suspected a thing?"

"Apparently, they were blindsided."

"Blindsided? He was the head of security! That is some serious dereliction of duty."

The company needed to get on top of this thing and distance itself from any scandals. Everyone sensed what was coming. There were those who argued Simon Marketing's case.

"It's not like Simon Marketing itself was involved. This Jacobson guy was scamming them, too," suggested one voice.

There was some scoffing.

"Well, what do we do?" McDonald's and Simon Marketing had a long history, and personal relationships had certainly been forged, but both sides knew what was coming.

McDonald's Corporation cut Simon Marketing loose two days after the arrests went down.

It was an unsentimental parting, the corporate world's version of a sanctioned mob hit. Nothing personal. Just business. Unfortunately, despite running promotions and marketing for other companies, there was no getting around the fact that Simon Marketing had put too many eggs into one Egg McMuffin. The McDonald's account made up 70 percent of Simon Marketing's overall business. The effects of the termination didn't take long to manifest. Simon Marketing was in a tailspin. There was no pulling out of it. If the company had been a real airplane with an actual pilot, writer Tom Wolfe's line from *The Right Stuff* would have been apt: "Shut up and die like an aviator."

Over a twenty-four-hour period, Simon Marketing's stock dropped an incredible 80 percent and a share was now worth a mere sixty-two cents. At the time, it was the largest one-day drop in financial history. A few days later, the company was removed from the New York Stock Exchange. It was over.

When the Jacksonville FBI field office first got on the case and began building their corkboard "murder board," it looked like a spindly sapling, but now, as more information continued to flood in, it had grown into a mighty redwood that detailed the entire scam. Uncle Jerry Jacobson's name and picture was at the top and the branches on the way down contained the names, faces, and connections between all the recruiters and the winners. It was a snapshot of a major criminal conspiracy. Laid out like this, it was stunning how detailed and broad the scheme was.

US Attorney Mark Devereaux's phone had not stopped ringing since the FBI had held a press conference announcing the arrests and the media pounced on the story. The sharp-dressed man from Florida was in demand. Everyone who had been scooped up in the bust, now facing years in the slammer, had gotten lawyers and were desperate to make plea deals. "We have information to trade!"

"Let's talk then," Devereaux would say. "I don't know what new information your client can offer though. Everything—and I mean everything—is on tape. We have him in the act. We have the whole thing pieced together. It's signed, sealed, and delivered."

"Yes, yes, yes. We're aware. But you know, my client has some information that nobody knows, not even the FBI. This is deep."

"Like I said, let's sit down and talk. We'll see," said Devereaux.

Devereaux started to play a game with himself. Before he took a call, he'd look at the area code to see if he could guess which suspect's lawyer was calling. It was a fun game and Devereaux, so intimately informed on the details of the case, was usually right. Once he got on the line, though, the fun stopped. He was looking for convictions.

Devereaux had a lot to work with. The group of eight that had been swept up in the original bust of August 19, 2001, and who had scammed McDonald's for a total of $13 million, were spilling the beans to anyone who listened, hoping for leniency. Now, thanks to the new information they provided, a total of fifty-three people were indicted across twenty-three states for mail fraud and attempting to cheat McDonald's out of a staggering $24 million.

Devereaux would see them in court.

A.J. Glomb, who had already done prison time for his drug-running operation, wasn't afraid of court or prison, but he had gone that route once before and wasn't looking forward to doing another stretch. In fact, he was strongly considering going on the run again. He was racked with guilt though. "I lied to all but two of the people I brought into the deal about how I really got the game pieces. They thought everything was cool—thanks to me—when it clearly wasn't."

To assuage his guilt, A.J. began making calls to the people he had recruited with the offer to testify on their behalf in court. His hope was that the court, upon hearing A.J. take the blame, would kick these folks loose with a slap on the wrist.

In theory, it was a noble and altruistic plan. In practice, it didn't play out.

"Hello?"

"Hey, man. It's A.J. Yeah, yeah, I know, I know. I'm really sorry. Look, I've told my lawyer I'm down to do this: I'll testify in court that you were duped. That I lied to you and you got caught up in this whole mess solely because of me. Just say the word and I'm there."

After several more calls like this, A.J. decided it was fruitless. They all decided to plea.

Gloria Brown lacked A.J.'s bravado when it came to doing time. Now she stared into the abyss and was overwhelmed by hopelessness.

Gloria had nowhere to turn. Despite being a so-called millionaire, Gloria knew she couldn't afford a lawyer. She and her sister called around using the phone book and found a public defender that became her godsend.

At a pretrial assessment at her house, a woman from the court laid out what to expect. "Gloria, you will definitely serve time. How much I can't tell you—it will be up to the court—but expect no less than two years. Can your husband take care of your son?" Gloria had only recently gotten married and her husband was in no position to take care of her son. It was hitting her hard. She was preparing herself to lose, not only her house, but her family. "Gloria, the best way to play this is for you to plead guilty and take whatever plea deal they offer," said the PD.

Gloria began to tremble. "Oh Lord. Oh Lord."

"If you plead guilty, the time you get won't be as much as what you'd get if we take this case to trial," the lawyer said. He also told her that since she had no prior criminal history, judges would tend to be more lenient with plea deals. Still, it was a little overwhelming for her.

Gloria felt a rising panic. What was going to happen to her? More important, what was going to happen to her son? She called her sister. "Promise me that whatever happens, you'll take care of him if I have to go away."

When her day in court finally came to plea, the showpiece for the prosecution was the footage from Shamrock Productions' "Reunion of Winners." As Gloria admitted, "I had a real bad feeling about that as soon as Amy Murray contacted me." When they ran the tape of Gloria's interview it was sad. What had initially played out as a comedy in that hotel conference room was now a straight-up tragedy. "McDonald's made me a *star!*" Gloria's extreme nervousness as she attempted again and again to deliver that line to Doug Mathews's directorial standards was heartbreaking. There was an uncomfortable intimacy in the footage. Everyone felt bad for Gloria.

Robin Colombo's guilt and regret for setting up and ultimately betraying her friend Gloria was severe, but she had more pressing concerns. There were the drugs, the criminal charges for credit card fraud, her own child custody issues, and the general messiness of her day-to-day life. Finally, like a rotten cherry on top of a shit sundae, was the news that her father, Buddy Fisher, had also been caught up in the arrests and had been indicted for taking her late husband Jerry Colombo's offer to "win" a million dollars from the McDonald's Corporation.

Buddy Fisher's capitulation to his own greed had left a smoking crater where his life and sterling reputation once stood. Fisher, Robin Colombo's father, was a lifelong navy man and had risen to the rank of master chief petty officer, the highest rank an enlisted swabbie could hope to reach. It was a position that bestowed honor and integrity upon the sailor who held it. Buddy was also a family man who strived to build a home that ran as tight as any naval vessel.

And he had thrown it all away for some easy money.

The fallout from the decision to accept the winning Monopoly game piece from Jerry Colombo plunged the Fishers into turmoil. Robin's mother, especially, was distraught. Buddy had never even told her about getting the winning token from Jerry. "How could this have happened?" Mama Fisher cried before breaking down in tears.

Buddy's reputation would never recover from this. The undercover video Shamrock Productions had shot was so startling—he sweated, stumbled, and looked like a boob—he really had no option other than to enter a guilty plea.

For years after the McDonald's Monopoly fraud case was finally closed, Buddy's videotape was played again and again in training seminars at Quantico and various FBI field offices as an example of what someone lying on camera looks like.

- 24 -

KNOCKED OFF THE FRONT PAGE

SEPTEMBER 2001...

The case made headline news across the country. On the front page, above the fold in twenty-point bold typeface, the papers screamed: McDONALD's MONOPOLY FRAUD!!! At breakfast tables, on commuter trains, in cabs, on park benches, at the watercooler, in the break room, the country was fascinated by the story of a long-running rip-off of an American institution.

That was just print. Television news saw the story as its own Happy Meal, something an audience would eat up and come back for more. Everybody knew McDonald's. The story really captured the American imagination.

Overnight, the perps became quasi-celebrities, standing at some weird junction of pop culture, true crime, and business news. The media was all over the story and they wanted color. If there were a bigger cast of flamboyant characters, heroes, and villains, they could only be found in outtakes of the burgeoning reality TV genre that was tightening its grip on the national consciousness.

It wasn't a great development for A.J. Glomb. He had been released from custody and was back home. Always a natural outlaw, A.J. placed a high premium on being anonymous and low-key. "The nail that sticks out is the one that gets the hammer." A.J. had long tried to pass through the world without attracting too much attention. It was a rule he had followed since his days as a drug smuggler and, later, as a fugitive. There was no laying low for A.J. now. Reporters and news crews crowded the sidewalk in front of his house.

"A.J.! A.J.!"

"Over here! Over here!"

"Can we ask you a few questions?"

"Aw, c'mon, A.J. Don't be like that!"

"A.J.! A.J.! Come back! Come back!"

Glomb couldn't leave his house without being overwhelmed by the crowd. It forced him to do the one thing A.J. Glomb would have never done under normal circumstances: he called "the Man" in the hope the cops could clear the sidewalk and give him back some of his privacy.

In the United States District Court for Florida's Middle District, US Attorney Mark Devereaux was jammed. He set his briefcase on the prosecutor's table and took out stacks of papers held in cream-colored manila folders. He turned to the defense table. It was packed with attorneys representing the fifty-three individuals who had been indicted. Things would have to be split up between seven to ten defendants at a time to get through them all. If anyone entered a not-guilty plea, that would then lead to a trial. Devereaux—not wearing his sunglasses—narrowed his eyes and gave a look that was halfway between an Old West gunslinger and a rattlesnake. He wanted to convey that he was looking for convictions for everyone. No excuses. If you were swept up in this thing, it was his job to make sure you paid the price. There would be no discounts. It was go time. The defense side of the courtroom was packed with friends and family of the accused. The rest of the limited space was taken up by reporters from newspapers across the country. Outside the courtroom, the TV crews waited with their cameras. *This is going to be a long day*, thought Devereaux. There was a crazy energy in the air. The date was September 10, 2001.

The next morning, America changed forever after four commercial airliners were hijacked by members of the Islamic terror group al-Qaeda and used as missiles in kamikaze runs on American targets.

By noon that day, the casualties were staggering:

2,753 killed at the World Trade Center and surrounding area.

184 killed at the Pentagon.

40 killed in the crash into the Pennsylvania field.

2,996 killed in total, making the event the deadliest terror attack in human history.

The Jacksonville field office of the FBI, so focused on the McDonald's Monopoly fraud case, had new, pressing business. A bunch of goofs scamming a major corporation out of millions of dollars? Who cares? Did you miss what just happened? Saddle up, boys. We're at war.

There was immediate fallout. Suddenly, Americans were asked to show ID and sign in before entering their places of work or banks and other businesses. Security was ramped to ridiculous levels on domestic commercial flights; many of those precautions are still with us today. There were daily threat assessments issued in the form of a color-coded system. Cable news broadcasts consistently reminded viewers that today was "orange" or "yellow" . . . but things could turn "red" at a moment's notice. The message was "Be terrified all the time."

On the other hand, President George W. Bush told Americans to go shopping. On the evening of 9/11, the president went on national TV and assured the country that "our financial institutions remain strong." The US economy was, he told his audience, "open for business." He would later advise patriotic Americans to "get down to Disney World in Florida . . . Take your families and enjoy life the way we want it to be enjoyed." His vice president, Dick Cheney, took a more direct tone when he urged Americans to "stick a thumb in the eye of the terrorists" by keeping to their daily routines.

It was a solid plan, but it didn't slow the economic downturn that followed the attacks. Simon Marketing and Dittler Brothers, already reeling from losing the McDonald's account, both went under. Dittler Brothers was sold to Québecor, an international printing conglomerate that immediately axed two-thirds of the company's employees. Simon Marketing filed for bankruptcy, but it didn't provide any relief. The company shuttered almost overnight, leaving five hundred employees out in the cold. McDonald's, definitely unhappy with Simon Marketing's role in the fraud, brought a suit alleging breach of contract, fraud, and racketeering. Simon Marketing countersued for fraud and breach of contract, alleging the corporation deliberately destroyed the company—once valued at $768 million—by not telling Simon Marketing of the FBI sting operation. In the end, McDonald's paid a $16.6 million settlement to Simon Marketing.

The country had entered completely new territory. The reaction reached ridiculously hilarious levels. Political leaders across both aisles crowed about how the terrorists "hate our freedom." To underscore the importance of "freedom," when France opposed the US's dubious plan to retaliate for the events of 9/11 by invading Iraq in 2003, Republican Bob Ney, chairman of the Committee on House Administration, changed "French fries" on the menus of three Congressional cafeterias to "freedom fries." McDonald's continued to use the more elegant term "fries" and avoided the ridicule that Ney managed to conjure with his stunt.

With terror in the air and paranoia and fear running wild through much of the country, the entire FBI was pulled off burger-related crimes and redirected to counterterrorism. Terror was on the front burner now. Fraud just seemed so . . . quaint in light of the new era the country had entered.

Jacksonville FBI caught flak during this time because it was uncovered that three of the 9/11 hijackers spent a couple of weeks in Jacksonville a year before the attacks, which predated Operation: Final Answer. But you also have to remember that before 9/11, the world was completely different. Special Agent Sean O'Donovan, who'd worked counterterrorism before 9/11, said, "There wasn't a whole lot to do because there wasn't a lot we could do before 9/11." Forty-five days after the attacks, the Patriot Act was passed. It gave agencies like the FBI expanded authority to monitor phone calls and email communications and trace bank and credit reporting records all in the name of safety from future terror attacks.

Back in Jacksonville, Doug watched Rick Dent disassemble their murder board. He sighed, "On to the next."

"It was a successful operation. You should feel good about it," Dent told him.

"It just feels like a letdown. Not that we weren't successful but it feels like the party's over, doesn't it?" asked Mathews.

"We completed the investigation, rounded up the conspirators, and brought it to court—"

"And crushed a successful undercover operation," Mathews interrupted. He pulled A.J. Glomb's picture off the board and put it into an envelope. "There ain't no way in hell you would have thought to do that."

Dent cracked a smile agreeing with Mathews. "Well, Doug, just keep being you. And while you're at it, I've got some notes on a 302 I saved just for you." Dent handed Mathews a thick stack of papers. "Just pretend you're me and make these perfect."

Although he found himself in trouble and facing time, A.J. Glomb still couldn't help but feel a sense of relief. Without the constant media attention, he was suddenly, thankfully, anonymous again.

Mark Devereaux, who had been all set to prosecute and convict all the players swept up by the FBI during the sting, now found himself at a crossroads. All his resources in the FBI and the Department of Justice were directed to get on top of the terror situation and make things safe in the homeland. Whatever resources he had going into the case on September 10 were gone after September 11. Suddenly, he found himself facing down fifty-three defendants, each with their own legal counsel, all by himself. He had been in one-sided battles before, but nothing like this.

You Deserve a Break Today:
HOW'S HE DOING IT? PART 3

The Delta Airlines A310 wide-body plane shrieked out of the sky and began its downward glide to the sunbaked runway at Des Moines International. There was a soft ping as the fasten seat belts light came on. Jerry Jacobson and Hilda Bennett sat together. They both experienced that odd, sinking feeling in the stomach that sometimes accompanies a landing. Jerry began pumping his right foot. The ball of his foot glued to the floor of the plane, his heel went up and down. His knee bounced noticeably. He gave an uncomfortable sigh and shifted in his seat. Hilda looked over at him. Every single time, she thought. Like clockwork.

"Are you okay?" Hilda asked him.

"Yeah. I'm fine. Fine. Stomach's a little fluttery," Jerry said, his knee still bouncing.

"Should I call the stewardess? Ask her for a mint or maybe some gum?"

"No, no. Same thing as always. My stomach gets, uh . . . overactive . . . when I fly."

"Have you had anything to eat today?"

"No."

"Maybe that's the problem," said Hilda.

"Yeah, maybe," said Jerry.

After the plane landed and the passengers deboarded, Jerry and Hilda walked down the terminal's concourse. Jerry's briefcase was still attached to his wrist by a chain and a handcuff. As they passed the men's room located in Delta's lounge—which Doug Mathews labeled "the Crown Room" because it was nicer and more private than the concourse restrooms anyone could use—Jerry paused.

"Hey, uh—"

"Go ahead," Hilda said.

"Thanks, thanks," Jerry said. "I'll only be a sec."

"When ya gotta go, ya gotta go."

"Ain't that the truth?"

Hilda was by the book. The security protocol—developed by Jerry himself—specified the pair was never to be apart as they made their way on their journey. A bathroom break was an emergency, Hilda reasoned. Besides, Jerry had developed the system. She assumed that as head of security Jerry Jacobson knew what he was doing—and was above suspicion. While she wasn't keen on the idea of separating, even if only for a few minutes, what could she do? The only option she had was going into the restroom with Jerry and being present while he took care of business. The thought made her shudder. She saw a gift shop across from the lounge and said, "Okay, Jerry. Hurry up. I'll be in the gift shop. Come and get me when you're done."

"Two shakes," assured Jerry. "Thanks."

Hilda watched Jerry scurry to the restroom. Poor guy, she thought. She went to the gift shop and killed time by looking at a table well stocked with Beanie Babies, the popular plush toys that had become collectible among a devoted fan base during the second half of the 1990s.

In the bathroom, Jerry rushed to an empty stall, shut and locked the door, unbuckled his belt, and dropped his pants so they pooled around his cowboy boots. If anybody passed by and looked at the space beneath the door, they'd think Jerry was just another diarrhetic flier catching some relief during his travels.

Jerry took a seat on the throne. He placed the brief-case on his lap. Using the barrel combination locks on either side of the case's handle, he deftly dialed in his own number as well as Hilda's, which he had gotten ear-lier at the Dittler Brothers facility simply by sneaking a peek as she entered the combination during their reassur-ing display for company executives.

Jerry popped the lid of the briefcase and saw the hologram-sealed envelope he and Hilda had signed in front of the Dittler Brothers honchos. He smiled. If this were a movie, the soundtrack might have played some sort of heavenly musical swell. This was what it was all about. The holy grail of McDonald's. It was almost an object of veneration.

Jerry carefully unsealed the signed envelope and removed the seed pack that contained the high-value win-ning game pieces. There was a number on the outside of the seed pack. Could have been ten or fifteen, twenty-two, or thirty, but usually less than fifty, which was the number of game pieces included. But only one was the winner. This was to further protect it when it was placed. He held the empty envelope in his mouth while he slipped the seed pack into a secret pocket he had installed in his Western-cut jacket. From another pocket, Jerry grabbed an identical seed pack—only these game pieces were "common." At most, some were worth a free order of medium fries. The rest advised the player to try again. These had been easy to acquire. The floor of every Dittler Brothers facility was littered with them. He counted out the exact number included in the winning seed pack and placed it back in the envelope. Finally, Jerry took out the key item, the one that would sell the scam: a brand-new, shiny, genuine, and legit hologram seal.

Jerry applied the new sticker to the envelope that held the common game pieces, careful to line up the strokes of his and Hilda's signatures before he resealed the flap. By the time he finished, no one would be able to tell it had been tampered with. Done.

Placing the envelope back in the briefcase, Jerry shut the lid, closed the latches, and spun the combination barrels to lock it. Jerry pulled up his pants and buckled his belt. Before he stepped out of the stall, Jerry flushed the toilet and heard a satisfying whoosh. Mission accomplished.

The whole operation had only taken four minutes.

Jerry opened the door and went to meet Hilda at the gift shop. She was still engrossed by the Beanie Babies display and was startled when Jerry popped up behind her and said, "All better. Let's go."

- 25 -

A JUDGE, A SHOWDOWN, AND DOUG MATHEWS AND THE WONDERFUL FRENCH FRY SUIT

AUGUST 2002...

Twelve sober citizens filed into the jury box in a courtroom inside the federal courthouse in Jacksonville. Each had gone through a rigorous jury selection process and had been carefully chosen by counsel for neutrality, lack of prejudice toward McDonald's, the defendants, or anything even tangentially related to the case. The twelve had also been unable to come up with any valid reasons why they should be excused from their sacred civic duty. This was serious business and the faces of the jurors reflected that. There was not a smile among them. They took their seats.

Out of fifty-three defendants, forty-six—including Jerry Jacobson—had pleaded out. In exchange for a guilty plea, they were awarded sentences and fines on the lighter end of the sentencing guidelines. But seven defendants had entered not-guilty pleas and demanded their day in court. It was a risky move. Even if the defendants were truly innocent of the charges, courts generally would hand down tougher sentences if they were found guilty by the jury. Many completely innocent people are currently behind bars because they rejected a prosecutor's offer and wanted their trial . . . and lost the case.

George Chandler was willing to take that risk. He remained adamant that he had only gotten involved because he had been willfully tricked into turning in the prizewinning piece by his foster dad, Dwight Baker. George insisted he had truly believed he was helping out someone in a bad situation by the lies spun by the man he trusted most in the world.

Also fighting the charges was Ronnie Hughey, the Rolex-wearing real estate developer who counted himself as another victim of Dwight Baker. Hughey had earlier recruited a friend, Texan John Davis, the last "winner" in the fraud scheme, and Davis was also fighting the charges. Mrs. Davis, back in the couple's suburban home, fretted about her husband's fate. She was still finding stray pieces of confetti from the visit by Shamrock Productions. That left four other defendants, Jerome Pearl, John Henderson, Thomas Lambert, and Kevin Whitfield who, like the Professor and Mary Ann in the first-season version of the *Gilligan's Island* theme song, were simply designated as "and the rest."

Mark Devereaux sat at the prosecutor's table and busied himself with the manila folders that covered the entire surface of the table. Special Agent Rick Dent joined him at the table. If he had any emotional involvement in the trial, it wasn't discernible on his face or through his body language. Rick Dent, as always, was practically a cipher: stone-faced and blankly neutral. He was impossible to read.

As Devereaux riffled through his files, he was interrupted by a tap on the shoulder. He turned to see the recently arrived

Special Agent Doug Mathews in the golden French fry suit he had worn in the FBI's first meeting with the McDonald's executives. "We ready to kick some ass today, Mark?"

"What the fuck are you wearing?" hissed Devereaux.

"What?" asked Mathews, genuinely confused. "The guys at McDonald's loved this suit!"

"This is a courtroom," seethed Devereaux. "You're making a mockery of . . . of . . . *the process*. Go home and change! You're going to make a bad impression on the jury in that getup. Go!" Defeated, Mathews left.

He took his seat next to Rick Dent, who had not reacted at all to the kerfuffle at his table. He didn't even react to Mathews's suit. Dent merely nodded as his young partner sat down.

The bailiff called the court to order and everybody rose to greet Judge Henry Lee Adams Jr. This may have been the government's case but it was without doubt Judge Adams's courtroom.

Adams took his seat at the bench and announced that the court was now open for business. With his ceremonial entrance out of the way, things were ready to begin.

The US attorney stood and took center stage to deliver his opening statement. Devereaux carried a vast amount of legal knowledge in his head but also knew that when it came to a jury trial, a little showmanship certainly didn't hurt. He wanted to impress upon the jury the importance of the case. As he stood in court, a change came over him. He became more relaxed and confident. This was his jam. This was who he was. He owned the floor. He explained to the jury that this was no Mickey Mouse civil or state court. This was federal court and it was no joke. "Comparing civil or state court to where we stand today is like the difference between playing football in high school and being in the NFL," he explained in terms the jury could easily understand.

Devereaux went on, avuncular at times and prosecutorial at others. The floor of the courtroom was his stage, and he was goddamn Tom Jones up there. The jury was getting a show and it responded with rapt attention. There was an undeniable vibe in the room. The jury was slipping right into Devereaux's pocket. They were his.

He was so effective, by the time he had finished his opening remarks, defendants Lambert and Whitfield changed their pleas to guilty. That left defense attorney Curtis Fallgatter with five defendants. He wasn't about to let this go. He had come prepared for a fight. Devereaux knew he needed to watch his step. Fallgatter was a known quantity to the prosecutor and Devereaux respected his opposite's skills.

Fallgatter may not have been quite the sartorial dandy that Devereaux was, but he was his equal in every other way . . . and those were the ones that counted. He had the courtly manners and measured delivery of the stereotypical Southern gentleman. He had once been an assistant US attorney for the Middle District of Florida, a position from which he once hired Mark Devereaux at the US Attorney's Office and, for a time, had been his boss. Like Devereaux, Fallgatter had also been in the JAG Corps. Each knew the other to be brilliant and cunning. It was a showdown like in an old Western where two equals, actually close friends, met on a dusty street to face each other with six-guns at high noon. They had already been in communication about certain aspects of the trial, most of them centered around George Chandler, who sat next to Fallgatter at the defense table, taking notes on the yellow, blue-lined pages of a legal notebook.

Chandler maintained his complete innocence in the matter and Fallgatter wholeheartedly believed him. Having heard Chandler's story, he called Mark Devereaux before the trial was set to start. He called on the US attorney's private line. They had a long history of working and socializing together. Their families were friendly, and they had shared more than one summertime cookout. Each knew the other was a formidable opponent, but Curtis Fallgatter believed he could set things straight for his client with this simple phone call.

"Mark! How are you, sir?" Curtis said as soon as Devereaux took the call. "Been a little while."

Devereaux knew that Curtis wasn't calling out of the blue to just chitchat, but like all well-mannered Southern gentlemen, he played the game. "It sure has, Curtis. How've you been? How's the family?"

"Aw, they're good, they're good, Mark. Thanks for asking.

"Now, let's quit fuckin' around with all this good ol' Southern hospitality horseshit. Why are you really calling me?" pounced Devereaux.

It didn't throw Fallgatter. In addition to hiring Devereaux at the US Attorney's Office, Fallgatter had also trained him. He knew the prosecutor's moves. The flipside was that Devereaux knew all Fallgatter's strategies, too. "Mark, Mark, come on now. You know, this kid, this George Chandler, man, he's the real victim here."

"How so, Curtis?"

"Well, for one, he was tricked. The kid's a ninth-grade dropout. He has a great mind for business, but he's a little naive in other areas," Fallgatter continued.

"Naive?"

"Well c'mon, now, Mark. This guy Dwight Baker was his foster father. He trusted and believed Baker all the way. Kid had a terrible home life. Baker and his wife took him in when he was still a teen. They gave him some kind of stability and they nurtured him along. Who knows what kind of terrible shit that poor kid would have gotten into if it weren't for the Bakers?"

"Looks like the Bakers got him *into* some serious trouble, rather than keeping him on the straight and narrow," countered Devereaux.

"That's your interpretation, Mark. Come on. They were active in the same church, for cryin' out loud. Besides being the kid's foster dad, Baker was also an elder in their church. How could George *not* trust him?" Fallgatter asked.

"So what you're saying is . . . " Devereaux continued to drag out the conversation.

"What I'm saying is we can clear this up right now pretty easily. You can drop the case. Look, George is completely innocent. He absolutely believed Baker. George was fooled. He didn't know the game pieces were stolen or embezzled or however you want to call it. He's innocent," Fallgatter insisted.

There was a pause on the line as if Mark Devereaux was considering the pitch. "Curtis, listen, I'm not willing to do that. First, a lot of people were tricked into participating in this scheme," Devereaux began. "But that's on them for not doing their due diligence."

"Now, now. Hold up a minute. This guy Jacobson goes out and recruits about ten people to get involved in his scam. Those ten knew what was up, no doubt about it and I won't dispute you on any of that. They *knew* the winning pieces were stolen. Now, these ten go out and rope in—trick, in other words—friends

and relatives to cash in those pieces. I won't deny that some of
those people the recruiters looped in also knew what they were
doing was illegal, but George—maybe you could say he was
willfully ignorant when it came to his foster father, that he had
a blind spot there—was still a victim of trickery," Fallgatter
explained.

"Curtis, I have fifty-three defendants. Are you trying to say
they were all 'tricked' and I should drop all the indictments?
That ain't going to happen," Devereaux assured him.

"I'm not saying 'all,' c'mon. But let's do the math. About
forty of those people were absolutely, without a doubt, unequiv-
ocally duped by Jacobson and his team of recruiters. George
among them," insisted Fallgatter.

"So you say. You believe him. I don't."

"Fair enough," countered Curtis Fallgatter. "But what are
you really driving at here? Punishment? George's already suffered greatly over this indictment. His business is destroyed.
He had a million-dollar, million-and-a-half-dollar contract to
injection-mold farm equipment. That's gone. The banks have
all called in their notes. The indictment has basically wrecked
his ability to earn a living. He has no income. He can't pay his
mortgages. He's managed to keep a roof over his head, but
who knows for how long? Things are going from bad to worse
for the poor guy. He's a twenty-nine-year-old kid who's been
absolutely crushed just by the allegations of the indictment.
Are we seeking justice here or are we just going for brutal
retribution?"

"Curtis, I understand that Baker was his foster father and
that George has a blind spot when it comes to the guy, but am
I supposed to believe that George, this so-called business

genius, didn't suspect something was strange? A million bucks all so Dwight could help out some unidentified friend hide money during a divorce proceeding? Give me a fuckin' break. If he didn't know something was fishy, he should have. I'll see you at trial," said Devereaux.

The call ended.

In court, Dwight Baker stood before the jury and told the same story: "George didn't know *anything*," he insisted. "He was never part of any conspiracy." He said it with conviction and sincerity. Curtis Fallgatter believed him. After all, Baker was under oath. Mark Devereaux rolled his eyes.

Now, sitting in Judge Adams's courtroom, George looked nervous as he sat at the defense table next to Fallgatter. He doodled. He looked at the jury. He looked at the judge. He looked over at the prosecutor's table. All the while, he managed to retain what little shred of professionalism and stoicism he had left. He was facing serious consequences simply for trying to help his foster father, but he felt confident things would work out in his favor. However, Mark Devereaux was relentless in insisting that George knowingly participated in the scheme and deserved to go down just like everybody else involved.

George thought it unfair. He had never met Jerry Jacobson. If Jacobson had approached him and said hello, George wouldn't have known him. Jerry Jacobson was a complete mystery to him. The tension and anticipation in Judge Adams's courtroom seemed like it couldn't possibly get any higher for George Chandler . . . until Jerry Jacobson entered the courtroom.

The ringleader of the scam that took the McDonald's Corporation for millions of dollars over a period of years had cut a deal with Devereaux. Now, as a witness for the prosecution, and as a part of his agreement, Jacobson was about to spill the beans in Judge Adams's court. For the first time outside of closed-door meetings with his attorney and the FBI, Uncle Jerry Jacobson would tell exactly how he managed to pull off one of the longest-running rip-offs in American history.

You Deserve a Break Today:
HOW'S HE DOING IT? COURTROOM EDITION!

Jerry Jacobson entered Judge Henry Lee Adams's courtroom unassumingly, but there was no doubt who he was.
He was the cheese, baby. The ringleader. The mastermind. The boss. The big wheel. Uncle Jerry. The Wizard of
Oz out from behind the curtain and revealed to be an ordinary man—an ordinary man who knew all the secrets and
was now going to reveal them in court.

George Chandler could hardly believe his eyes. It was
his first time seeing the man who stood at the center of
all his troubles. This was the guy? George had built him up
in his mind and this older, absolutely normal-looking person wasn't what he'd expected. He had pictured a super-
villain like the Joker. What he got was Quiet Dude from
Down the Street.

Jacobson had cut his deal and was now working with
the government to fulfill his end of the bargain. Devereaux
treated him with respect and deference.

Devereaux pulled a chair onto the floor with great flair.
This was minimalist theater and the audience—the jury—
gave the drama its full and rapt attention. "Jerry? You've
told us how you were able to switch out the winning game

pieces and it's quite the story. But I think we'd all benefit from a little demonstration. I'd like you to show us— exactly and in detail—how you managed to make the switch."

Devereaux had earlier worked out this routine with Jerry Jacobson and rehearsed it carefully. A good lawyer doesn't want any surprises or stumbles in his presentation and he especially doesn't want them coming from his star witness. When Jerry Jacobson had pleaded guilty at his arraignment, he had agreed to be a witness for the prosecution. It was the smart move. The system would go easier on him in exchange for the plea and the information he would willingly supply.

With the prop chair in place, the stage was ready. The only thing missing was a spotlight with a yellow gel to add some intensity. "Okay, let's set the scene. This is an airport men's room. A pit stop on your travels with Hilda Bennett. You've just told her of your great and pressing need to use the facilities and you've left her looking at items in the gift shop. But now you're free and you've got to switch out those pieces. Go!"

Uncle Jerry Jacobson stood and walked from behind the prosecutor's table. He carried a prop briefcase with him. "Well, the first thing I'd do, naturally, would be to enter the stall." Jacobson approached the chair and pantomimed entering a toilet stall and closing the door. Jerry Jacobson wasn't a great actor, but he did alright. And that's exactly what Devereaux wanted.

Under Devereaux's questioning, Jerry revealed how, after entering the stall, he'd sell the subterfuge for anyone else who may have been in the lounge's restroom. He would make noises typical of those heard in toilet stalls. The jury was riveted. This wasn't some dry, boring recitation of past deeds. Jerry Jacobson made it come alive. He transported the jury into that restroom. To some, it must have felt they were in the next stall as Jerry demonstrated an unusual skill making toilet noises. The demonstration may have caused some giggles among the jurors.

As Jerry sat on the stand, he continued his demonstration, his testimony shaped into a narrative by Mark Devereaux's skilled questioning.

Asked about Hilda and her apparent neglect of security protocol, Jerry had nothing but praise for her. He said she was a great accountant and related how, when Simon Marketing decided to switch accounting firms, Jerry pulled a few strings, called in some favors, and used his position as head of security to get her hired with the new accounting firm.

When asked how integral Hilda was to his scheme, Jerry answered that while she played a vital part, she wasn't aware of it. He explained that Hilda didn't look too closely at things or dwell on any possible suspicions—if she even had any. He made it absolutely clear that Hilda was never a part of anything illegal. Besides, Jerry told the jury, his actions in the restroom were completed in under five minutes. After carefully lining up his and Hilda's signatures on the flap of the envelope, he'd reseal it with a new hologram sticker.

The tampered envelope went back into Jerry's briefcase, the briefcase was locked, Jerry pulled up his pants, and he left the stall to rejoin Hilda on the concourse. It was fast and it was efficient. In and out.

Devereaux asked about the hologram security stickers Jerry had mentioned. Here, Jacobson slipped into his security expert persona. He was engaged and enthused. This was his area of expertise. He explained to the jury that the technology sounded much more space-age than it really is. The biggest strength of hologram stickers is that they are hard to counterfeit. Depending on the security level required they can be very simple or they can be quite elaborate. Jerry explained how the ones used at Simon Marketing were made in China and had all the bells and whistles: fluorescent inks, hidden images and micro-text, and writing that can only be read under ultraviolet light. For little adhesive-backed doodads that came on a roll of plain old paper, they were very high-tech and almost impossible to duplicate.

That caused Devereaux to ask if Jerry had access to the stickers as head of security at Simon Marketing. Jerry chuckled. He was very clear that he did not. He explained that, because he was so integral to the various steps in the process, he'd be the least likely person from a security standpoint to have access to them. The potential for cheating would be too great, Jacobson explained. The jury chuckled.

The big question then was how did Jerry acquire them?

Jerry attributed it to fate. He didn't know how else to describe it. He told a story of how one morning he came into work just like always and went straight to his desk. Sitting right on top—it couldn't be missed—was a package addressed to him. He thought it unusual when he opened it to find a big roll of hologram stickers. They were not supposed to come to him, but there they were, the exact same hologram security seals that were such a vital part of the security system put into place for running the McDonald's Monopoly promotional game.

Then came Jerry's fateful move. He picked up the roll and held it in his hands. As he explained, his mind started to go to places it shouldn't have. He started to think of how, with these stickers, he could develop a scheme to fix or rig the Monopoly promotional game. He wondered if it could really be as simple as he envisioned. As it turned out, it was. Especially since nobody knew he was in possession of these seals.

Jerry felt it was fate that had gifted him with these stickers. The universe was talking to him and he was listening . . .

- 26 -

MARVIN BRAUN TESTS THE WATERS AND FLUSHES AWAY A MILLION BUCKS

SOMETIME IN 1989...

I t was a phone call, or maybe over several phone calls—Marvin Braun, Jerry Jacobson's stepbrother, doesn't exactly remember—Jerry came right out and asked Marvin if he was interested in an opportunity. Marvin listened as Jerry told him he had a $25,000 McDonald's Monopoly game piece and that "maybe" they might be able to do something with it. He later described the conversation as being mostly in generalities, but the gist was that there was an available game piece and it was Marvin's if he wanted it. Marvin indicated that he would be interested.

"I don't want to say it was a week later, a month later, six weeks later," Marvin says now. "But one day, Jerry showed up with a piece and said, 'Cash it in.'"

"As I remember it," says Marvin, "it was in an envelope, I think." Inside was a game piece worth $25,000.

The very next day, Marvin cashed in the game piece. "There was an eight hundred number on the piece and they gave me instructions. I went to the post office and sent it to McDonald's via registered mail."

As stepbrothers, Jerry trusted Marvin enough that he'd keep his mouth shut, which he did.

Not long after sending in his game piece, Marvin got his check from McDonald's. The whole operation was as simple as pie. No muss, no fuss. It was a rush. It was exciting to get a check in that amount, especially after not really having to do anything to get it other than making a trip to the post office.

It was also confirmation that Jerry Jacobson's scheme to rig the McDonald's Monopoly game would work. The two men split the winnings right down the middle.

Several months later Jerry offered him bigger game pieces. Marvin wasn't interested, nor did he need the money. He was doing well with a maternity clothing business he'd built and it was turning a healthy profit.

Marvin decided to see if a couple manufacturers he dealt with in New York might be interested in Jerry's game pieces. He knew they were the kind of guys who could be discreet and connected them with Jerry.

During the filming of our documentary series, we asked him who these unidentified manufacturers were. His response: "I'd rather not mention names." We often wondered if this was the first connection to Uncle Dominic, which led to Jerry Colombo. It was one of the many questions we had hoped to have answered if we ever interviewed Jerry Jacobson directly, but that mystery still lingers.

The excitement of the first deal had begun to wear off, and not motivated by the money, Marvin claimed to not know exactly what went down between Jerry Jacobson and the New York manufacturers. He also put a friend of his from Texas in touch with Jerry, but he stayed out of wanting to know what happened.

A few years later, Marvin and Jerry went out to dinner with their wives. A double date. While the ladies enjoyed their meal and chatted it up at the table, Marvin and Jerry went to the restroom.

Jerry checked to make sure it was empty before he handed Marvin a million-dollar game piece. Marvin eyeballed it and then told his stepbrother, "Jerry, I don't want anything to do with that. I don't want to be involved." By then, Marvin was over it and regretted doing it in the first place. He didn't approve of what Jerry was doing and was worried something bad would happen.

He gave him hell. "What are you doing, Jerry? No thank you," Marvin said, quite sternly. The first game piece for $25,000 was one thing. But a million dollars turns what could be a slap on the wrist into something more serious if anyone found out. Marvin was getting pissed. "You're pushing your luck. You're gonna get caught."

Marvin's warning didn't deter Jerry, who handed Marvin the baggie with the game piece hoping that once it was in his hands it would be harder for him to back out. "Do something with it. Do whatever you want: sell it, trade it, it's yours now," Jerry said.

What Marvin did next was straight out of a movie. He took the game piece from the baggie and held it up where they both could see it. Then he tossed it into the toilet bowl. In what felt like slow motion he reached to flush it. They both watched it swirl away down the drain.

There was no shock or anger on the side of Jerry. It could have been less emotional for him than when he flushed his dead goldfish down the toilet as a kid. In that moment Marvin told him to stop. Jerry agreed. He was done. At least that's what he let Marvin believe.

So the next time you hear someone say, "Don't go throwing money down the toilet," you can think of Marvin, who flushed a million dollars down one.

When Marvin learned of the federal takedown of his brother-in-law on the evening news, he got a sick feeling in the pit of his stomach. He knew this could be bad and was worried he'd get caught up in the whole thing.

Fear is a great motivator. The potential consequences of actions he took a decade earlier had Marvin Braun scared. He was also in disbelief that Jerry had continued with the scheme even after he had assured Marvin he would stop. He thought Jerry had lost his mind, had been corrupted by greed.

As he was working one afternoon at one of the several maternity stores he owned in Florida, two FBI agents walked in the door. He weighed his options and saw no way this would work out in his favor. He called a lawyer and turned himself in to the FBI.

– 27 –

RULES

t was high noon in Judge Henry Lee Adams's courtroom—
and it wasn't even eleven o'clock yet. Jerry Jacobson had
already given his testimony. The judge sat on the bench, not
saying much. The showdown was between the two attorneys at
the center of it all, Mark Devereaux and Curtis Fallgatter. They
were deep into an argument regarding the fine-print rules of
the McDonald's Monopoly promotional game.

Devereaux had set up a slide projector in the courtroom.
When the lights dramatically dimmed—Devereaux knew all
the tricks of presentation—he brought up an image of the rules
to the McDonald's Monopoly game. This was the dense block
of microscopic text that informed all who played the promotional game what was and what wasn't permitted. Most players
never bothered to read them.

Lights low, the courtroom now a cocoon disassociated from
the outside world, Devereaux made his point. There on the screen,
enlarged, was the stipulation that "game pieces are nontransferable." Devereaux read the words and paused to let the jury soak

in them for a while. He broke the silence when he repeated the line for effect. "Did you get that? 'Game pieces are nontransferable.' There's nothing in the rules that specifically says, 'Why, yes, you can obtain a fraudulently acquired—stolen, in reality—game piece from a friend.' You can't because it's not there. It's also not there that you can get a game piece from Uncle Jerry."

When Curtis Fallgatter took the floor, he countered, "Nobody ever reads the rules in these types of contests and promotions. Nobody. Not George Chandler, certainly. And now here's Mr. Devereaux—with his expert witnesses in games and the rules of games—going over these words like they were the Constitution of the United States of America. It was a *game*, ladies and gentlemen. Nobody who played that game paid attention to the rules. Who would have thought, in the deepest recesses of the human mind, that anyone who broke one of these rules would then have to face down the Department of Justice and the full might of the United States government?"

Devereaux retook the floor. "Let's go back to what Mr. Jacobson told us about St. Jude's receiving the anonymously donated million-dollar game piece. He said he sent it anonymously, but even so, it created a lot of media buzz. It's not often that someone would so generously donate that kind of money to a research hospital dedicated to helping terminally ill children. But, if you recall, Mr. Jacobson hadn't exactly gifted the hospital with a million dollars out of the goodness of his heart. The truth was that he had been looking to get the piece to someone he knew and with whom he could work, but these games had very specific start and end dates, and this version of the game was running out of time. But waste not, want not. Just because Mr. Jacobson or his associates couldn't find a participant to cash in that piece before the contest ended, why not just give it away where it could do a lot of good? And where could the dates of these promotions be found? In. The. Rules. There was a lot of publicity, as we've noted, regarding the anonymous gifting of a game piece worth a million dollars to St. Jude Children's Hospital. That doesn't happen every day, so understandably, it was big news. It went beyond local; this was a national news event. But one thing never got much publicity: McDonald's Corporation, following its own Monopoly rules, determined the winning game piece could . . . not . . . be . . . transferred. Couldn't be. A violation of the rules. So now what? With all the positive publicity of what a great thing this was—and well aware of how mean it would appear to deny a hospital full of sick children a million dollars it already thought it would receive—came up with a work-around. McDonald's paid out a million dollars to the hospital but as a donation, rather than the redemption of a winning Monopoly game piece. And, yes, by doing this, McDonald's also got the tax breaks that come with a million-dollar donation. So did the hospital. If it had redeemed the winning piece like an actual person, it would have been taxed as such. It was some technical fancy footwork, but there was a good reason for it: the rules. The rules—and a strict adherence to them—gave the game and the company integrity. The rules were not there just there for decoration. There were solid reasons for them. No matter how Mr. Fallgatter frames them, no matter that almost nobody who played the game read them, they were necessary, and they had to be followed."

Curtis Fallgatter believed George Chandler. And not just because he was acting as the young man's attorney. Fallgatter

272   JAMES LEE HERNANDEZ AND BRIAN LAZARTE

was, like almost everyone else who met George, impressed by his humility, his guileless nature, and his backstory. By all odds, George should never have made it given the circumstances of his early life. George had been destined to be a statistic. A cautionary tale. A sad, "Do you remember that kid who . . ." Even Dwight Baker, George's foster father and the man who roped the kid into the scheme with a lie, had nothing but good things to say about George in the courtroom.

"What you're telling the court is," began Curtis Fallgatter as he questioned Baker, "Mr. Chandler's knowledge of your scheme was incorrect, wasn't it?"

"Yes, sir, it was. I convinced him that an acquaintance of mine was going through a bad divorce and, because of it, was in some real financial trouble," Baker told the courtroom.

"Trouble? How so?" Fallgatter asked.

"That my acquaintance was in possession of a winning McDonald's Monopoly game piece worth a million dollars and if he cashed it in, his greedy, horrendous wife was going to take a substantial chunk of it—if not the whole thing—and leave him high and dry," explained Dwight.

"And this so-called acquaintance of yours, who was this fellow?" asked Fallgatter.

"He was nobody, sir. I just made him up like I made up the story I told George," Dwight answered.

"Your story was completely fabricated for the sole purpose of duping your own foster son to collect a million dollars? It was entirely faked?"

"Everything except the million-dollar game piece, yes, sir," Dwight Baker answered.

"Why did you not tell George what he was getting into?" asked Fallgatter.

"That was Mr. Jacobson," Dwight explained. "Mr. Jacobson insisted that we keep George in the dark about how the million-dollar game piece came to be in my possession. I made up a story about a fictitious friend."

"But George didn't just accept the story the way you told it, did he? He, indeed, did what we might call his due diligence, did he not?" asked Fallgatter.

"He did. He did," answered Baker. "And I lied to him. George wanted to know who this made-up guy was and why he was giving away a million-dollar game piece. George wanted the story to make sense. And while he's only got a ninth-grade education, he's very smart when it comes to business and finances. Like, genius level in my opinion."

"What kind of questions did George ask you about the proposed transaction?" Fallgatter asked.

"Oh, he was full of questions. 'Who is this guy?' 'How come I never heard of him if he's a friend of yours?' 'Why all the secrecy?'"

"And what did you tell him?" Fallgatter asked.

"Nothing. Absolutely nothing. And when I say nothing, I mean nothing. Jerry Jacobson insisted from the beginning that the fewer people who know about the system he had put in place, the better for all of us, for him. And I wanted to protect George as far as I could," testified Dwight Baker.

"George came into possession of that winning game piece by transfer, but he didn't know anything about the scheme Jerry Jacobson had crafted and which you were a knowing participant?" Fallgatter asked.

"Exactly," said Dwight. "We—I—made sure to keep George completely in the dark. He was convinced this all centered around some guy I knew who was going through a divorce and didn't want to be known to anyone. He was a babe in the woods. Innocent."

Pretrial, Fallgatter had become absolutely convinced of George's innocence. During their meetings, George repeatedly stated he didn't understand why he even had to go through this. "Mr. Fallgatter, I see people selling tickets and prizes all the time on eBay and other places. Are they all going to trial, too? When Dwight presented the opportunity of acquiring that game piece, I was convinced I was helping someone in need. I thought I was helping a friend of Dwight's. And I related to the guy's situation. I had my own marital woes. I had just gone through a painful and messy divorce myself, so I could relate to this guy's situation. I looked at it as an investment."

When George Chandler took the stand, Fallgatter walked him through his story for the jury. Clearly, George was under a great deal of stress. Every morning before leaving for court, George had to hug his son and reassure him that he would return that evening. The child was terrified that the system would swallow his father whole and that he'd never see him again. This was also one of George's major concerns, too. If he did go away, who would look after his family? But that wasn't George Chandler's only source of worry. He had basically lost all his revenue streams once news of the arrests broke. He'd lost properties he owned. Legal counsel—good legal counsel—was expensive and George Chandler was hemorrhaging financial resources.

And now Mark Devereaux was coming after the young man with the full might and power of the United States government all because of a violation of the fine-print rules of the McDonald's Monopoly promotional game that said the prizes were nontransferable. It was a tough break, Devereaux had to agree, but rules are rules and rules are practically sacred. Without rules, all we're left with is chaos.

But for someone who insisted upon rules and traditions in almost every matter from courtroom attire to McDonald's Monopoly, and the law itself, Devereaux ended up in violation of the regulations himself. There was no doubt that while Mark Devereaux and Curtis Fallgatter were commanding presences in the courtroom, the real star, the king, the man everybody needed to bow down for was Judge Henry Lee Adams Jr. This was his courtroom and if Mark Devereaux thought himself a stickler for rules, he was bush league when compared to Adams's dedication to them.

After Curtis Fallgatter had delivered his closing argument to the courtroom regarding George Chandler's innocence in the case, Judge Adams addressed the jury. He gravely instructed the jurors, "You can only find George Chandler guilty if you believe he *knowingly* was part of a conspiracy to defraud McDonald's." The judge might as well have said, "Are you kidding me with this? This man should walk." Fallgatter clapped a hand on George's shoulder. This was great for their case. He whispered into his client's ear: "They no longer have a case against you."

Mark Devereaux was not happy with the jury instructions, but he'd deal with it. He turned to discuss a point with FBI agents Doug Mathews and Rick Dent.

In doing so, he violated one of the major rules of etiquette in a federal courtroom: he turned his back on the judge. It wasn't deliberate. It was the heat of the moment. Judge Adams was a stickler for rules, too. He asked, "Mr. Devereaux, do you have a problem?"

Realizing his error, Devereaux tried to make it right. The punishment for such a violation could be a contempt of court charge. "No, your honor. I apologize. I was careless and meant no disrespect."

"We live by the rules here, Mr. Devereaux. I hope you will show more respect for them as we move forward," cautioned the judge.

"Yes, your honor. I'd like to request a brief recess to discuss the case against Mr. Chandler with my colleagues," Devereaux said, indicating Dent and Mathews.

"No recess, Mr. Devereaux. Let's proceed to your closing arguments," said Judge Adams. There would be no dismissal. The jury would decide George Chandler's fate.

With that, Devereaux couldn't see a way to cinch the case against Chandler. In desperation, he took a shot at a strategy on the fly. He had noticed that there were several women in the jury box and he thought he knew a surefire way to appeal to them. "George Chandler can claim he was not part of a fraud ring," began Devereaux. "But he still knowingly attempted to defraud someone. Based on the story he had been told by Dwight Baker, George purchased his million-dollar game piece not only to enrich himself, but also to keep the money away from a woman in a divorce. While this story and the woman herself did not actually exist is beside the point. As far as George Chandler knew, he was an active participant in defrauding this woman of what was rightfully hers."

"Objection!" interrupted Fallgatter as soon as the words left Devereaux's lips. "This so-called cheated, defrauded woman does not exist! Did not exist! It's a ridiculous argument, your honor!"

Judge Adams cleared his throat. "Sustained," he said. "Ladies and gentlemen of the jury, please ignore that last statement from the prosecution." It was a decision made on solid legal grounds, but the jury had already heard the words and Devereaux hoped he had planted a seed in the minds of the female jurors. After receiving some instructions from Judge Adams, the jury filed out to deliberate. As Curtis Fallgatter noted, "You can instruct a jury to strike, but you can't unring that bell."

When they returned, they delivered guilty verdicts to all the defendants but one—and that one was not George Chandler who now appeared to be in a state of shock. When he had left home that morning, he had once again assured his tearful young son that everything would be all right and that Daddy wouldn't be going to jail. Now he had to go home and tell the kid that was no longer true and he would likely be going away for a while. Tears welled in his eyes.

Dejected and despairing outside on the courthouse steps, George felt Curtis Fallgatter's hand clasp his shoulder. "Do you want to fight this, George? We can fight it and I believe we can win on appeal," he told George. "Come with me and we'll talk."

Across the street from the courthouse in Fallgatter's office, the two men sat and contemplated the next move over glasses of whiskey. "I would like to fight it," said George. "But this whole thing has already wrecked me financially, Mr. Fallgatter. I'm broke. I have no idea how I'm even going to keep a roof over my head going forward."

"George, I feel so strongly about your case and your innocence; I don't want you to worry about that. We'll work it out later. Let's get to work," said Fallgatter.

"I'm ready. And if it's the last thing I ever do, I will pay you back every single dime, Mr. Fallgatter. Thank you. Thank you." George fought back tears of gratitude.

– 28 –

THE BALLAD OF GEORGE CHANDLER

JULY 2004...

"Your dad's going to prison! Your dad's going to prison!" A group of children surrounded a boy on the school playground and taunted him with a singsong chant: "Your dad's going to prison!" They formed a tight ring around the kid that left him with no escape route. The chant drew the attention of other children and they circled like sharks smelling blood in the water. The kid in the middle, outnumbered, overwhelmed, and facing his own problems and worries at home, crumpled to his knees.

A noon aide—a local mom donating her time to the school—saw the commotion and walked over, whistle clenched between her lips. She was ready to blow a few short, sharp blasts to break up whatever the kids were up to. When she saw who was being picked upon, she shrugged and walked away. *The kids' ll sort this out themselves*, she thought. The child in the middle of the circle saw salvation slip away. "This is for Ronald McDonald!" said a tubby older boy who landed a roundhouse punch to the back of the kid's head. The other children cheered.

As suddenly as it started, it was over. The gang had made their victim cry and their fun was apparently over. The bell rang and noon recess ended. The children raced back to class. The child who had just spent another brutal lunch hour picked himself up, dusted himself off, and angrily wiped away his tears. His problems were bigger than merely getting stomped and taunted on the patchy grass of a school playground in Walhalla, South Carolina. Back at home, his father, George Chandler, found guilty of taking part in Jerry Jacobson's long-running scheme to defraud the McDonald's Monopoly promotional game, faced the real—likely—prospect of losing a few years to the system. Although he claimed he had been duped by the person he trusted most in the world—his foster father Dwight Baker—the jury hadn't believed him and handed down a guilty verdict. Now, George fought the case on appeal. His attorney, Curtis Fallgatter, believed so strongly in George's innocence—that he had been victimized by Jacobson and Baker just as much as McDonald's itself—that he was now working the case for free.

It wasn't going well for the Chandler family. George faced the possibility of spending the next five years in prison plus fines and restitution. Many people sentenced to federal prison did their whole bit before an appeal was granted. Out of those who had been allowed to appeal their cases, a paltry 2 percent of those cases won. To say the odds were stacked against George Chandler was selling the situation short. Things looked grim.

While George was, according to anyone who knew him, a savant in business, it was of no use now that he had lost a million-dollar contract for work and was struggling to pay his mortgage. George was barely hanging in there.

Worse, the local Walhalla newspaper had a field day running headlines about George Chandler's guilty verdict . . .

but didn't devote much coverage to the more mundane: LOCAL MAN FIGHTS CONVICTION ON APPEAL. George and his family were suddenly outcasts in their small, insular Southern town. The children—especially George's son—took a lot of abuse despite not having anything to do with the case other than having George for a father.

To his credit, Curtis Fallgatter was true to his word. He remained firm in his belief that George was innocent and that, eventually, his name would be cleared. Fallgatter navigated the byzantine rules and formalities of the appeals process, and, finally, after two years battling in the courtroom, he defeated his old friend and rival Mark Devereaux whose previous conviction and courtroom victories were overturned. George Chandler was acquitted.

It was a bittersweet victory for George. While his name was cleared, it didn't rate the earlier negative press he had received. To the people of Walhalla, he was still George Chandler, the real-life Hamburglar who stole a million dollars from the McDonald's Corporation, America's most beloved fast-food institution. George told anyone who was interested, "I've spent my life trying to rebuild my damaged character and find a way to provide for my children," he said.

In addition to the appeals process, George Chandler's life had undergone major changes. He had divorced his first wife, found a new one, and added more children to the mix. He was now a father of seven, with his youngest children not having a clue of what their dad had been through.

The older children weren't as lucky. George's oldest daughter, a budding ballet dancer, was cruelly teased just like her brother had been. At her dance classes, it was rare for a lesson to pass without a group of mean girls taunting her with the accusation that the only reason she was able to afford ballet classes was because her father was a crook. Despite that, she was delighted and proud when George showed up to one of her recitals in a pink tutu so he could dance with her. He was her hero. But no matter what he did, no matter what he said, George's reputation—and the family's—was shot in Walhalla. It was never going to recover, George concluded. It was time to move on.

George pulled up stakes and relocated the family to a farm some distance from Walhalla and Fair Play. There, on a property that featured emerald-green pastures, a fishing pond, and placid, cud-chewing cows, George took up the life of a cattle rancher. It was a huge undertaking and a complete change of lifestyle. It must have agreed with George because everyone noticed the transformation in him.

While enduring life through the appeals process, George walked and talked like a man about to face a firing squad at dawn. He shuffled, rather than stepped. His head hung between his shoulders like he was trying to avoid the rain falling from the personal black cloud that voided itself right over his head. Now, after the move and the change of careers, he rode the property on the seat of his John Deere belting out church songs like "Amazing Grace" and "Leaning on the Everlasting Arms." He'd dismount to check out his cattle. He knew nothing about them other than what he read and what he was able to glean from other ranchers. But that wasn't a problem. George had always been a quick study and the local ranchers were happy to help the eager young guy who was always ready to return any favors he received with hard work and his time.

"I'm new to all this," George would tell a neighboring farmer.

"We all are, at first," said some grizzled cowboy, sweat dripping down his neck and face and carving little rivulets into the powdery silver dust that had collected on his skin.

"I got this cow over here with a bum leg," George would say. "She's getting worse every day it seems. I've been putting on an ointment and giving her antibacterials, but she doesn't seem to be getting any better. Do you have any experience with this?"

"Oh, son. You don't want to spend too much time on something like that. Ranching's a tough proposition sometimes. Harsh. Cows shouldn't be costing you money besides basic care. You just gotta be prepared to put 'em down."

"Put her down? Oh no. I can't do that. I've been through some stuff, too, and if it weren't for one guy believing in me, I don't know what would have happened to me. I try to pay it forward now. I think I'll call the vet," George speculated.

The older rancher smiled. "That tender heart of yours is admirable, kiddo, but it'll end up costing you an arm and a leg."

"It'd be worth it," George would say with a smile. "Every life deserves a second chance."

"Well, son. I'll have to think on that for a while, but you make sense in a spiritual way."

George had also made a major change in matters of faith, too. He had been raised among the Latter-day Saints; from the poor, chaotic, challenging home he'd had with his birth parents to the more stable environment provided by his foster parents, the Bakers, the LDS had been all he had known. After the trial, he reexamined the church and was disillusioned.

George ended up taking the family to the welcoming arms of a local Baptist church—it didn't get more Southern—with a mostly Black congregation. George and his family loved it. It was communal, it was loving, and the people were salt-of-the-earth types. The Chandlers loved the potlucks, the social events, the camaraderie of the new church, but if you were to have asked George what he loved the most, he would have said, "The music."

It was true. The singing during services was stirring. It could be wildly joyful one moment and then melancholy and mournful as the darkest hour of night. It was like the Lord's Top 40 countdown every Sunday and George wouldn't miss it. He'd pile the family into two cars to get them all there. As the only white faces in the pews, the Chandlers were a curiosity at first, but the congregants grew to love the Chandlers as they got to know them. George even joined the choir. He wrote a song. He approached the choir director one day.

"Choirmaster? Just want to thank you again for allowing me to join the group. It means a lot to me," George told him.

"You have an ear for it, Brother George. We gonna get you to sing a solo one of these days, yes sir," the choirmaster told him.

"That's what I wanted to talk to you about," George said. "I don't know if you know about my past, but the last few years have not been the greatest."

"Ah, the trials of life," agreed the choirmaster.

"Literally," said George. "Anyway, the thing that got me through was the Lord and this church. The Lord's always guided me and I hate to think where'd I'd be if I didn't have Him in my life. I wrote a song and would like to sing it one of these days . . . with your permission and help, of course."

"Let's hear what you have, son," the choirmaster directed. After a few weeks of rehearsal, the choirmaster had made a

beautiful arrangement and George was ready to belt. His children beamed as George stepped to the front of the choir and
sang his song. By the time he reached the final measures, there
wasn't a dry eye in the house. Everyone cried tears of joy.
George Chandler had been through it, indeed, but he hadn't
been broken. The Lord watched over His servant. No matter
how bad things had been, they were moving in the right direction now and the Chandler family could see a little light at the
end of a long dark tunnel and it was growing bigger and brighter
by the day.

While he weathered the appeals process and worried about
the future, George tried to keep his mind limber. He learned by
trial and error—and there were a lot of errors along the way—
how to run a farm and how to care for livestock. It was hard
work, and he knew virtually nothing about agriculture and
animal husbandry when he started. George kept at it, though,
and his skills improved incrementally. Within a few years,
George had it wired and the farm started to turn a profit.

One day, as he pored over files from his latest cases, Curtis
Fallgatter's office phone rang. It was his assistant. "Mr. Fallgatter, there's a man here who says he needs to see you."

"Does he have an appointment?" Fallgatter asked. He was
busy and the last thing he needed was an unannounced visit
from anyone.

"He says it's urgent. He's insistent."

Seeing it was nearly noon and he'd be taking a short lunch
break anyway, Fallgatter said, "Sure. Send him in."

When the door opened, Fallgatter was floored. Standing
before him in cowboy clothes, with a ten-gallon Stetson held in
his hands, was George Chandler, a big grin plastered on his
face. "Hi, Mr. Fallgatter. How you been, sir?"

Fallgatter got up from behind his desk and greeted George with a handshake. "George! It's good to see you!"

"I hate to interrupt you like this, Mr. Fallgatter, but I need to take care of this." He handed an envelope to the attorney.

Curtis Fallgatter opened it and was speechless. Inside was a cashier's check made out to him for the complete amount of the pro bono work he had done that eventually led to George's acquittal. "I-I don't know what to say. Do you have any idea how unusual this is?"

"Not really," said George. "But I told you I'd pay you back in full one day . . . and that day has arrived."

His obligation now fulfilled, there was still an unresolved issue tugging at George Chandler's emotions. That was the relationship he'd had with his foster father Dwight Baker. Given his history, it was understandable that George had a visceral need for a father figure in his life. But what does a man do when he's been duped and used by the one he called Dad?

As a Christian, George had God the Father to guide him and watch over him—so George didn't feel orphaned—and if there was one thing Christians valued it was the concept of for-giveness. It still took George a full decade to reconnect with Dwight Baker.

He made the trip back to Fair Play with the specific goal of forgiving—in person and face-to-face—the man who had betrayed him. On the drive, George watched the countryside slide past his windshield and his mind wandered back over the story of his life and its major beats. There were a lot of them, he realized, and he was thankful and grateful for them all. There were the obvious things, the good things, he believed his God had bestowed upon him: his children, his new life as a cattle

rancher, his church, his faith. But George was also grateful for
the defeats and troubles he had suffered, too. There were a lot:
his birth mother throwing him out when he was still a kid; the
grinding poverty of his earliest years; being tricked into
defrauding McDonald's and losing everything; and then the
long climb back from all the negative publicity and fallout that
resulted from Jerry Jacobson's scheme. In them he found what
he believed to be some measure of wisdom. Master seminars in
how to recover from bad fortune and fate . . . even though
George believed God guided all things. *I'm exactly where God
wants me to be*, George thought. And whenever He shuts a door,
He opens a window.

But as the miles rolled by, George felt butterflies in his
stomach. God might direct all things, but that didn't guarantee
they would go smoothly or be pleasant. George truly did not
know how his meeting with Dwight would proceed and he was
scared and nervous. Dwight had played a huge role in his life
and had betrayed him. George only knew one thing: he wanted
to forgive Dwight. Behind the wheel of his pickup, barreling
down a two-lane blacktop country road, George lifted a prayer
to his God: "Lord, please help me to truly forgive Dwight
Baker, to be shut of this thing. I don't want to go to my grave
with hate still in my heart."

At home, in his kitchen, Dwight nervously awaited George's
arrival. He had been racked with guilt for the past ten years.
The court had given him three years of probation and he was
on the hook for paying back the money he had scammed from
McDonald's. It would take a while to make things square. He
was making payments of fifty dollars a month. His children
had yet to forgive him for all the trouble and shame he had

brought upon the family. Something that still weighs on him today. Dwight, who had sincerely loved being a part of the LDS, was stripped of his membership and position. Excommunicated. Cast into the wilderness. Alone.

He had met with LDS leaders weekly, and later monthly after the arrest. It was a serious matter, and he felt obligated to protect the church as best he could.

Dwight was a local business leader but his core identity—even as he possessed a bit of larceny in his heart—was that of a Latter-day Saint. To avoid excommunication Dwight needed to repent. Yet he also understood that being excommunicated was not a punishment, but in fact a blessing. The expectations to live up to the covenants are no longer a reminder of one's failures.

After being given several opportunities to repent, Dwight chose not to. He wasn't ready. He was still working on forgiving himself and felt the road back, which included repentance, would happen on his and the Lord's schedule.

From his seat at the kitchen window, he saw George pull up in front of the house.

He greeted his foster son from the porch as George stepped down from the cab of his pickup truck. "George! How've you been! You're looking good!"

George was reserved. "Hello, Dwight. You look good, too." He wasn't being completely truthful. A decade had passed and Dwight showed every one of those years. Time and the weight of excommunication had taken their toll. Dwight looked old and gray to George now. A figure of pity.

Dwight slowly navigated the front steps of the porch and George met him on the front lawn. Without hesitation, George enfolded him in a bear hug and squeezed. "I forgive you, Dwight.

I truly do. I'll never be okay with it, but I can drop it and put it behind us. I don't want to live my life with even a spark of anger smoldering in my heart. I'm letting it go. It's over."

Dwight was overcome. He fought back tears. He had lost so much by taking part in the scheme to defraud McDonald's, and now, a man whose life he'd almost ruined was hugging him and forgiving him. It could have been a tear-jerking country song.

"The worst part of all this isn't what happened to me. That was my own damn fault. I was greedy. I took the easy route. But you didn't deserve any of what happened to you, George. The worst part is that everyone around me, everyone I cared about, had to pay the price for my bad decisions. I'm sorry, George. I'm sorry."

- 29 -

GO TO JAIL, DO NOT COLLECT $200

LATE 2001-2002

Gloria Brown, single mom, could not have agreed more with Mathews's and Dent's summation of the McDonald's Monopoly scam. The entire experience was traumatizing and a challenge to relive for the first time on camera during our interview. "Oh, why did I ever let myself get involved in this thing?" she lamented. "I knew it was wrong. I knew it. And once I was in, there was no going back. I was just trying to get by. Everything was such a struggle. It was probably the worst move I ever could have made. What a risk I took. I had no idea. I almost lost it all. It's the biggest regret of my life. If it wasn't for the public defender, I would have gone to jail and what would have happened to my son? I don't even want to think about that. I'm not a bad person." Gloria said, as she broke down in tears.

Florida's golden sunshine poured into the Jacksonville coffee shop from a low angle and bathed the room in a honeyed glow. This place was old-school Googie style: lava-rock walls, cream-colored Formica, pressed aluminum, seafoam-green Naugahyde. Coffee steamed in brown ceramic cups next to sweating glasses of ice water. It wasn't quite eight o'clock, but the crowd was already arriving for the various breakfast specials: two eggs any style, choice of bacon or sausage, choice of grits, hash browns, tomato slices or fresh fruit, choice of toast or biscuits, and, because it was Florida, white sausage gravy upon request.

Already seated at a table, his sunglasses cutting the glare of sunlight streaming into the dining room, was a well-dressed man with a neatly clipped mustache. His tie even matched the seafoam-green Naugahyde of the dining room, although it hadn't been planned. He sat impassively as he scanned the room and took occasional glances at the laminated breakfast menu. Suddenly, something caught his eye and he raised a hand.

A just-arrived diner saw him, nodded, and made a beeline to the table. He was dressed in a much more casual way: gray slacks, black socks under black sandals, a blousy navy velour crew neck shirt, and a pair of orange-tinted sunglasses. His head was shaved smooth. He slid into the booth with a big grin on his face.

It was a friendship as unlikely as any, the prosecutor and the perp, yet here they were on good enough terms that they were both comfortable teasing the other in that age-old male bonding ritual known as "bustin' chops."

Marvin Braun, mastermind Jerry Jacobson's stepbrother and the first person to cash in a stolen McDonald's Monopoly game piece worth $25,000, wore a big grin on his face. If there was lingering resentment over his conviction, he didn't show it. Thanks to Mark Devereaux's efforts, Marvin ended up serving two years under house arrest, or, as it was known in Florida, "community control." He was monitored by a heavy plastic ankle bracelet containing an electronic global positioning system that would alert law enforcement if Marvin violated the terms of his sentence.

Mark Devereaux, who usually did not care what happened to the people he helped convict after the conclusion of a trial, had been impressed with Marvin. In his eyes, Marvin had stood tall and filled in the FBI on how early Jerry Jacobson's scheme had gone into effect. In doing so, he provided a lot of information law enforcement would never have learned otherwise. He was the first person to turn himself in when Jacobson's scheme finally unraveled. Upon their first meeting, Devereaux in his no-nonsense style had warned Marvin straight up, "I can't stress this enough: don't ever lie to me. Lie to me, and I'll see to it that you serve every second of your sentence in federal prison."

Marvin took Devereaux at his word. "The guy scared me shitless," he'd say later. While he didn't know the actual process of how Jerry Jacobson acquired the winning game pieces, he was able to provide enough "substantial evidence" in the prosecution of Jerry Jacobson that two years of community control would be a better option for justice than throwing an old man behind bars. He pleaded guilty to one count of mail fraud. He also had to pay back $625,000 restitution to McDonald's. As they worked together during the case, a friendship started to develop.

Marvin had not seen or talked to his stepbrother Jerry Jacobson since the trial ended in 2001. It made family get-togethers a little awkward.

At trial, Jerry Jacobson detailed the intricacies of his crimes and admitted that he had boosted, at his best recollection, as many as sixty McDonald's Monopoly game pieces, and for each one of these received kickbacks of $45,000 or $50,000. In total, the scheme netted him, at his estimate, about $3 million over the ten years he had rigged the contest.

There was fallout. Disappointed, resentful McDonald's Monopoly players felt the opportunity to legitimately win a million dollars or some other high-value prize had been stolen from them personally. "Fuck McDonald's! They did nothing to stop this Jacobson guy. Hey, I've been a loyal customer for years. My family could have used a million bucks. Hell, I could have used a Viper in my driveway. Can you imagine? I could have been the coolest guy on the block. Now I'm just the guy with a sack of cheeseburgers and fries . . . but they're from Wendy's because, again, fuck McDonald's."

These people could have been dismissed as cranks and malcontents, but they were vocal and there were enough of them to create some concerns in the boardroom of the McDonald's Corporation.

In the end, what McDonald's came up with was a $10 million "instant cash giveaway." That amount was distributed among fifty-five randomly chosen winners. It was a low-key contest and didn't generate the word of mouth and excitement that the Monopoly games did. After the money had been quietly distributed and the contest was over, McDonald's brushed its hands and walked away. It was over.

The FBI had some opinions on the case. Doug Mathews and Rick Dent both believed it was possible that there were perhaps dozens more people who had fraudulently cashed in game pieces and were involved in the scheme but who couldn't be clearly linked to the case.

"It was totally likely there were others," speculated Doug Mathews. "As we learned through this process, the biggest challenge in every case is needing evidence to prove there was wrongdoing. What else could we have done? We're lucky we got as far as we did."

And they did get pretty far. One of the details we love about this story is thinking about how it all got started with Agent Mathews's curiosity about that Post-it on Rick Dent's computer. Would Dent have eventually gotten around to it? By the time he had, would the latest game already have been in motion? Would the informant have changed their mind about talking had Dent called a week or a month later? There were so many questions we couldn't help but wonder. But along the way, the question of who made that initial call was always there: Who was the informant?

– 30 –

SPECULATING ON THE INFORMANT

The America of the early 1900s was a product of the rapid
industrialization of the Gilded Age. In the 1870s to 1890s,
vast fortunes were built and hoarded by the few, creating a
near-feudal system in which people like John D. Rockefeller,
George Westinghouse, Thomas Edison, Elisha Otis, Andrew
Carnegie, and John Pierpont Morgan were the economic over-
lords. Their images were enshrined in portraits that showed
them mustachioed and glowering. *Look on my Works, ye
Mighty, and despair!*

Lizzie Magie, a progressive feminist from Washington,
DC, was deeply concerned by the disparities she saw. She
wanted to preach the good word about the dangers of the lop-
sided economic system but knew nobody liked lectures. She
also knew that everybody liked to play games. She developed a
board game that involved acquiring property and collecting
income from it. While she was an astute game-maker, she was
absolutely terrible when it came to naming her product.

Calling it The Landlord's Game, Magie took out a patent on her handmade game in 1903.

Magie developed the game so that it could be played in two ways. One option was the anti-monopolist version that allowed all the players to build wealth. The other option—and the one that most people liked—was the monopolist version, which reflected the era's brutal and unrestrained capitalism. All players were out for themselves with the goal to acquire all the wealth and, most important, crush any opponents. Magie explained her game in intellectual terms. The two versions of the game presented the dilemma of the American system: Do you enrich society or do you enrich yourself?

A man named Charles B. Darrow, an out-of-work engineer, knew where he fell in that equation. He had been introduced to a version of The Landlord's Game at a dinner party and loved it. He saw the potential for making a fortune off Magie's game, so he brazenly brought it to Parker Brothers as his own creation. The company, later learning of Magie's role in the game's development, offered her five hundred dollars for the patent.

Magie believed this meant the company would manufacture The Landlord's Game and society might become a better place because of it. Then, one day, she saw the game for sale in a toy store and realized she had been scammed. Not only had the name been changed to Monopoly, but the anti-monopolist option had been removed. Greed and ruthlessness were virtues within the framework of the new game. There was one winner and multiple losers, just like in the real world. And in that real world, Charles B. Darrow went on to earn millions off Monopoly, while Magie got a five-hundred-dollar check—and no royalties—for her role in its development.

The contestants playing McDonald's Monopoly didn't fare much better than Lizzie Magie. Many of them went through some deep, dark times, perhaps none more so than Robin Colombo, the widow of Monopoly scamster Jerry Colombo. She was a frequent visitor to Jerry's grave at Jacksonville's Arlington Park Cemetery. Chain-smoking at the grave, Robin could be seen crying and occasionally kissing the headstone. "I'm doing better now, baby," she'd say to the granite headstone. "I'm doing good. Just trying to stay out of trouble and do right. I miss you." And then she'd dissolve in tears.

Frankie, the son she'd had with Jerry, was living with his grandparents and she was an outcast from the Colombo family. They blamed her for Jerry's untimely death. Frankie bounced between the Colombos and the Fishers, Robin's family, while she was either incarcerated or suffering the effects of her drug addiction. When he was nine, Nana Colombo called him into the living room where she was going through a scrapbook. She held it on her lap like it contained the secrets to the universe. "Hey, kiddo, did you ever see this picture of your dad's car?"

"No, Nana, never."

"Do you think you're a big enough boy to see one now?"

"I'm not a baby," Frankie reminded her and peeked over her shoulder at the open page of the scrapbook. The kid visibly blanched at what he saw. There was a laminated newspaper clip that showed Robin's flattened Ford Explorer.

"Just think," said Nana. "If your mother had a better car, your daddy might still be here with us."

Because he was so young when the accident happened, Frankie had no memory of it. His only recollection of his dad was playing with him on the kitchen floor, banging pots like they were drums or play-tussling at karate and wrestling. Seeing the picture—and constantly hearing the propaganda against his mother—created a hole in the kid's heart. Raised by committee, Frankie was developing into a troubled young man.

When he turned seventeen, and with Robin in between stays at the county jail or in a rehab program, Frankie turned up at her doorstep. "Hi, Mom."

"Oh, Frankie!" She embraced her son. Right away, Frankie could tell that although Robin may have been a free woman, that just meant she wasn't in jail or in detox. She was still a slave to her worst impulses and the drugs.

Frankie was searching for answers to better understand the woman who he had heard so much about but who he didn't really know. Despite the drugs, the instability, and the absolute squalor in which Robin lived, Frankie decided to stay.

It wasn't the best decision.

Before long, Frankie was living the same lifestyle as his mother. There were drugs, petty crimes, and a hardening attitude about the world. The kid couldn't take it. Few could. He found himself in the lowest and darkest moment of his life. His future faded from possibility as he contemplated joining his father. But was suddenly smacked with a feeling of clarity. He'd say later that in the moment he felt the presence of his father and knew everything would be alright. The next day, after a night's sleep, Frankie cleaned up. No more drugs, no more crime, nothing but the straight and narrow from now on.

To Robin's delight, Frankie eventually got married and made her a grandmother . . . even though she likely hated the term. Sensing a new beginning for her and her family, Robin reached out to Gloria Brown. Gloria, who had already suffered a lot from listening to Robin's advice, was wary at first, but the two women eventually rekindled their friendship.

During the filming of *McMillion$*, there was a scene that didn't make it into the final cut. Lee Cassano, who was recruited into the McDonald's Monopoly scheme by Jerry Colombo and then put on the hook for paying the taxes on her cash prize, met with Robin. She had something she wanted to get off her chest. The two women sat on a porch and reminisced about the late Gennaro "Jerry" Colombo.

Lee dropped what she thought would be a bombshell revelation. "I was the one that got the whole investigation started by calling the IRS and reporting everything I knew about you and Jerry," said Lee.

Robin's eyes narrowed to slits. "What the fuck are you talking about?"

"There would have been no investigation if I hadn't called the IRS. That's where it all started," Lee said with authority.

Robin wasn't sure about that explanation. "You never called the FBI?"

"No. Why would I do that?" Lee wanted to know.

Robin had said in previous interviews with the FBI that both her husband, Jerry Colombo, and her husband's partner in crime, "Uncle" Jerry Jacobson, had promised her a winning McDonald's Monopoly game piece that she never received. Robin also had a history of threatening to inform on Jerry Colombo whenever she got upset with him. Their very public battles at Jerry's Church of Fuzzy Bunny's were legendary. She denied being an informant despite seeming likely for the role.

Holding court on a tuck-and-roll red velvet couch, in the center of a blue-gray swirl of tobacco smoke, she said, "Me? The informant?" She let loose a crow-like laugh. "Honey, you gotta be kiddin' me! I was neck-deep in the operation. I'm not gonna inform on myself, now am I? That wouldn't make any sense."

Robin did have a strong opinion on whom she suspected. "I think it was Jerry's younger brother Frank. He and his wife were pissed that they never got the million-dollar game piece Jerry had promised them. It was revenge."

When FBI Special Agent Doug Mathews heard Lee's story during the making of our documentary *McMillion$*, he couldn't help but laugh. "The IRS? Are you kidding me? That's what she said? Get real. First, the IRS is slow. Also, if the IRS was involved all the coverage we read from all over the country would have said something about 'In a joint operation with the FBI, the IRS cracked the case of the McDonald's Monopoly fraud case.' They would've been right there with us. Go back and look. Nobody, no news outlet, ever said anything like that. They called Rick Dent who wrote their number down on a Post-it—and who didn't follow up on it. I did the initial investigating and eventually met with the informant. It's FBI policy to not reveal the names of our informants. Mystery tags my fun meter. It always has. My lips are sealed."

So if the informant wasn't Lee Cassano, who was it? That question hung heavy among all the people who had taken part in ripping off McDonald's Corporation.

Dwight Baker, always in the mix, had his own self-centered theory. "It was me," he says. "Or at least my fault," said the shady Mormon businessman. "You see, I had a business associate who was as crooked as they come and *he* was under investigation by the FBI for something, I'm not sure exactly what. But anyway, one day I'm out in the driveway and I see the telephone pole across the street has some kind of blue metal box attached to it. I think the FBI was using it to monitor that guy through our phone conversations. In the course of doing that, they learned of the McDonald's scam through calls Jerry Jacobson made to me."

Upon learning of Dwight Baker's theory, FBI Special Agent Doug Astralaga who had been such a vital part of the Shamrock Productions undercover team, laughed and shook his head. "Well, all I can tell you is that the whole thing went down because of a single person, but I can't tell you the name. I can tell you, without a doubt, that the investigation didn't start because of a wiretap. It wasn't Dwight," Astralaga insists to this day.

There was some speculation that Marsha Derbyshire, Jerry Jacobson's ex-wife who had nursed him through his bout with Guillain-Barré syndrome, may have been the informant. After all, she had been the head of security at Dittler Brothers from 1987 through 2000, and may have had some hard feelings over a land deal she had been involved in with her ex-husband and Dwight Baker. She had invested $50,000 in the project on one of Dwight Baker's properties. "When I found out that Dwight was involved in the scandal, what went through my mind was that Jerry never paid my fifty thousand to Dwight Baker. I'm pretty sure that Jerry gave Dwight Baker a ticket. That's what happened. I'm the only one that gave any money for this little piece of land that ended up costing me out the wazoo," she said. Marsha went on with her suspicions. "Did my fifty thousand pay for the ticket that Dwight Baker got since Jerry didn't pay that money to Dwight Baker for the land? Or did Jerry just trade half of my lot and gave Dwight a ticket and I paid the fifty thousand to cover it all? I probably bought the ticket for Dwight," she said with a slightly bitter laugh. "It seems like Jerry took my fifty thousand dollars and put that toward the land and then he paid Dwight with the ticket." Did Marsha drop a dime as revenge for a land deal gone bad?

When asked again about the identity of the informant, Doug Mathews only had this to say, "Look, that is sacred, protected information. I can't reveal the identity. Can you imagine what would happen? Informants need anonymity and they need to know that the FBI would never expose them like that. We rely on informants a lot of the time. What's going to happen if they suddenly start to think we'll sell them out down the line?"

Rick Dent offered some commentary in his usual taciturn way. Questioned about whether he knew the identity of the McDonald's Monopoly informant, he answered simply, "Yes." Asked to expand and elaborate, he said, "No."

Mark Devereaux, the US attorney, was tight-lipped, too, although he did drop a hint: "To the best of my recollection, it was someone who was supposed to have received a million-dollar game piece from Jacobson and then didn't. That person was upset and dropped a dime to the FBI in an act of revenge. At least that's how I remember it," he said.

If Devereaux's memory was correct, that narrowed the field of potential informers to just three people.

First up was Robin's daughter from a previous marriage, Jennifer. Her stepdad, Jerry Colombo, perhaps hoping to strengthen the shaky foundation of their relationship, had promised her a winning game piece when she turned eighteen. She never received it. Had she dropped a dime to exact some revenge?

The next two on the list of possible informants were the late Jerry Colombo's brother Frank and his wife. They had been promised a million-dollar game piece—free, with no required kickbacks—for their wedding day, but it had never happened because Jerry died.

In a sunny kitchen, Frank Colombo and his wife, Heather, sat for our interview where we asked about Robin's theory. Frank said, "You know, we carry a lot of baggage just having the last name Colombo. We're always under suspicion. Always have been. I never wanted that lifestyle. I never wanted to be part of a crime family."

So who was the informant? As filmmakers, we're interested in motivation. What drove all this? What led the players in this saga to do what they did? Take Jerry Jacobson, for example. Here's a man who had been in law enforcement and who later worked in security. Crime wouldn't seem to be a good fit for a guy like that, but he still crossed the line. Did he do it to fund his numerous alimony payments? After all, he had seven marriages under his belt. Was he worried about the potential return of his Guillain-Barré syndrome, leaving him incapacitated and unable to work? It might be good to have a solid nest egg for just such a rainy day should it ever arrive. Was it a way to acquire a sense of power? Could it have been something similar to A.J. Glomb's excuse, that he did it because he was bored?

Mark Devereaux had his own take on things: it was simply greed. As he told us, there are a lot of reasons and rationalizations people will use to justify their actions, but when all those are stripped away, what we're left with is greed. That's it. And when we finally learned the identity of the real informant—read on—it made sense.

EPILOGUE

THE INFORMANT IS REVEALED

2024...

To make a six-part documentary series takes some time. We filmed over the course of a year or more. We also shot cinematic re-creations to help transport the viewers back in time and put them in the shoes of our characters. One of the last things we did when filming our interviews was to return to Frank and Heather Colombo's home . . . somewhere in Florida.

We decided to spend a little extra time to get to know them—and understand why they now had ten beautiful custom-built cars in their driveway. We also hoped they would answer the mystery that had been gnawing at us this whole time: *Who was the informant?*

But first, the cars. They were "drifters." Candy-colored, Japanese specialty racers with spoilers, wings, ground effects, special tires, overbuilt brakes . . . these rides were straight out of the 2006 movie *The Fast and the Furious: Tokyo Drift*. They were built to "drift"—taking corners at impossibly high speeds by allowing the car to slip into a controlled slide. It requires skill and guts. One little miscalculation and it was all over. The only thing standing between the driver and disaster was a mastery over the laws of physics. If you don't know the sport, we encourage you to check it out. What was crazy to us was that they did all this as a family, with Frank, Heather, and their son, Vinnie, keeping the family bonds strong through speed and adrenaline. Each of their cars were bespoke Nissan Zs. Also in the driveway was a big, imposing Hummer that dwarfed the drifters.

We weren't sure how drifting fit into the story we were telling, but we certainly thought it was cool and later we discussed developing a show with them about it. For the record, we still think it's a great idea.

So when they took us for a drive up the street we stopped to pick up some coffees and we decided to roll our camera— probably because we were at McDonald's—and we did a double take when they asked for their coffees with ten creamers and ten sugars each. Noticing the looks on our faces, they cheerily explained, "It's basically like a latte." That's debatable, but who are we to judge?

This is the beautiful thing about filmmaking: sometimes you have no idea what someone is going to do or say when the camera is rolling. You hope to capture gold, but that rarely happens.

Instead, it dropped into our laps when Heather responded to a very simple question we put to the two of them. We asked, "Let's circle back for a second to the informant. We've heard that there was a woman who was a winner of a million-dollar piece that Jerry—your brother Jerry—collected his cut of a hundred thousand dollars. Out of that, he was going to pay her fifty thousand to pay the taxes she would incur on the win. But because your brother passed away after the accident, she wasn't able to get that fifty thousand to pay taxes and she called the

IRS to explain the situation. In doing so, she revealed the whole story. Is it possible that this woman was the informant?"

Frank answered without hesitation. "I would say no."

Heather left a window open though. "Could this woman have also called the IRS?" she said. "Sure. Possibly. And it could have come about at the same time that the informant would also call the FBI. But was this woman the only informant? Absolutely not. No."

Frank offered, "If I knew who we were actually talking about, I could maybe look into it a little bit. But if it's anyone associated with Robin—Jerry's widow—I'd say it was complete bs."

Then Heather jumped in and, in a little bit of crosstalk with her husband, dropped something that caught our attention. "I don't think anyone thought for a second that it was gonna get as big as it did. And it got really big, and it got really big really fast. I said, 'I don't want to be caught up in this.'"

At one point, Frank and Heather had been promised a million-dollar game piece as a wedding present; Heather would just have to claim it under her maiden name.

She continued her story. "Had I taken that McDonald's and cashed it in, I, honestly in my heart, believe she still would've called the FBI and I would be in prison . . . "

"The informant was who?"

Heather takes a breath, then said, "The informant was Frank's mother."

Our mouths fell to the floor. We were not expecting this angle. Ma Colombo the squealer? This whole time we had thought it could be Frank.

Ma Colombo, who had never approved of Robin as either a wife to her son Jerry or as a mother to their son Francesco. But calling the FBI? What would she have to gain?

Heather laid it out. "It was to save her grandson, Jerry's kid, from Robin's bad influences. That's what it was all about. In a way, she was saying, 'You took my son, so I'm going to take yours.' She actually said those words at one point. So she had something to gain: Francesco. She had a reason to go to the FBI and to rat everyone out. Francesco was what she was getting out of it." Heather and Frank went on to explain that they believed if this is how things really went down, Ma Colombo never expected her call to the FBI would kick off an investigation into what was a nationwide scam that went on, undetected, for years. She was just trying to hamstring Robin and gain custody of Francesco. At the time, Robin was serving time for check fraud. Ma Colombo knew if she dropped a dime on Robin and could implicate Robin's father, Francesco wouldn't be allowed to stay in the custody of either of them. That would leave the Colombos as the child's guardians. She had no idea how big the McDonald's Monopoly fraud actually was or how many people were caught up in it. It was, as Mark Devereaux summarized, an example of greed. Ma Colombo wanted her grandson all to herself. She had no idea how big the fraud really was or how many people it touched.

Back at the Colombos' home, we were wrapping up our interview in the kitchen when their son, Vinnie, came walking in wearing his McDonald's uniform. It was unexpected. James and I both knew at that moment that we had just been presented with the ending for our documentary.

And now we've arrived at the end of our book.

Behind the scenes, we got in touch with Robin Colombo. Like us, she had believed that Frank Colombo had been the informant. That it was Ma Colombo acting out of spite and revenge against Robin didn't seem to us the kind of thing she would want to learn from HBO . . . even if Robin herself was a huge fan of *The Sopranos.*

We were surprised how she took the news. Over the years, she and Ma Colombo had become close in one of those crazy turnarounds that often happen in families. The hard feelings of the past had gradually subsided as both women realized that family was more important than grudges and revenge. She told us she had suspected Ma's involvement all along, but couldn't be sure. Now she was convinced. Later, Robin told us that she called Ma to confront her with her newfound knowledge and that Ma had cried and admitted the whole thing saying, "I wanted to tell you for *years* . . . " Robin told us that, in the moment, she had forgiven her mother-in-law and they remain close.

While Robin had forgiveness for her mother-in-law, there are still people to this day who will never forgive Jerry Jacobson. He had ruined their chances of winning big—even if in a totally straight game those chances were infinitesimally small.

To offset things, and to the company's credit, McDonald's did try to make things right. It ran a contest that distributed $25 million in random giveaways of cash and prizes. We were given the opportunity to look at in-house archival footage of the event. It didn't look nearly as fun or exciting as the tainted Monopoly promotions.

After all of our research and documentation of the scandal, one of our biggest takeaways was that it was easy for Jerry Jacobson and others caught up in it to believe that what they did was commit a "victimless crime," but that wasn't really a very clear-eyed—or honest—take on the situation. We have to assume Jerry believed if he were caught, Simon Marketing would just fire him and sweep the whole thing under the rug for fear of hurting the company's reputation and its bottom line. During the trial, Jacobson also claimed to have evidence he thought would save him if busted: he said he had proof that McDonald's and Simon Marketing purposely stopped anyone from winning their games in Canada. McDonald's flatly denied this allegation. Assistant US Attorney Mark Devereaux shared that he and the FBI had looked into it and found nothing, adding that it was a "totally unsupported claim by Mr. Jacobson. Why in the world would McDonald's not want somebody in Canada to win? Don't you think people in Canada are going to spend money in their restaurants?"

Nobody involved expected the FBI to blow the scam wide open and eventually force it into the public eye. The FBI maintains that the real victim was the American public, which never had a fair chance to win the big prizes offered in the contest. In a lot of ways, McDonald's was also a victim, having been duped into believing all those coming forward to collect prizes and appearing in local newspapers or on broadcast news were legit. While the corporation lost millions, it's hard for a lot of people to have sympathy for a company that was making *billions* of dollars every year. However, the fraud compromised the company's reputation and basically destroyed the legitimacy of a promotion that had greatly helped its bottom line and was beloved by people everywhere. Then there are all those people who ended up as federal criminals. Their families, their kids were all touched by the stigma of the crime even though they had nothing to do with it. We see them as victims, too. And while you might say you can't find it in your heart to feel sorry for any of the perpetrators because they did the crime and have to pay the price in the name of justice, remember that in a number of cases they were screwed. Most of those who claimed the stolen game pieces got paid in installments and many of them never even received the initial payment. It didn't matter. They were still ordered by the court to pay restitution—and are likely to still be paying it off. The rule at play here is that restitution is based upon *intended* fraud, not what they actually received. They were duped into believing their participation in the scheme would have no negative consequences. After all, "somebody" had to win. Gloria Brown, for example, believed God had presented her with an opportunity to lift herself out of difficult financial straits. On top of that, when you think about all the people who lost their jobs at Simon Marketing and Dittler Brothers, it's clear a lot of lives were negatively affected by this scheme.

This story has had some interesting silver linings. George Chandler found love and remarried; Mark Devereaux has fully retired and spends all his time with his grandkids and lovely wife, Diane; Robin Colombo and Gloria Brown have written books; and Chris Graham is an FBI media consultant. The documentary series of *McMillion$* premiered at the Sundance Film Festival on January 28, 2020, and brought together Gloria Brown, her sister Balecia, Mark Devereaux, Chris Graham, Rob Holm, and Amy Murray—all in the same room talking, reflecting, making peace, and genuinely reconnecting. As filmmakers, it was a surreal yet inspirational sight.

As for Doug . . . well, he loves his sense of mystery but we can say that he's still out there busting bad guys. This project has had such a profound impact on us, with Doug being a big part of that. So when it came time for us to name our production company, we went with the logical choice: FunMeter.

Most of the "criminals" in this story were merely good people who made bad choices.

In the end, you have to ask yourself if a friend or family member came to you and presented a way for you to win a million dollars that only required you to tell a little white lie and kick back some of your winnings: *Would you do it?*

Oh, and just in case you're interested, we've heard that McDonald's might be bringing its Monopoly promotion back soon. But don't get any bright ideas, and keep your greed under control. Doug Mathews just might show up at your door with a fully loaded confetti cannon and a set of shiny handcuffs.

And then we'll call you for an interview.

ACKNOWLEDGMENTS

Writing this book was a four-year endeavor, in part because it wasn't a financial decision. We've always believed in this story with all of our hearts and knew there was more to say. We are grateful to Grand Central Publishing for supporting that vision and to our editor Suzanne O'Neill for hand-holding us through a new experience and being supportive of us getting it out there on our time line.

We'd like to thank Michael Albo for helping us channel the pages and pages we wrote and diving into the endless amount of interviews and legal transcripts.

To our book agent, Richard Abate, who was a guiding light through the wild world of books. From our first call with you, we knew that we were in good hands.

This wouldn't be possible without the support of Mark Wahlberg, Stephen Levinson, and Archie Gips and everyone at Unrealistic Ideas. We can't thank you enough for being such amazing creative partners on this journey.

Thank you to everyone at HBO, especially Nancy Abraham and Lisa Heller, who believed in two unknown filmmakers based on our passion and vision. We are forever grateful.

A supersize thank-you to McDonald's for opening your doors to us and cooperating in a way that most large corporations would never permit. You truly are Americana.

To the FBI—especially FBI Jacksonville, the Department of Justice—specifically the Middle District of Florida, and all the law enforcement professionals who trusted us to tell this amazing story. Every single day they work tirelessly to protect us from evils we can't even fathom.

There was a long list of people we wanted to speak with who chose not to participate in this project. We understood the fears and concerns they had and to this day, we wish them well. To that point, we are extremely grateful for all those who did make time for us. A very special thank-you to Robin, Jennifer, Frankie, Gloria, Balecia, A.J., Dwight, Russell, George, Frank, Heather, Marvin, Lee, Marsha, Brian, Curtis, Ed, and Janice along with your families, friends, legal teams, and, sometimes, pets. For many of you this was one of the worst, if not the worst, thing you've experienced. We appreciate your trust in us. The mass amounts of compassion that has poured out since the documentary was released proves that no one should be judged by one decision.

There aren't words to describe how thankful we are to the entire *McMillion$* documentary team. Everyone put their heart and soul into this and it shows. A special thank-you to Shannon Pence who not only was a supervising producer on the series but also helped with fact-checking this book.

And last, all our reps at UTA, Entertainment 360, and Raymond Legal. No matter where you joined us on this journey, you've helped us in countless ways and we are so appreciative you are in our corner. Kellen Alberstone, Grace Royer, Brian Levy, Darin Friedman, Jordan Lonner, Brian Raymond, and Sean Faussett, a huge warm thank-you!

JAMES LEE HERNANDEZ

To my parents, Jim and Jamie Bandelin. I am so fortunate to have such great role models. You've both always encouraged me to push the limits and never acted as if my dreams of being a filmmaker were insane, even if you were secretly terrified. I wouldn't be here without your love, patience, advice, and laughter. I also have to say thank you, Mom, for taking me to McDonald's and letting me play the Monopoly game, even when money was tight.

To my Chicago family. I love you all so much. Thank you for keeping me grounded and for always making me smile. Also for being such inspirations when it comes to hard work. Growing up, I just thought everyone started their own business. I can't wait to hit Vito and Nick's with all of you soon.

To my Hernandez family. All of you have set such an amazing example for me in life. You showed me that there's a way to be artistic while also being driven and focused. I'm grateful for the warmth and compassion I've felt all of my life.

To my Bandelin family. All of you have been such rays of sunshine. I appreciate the love and support I've felt from all of you from day one and can't wait for more karaoke on Christmas Eve.

To my friends. I'd name you all but there's a word count limit. I'm extremely lucky to have such a tight-knit group. We've been through so many of life's ups and downs. Thank you for encouraging me on this wild journey. You've given me strength in ways I can't fully explain.

To Brian Lazarte. The story of *McMillion$*, and everything since, continues to be the ride of a lifetime. Thank you for having faith in me when I told you about this crazy idea and for being a rock when I was low. It's awesome being able to experience all of this together. What we've built at FunMeter is one of the greatest joys of my life. Also, a big thank-you to Iris Ichishita for hiring me all those years ago. Thank you for your mentorship and for linking me with Brian.

Thank you to team FunMeter! Brian and I are beyond lucky to be working alongside you to build something that is rare in this industry. You're all such beautiful, talented people and inspire me daily.

Last, and definitely not least, to my grandma Irene Barry. Thank you for teaching me so much in life. For showing me the importance of fun and laughter. That family and friends mean everything. One of my only regrets with all that's happened since *McMillion$* is that you weren't here to see it. But I know that you, Elvis, and Sinatra are watching on.

If you're reading this and have a wild idea, something that's calling to you but might seem insane to anyone "normal," please let me encourage you to take the leap and go after it. *McMillion$* was made out of thin air. If I can do it, so can you.

BRIAN LAZARTE

There have been many relationships, mentors, and champions of my creative pursuits over the years that have helped lead me to this achievement. You all know who you are and I thank each and every one of you. Beyond everyone mentioned collectively, there are a few personal names I must single out.

Iris Ichishita. My incredible wife, life partner, and mother to our children. There are not enough thank-yous to express my gratitude for all you have done for me. You deserve immense credit for my many successes. Without you, I would never have met James, and this book would not have been possible. Our HBO documentary series *McMillion$* would not have been made, and the countless creative pursuits you've witnessed me chase would not have been as rewarding without your support. I would not be the man I am today without you. Your intelligence, charm, talent, and wit appear effortless. After all these years, I remain in constant admiration of the quality of your character. Your honesty and authenticity serve as my model for becoming a better person, a great father, and remaining genuine. I am incredibly grateful and appreciative of the life you've helped us create. I love you and thank you!

Blanca and Dave. My incredibly loving and supporting parents. For the many sacrifices you made to help me pursue my interests, the many headaches I put you through, and your continued love, thank you. Your work ethic and kindness have been a guiding force in discovering what I'm capable of and finding goodness in others. May the two of you and both my sisters know how much I love you all. You all played a major role in shaping who I've become.

James Lee Hernandez. My cowriter and creative collaborator since 2017. This story wouldn't have happened had you not been looking at Reddit one day and read that TIL post. I'm forever grateful that you thought of me and reached out to Iris. I don't think either of us could have predicted how the story would explode the way it did or where we'd be today, building a company together (FunMeter) and continuing to find creative projects to collaborate on together. You are sharp, funny, and continue to impress me. I'm honored to be a part of this journey with you!

My many teachers, professors, and educators. You all saw something in me to help me grow and discover my many strengths. You also helped me improve upon my weaknesses. You inspired me and passed on the tools and knowledge necessary to find my way in the working world. I'm grateful for each and every one of you. A special thank-you to Kevin Burke from the University of Cincinnati, CCM, for being so encouraging, passionate, and dedicated to seeing all your students excel. You played a crucial role in my creative growth and current path.

Tom Segura. My cousin/brother. Your creative and professional ambitions continue to inspire me. I remember how your eyes lit up the first time I mentioned this story to you. From offering to do our bonus podcast episode to inviting us to *Your Mom's House* podcast with your wife Christina P., and finally introducing us to Richard Abate, who helped make this book possible, I couldn't be more grateful and thankful for your support! Thank you, cuz! Love you.

ABOUT THE AUTHORS

JAMES LEE HERNANDEZ is a multi-Emmy– and PGA Award–nominated Latinx filmmaker, Signal Award–winning podcaster, and co-founder of FunMeter, a TV and film production company specializing in stranger-than-fiction stories. Hernandez directed, edited, wrote, and executive produced the five-time Emmy-nominated HBO original documentary series, *McMillion$* (Sundance 2020), alongside Brian Lazarte. Next, Hernandez wrote, directed, and executive produced the Apple TV+ original documentary series, *The Big Conn* (SXSW 2022), again with Lazarte, and produced the award-winning documentary *The Herricanes* (SXSW 2023). He also executive produced *Lolla: The Story of Lollapalooza* (Sundance 2024) for Paramount+ and co-hosted the Apple Original podcast *Scamtown*.

BRIAN LAZARTE is an Emmy-nominated producer, director, and editor. His work has been seen since 2005 on major networks and streaming platforms, including a variety of award-winning documentaries and series. Most notably the five-time Emmy nominated *McMillion$* (Sundance 2020) for HBO and *The Big Conn* (SXSW 2022) for Apple TV+, which he wrote, directed, edited, and executive produced alongside James Lee Hernandez. He is a Signal Award–winning podcaster as well as a founding partner of FunMeter, a TV and film production company specializing in stranger-than-fiction scripted and unscripted content.